W9-CMZ-941

THE GIFT OF
SHAMANISM

"Itzhak Beery's *The Gift of Shamanism* offers clear teachings as well as riveting testimonials about what becomes possible when we walk this path with humility, reverence, and discipline. He is to be commended as he has created very good medicine. I love this book!"

HANK WESSELMAN, PH.D., ANTHROPOLOGIST AND
AUTHOR OF THE SPIRITWALKER TRILOGY
AND COAUTHOR OF *AWAKENING TO THE SPIRIT WORLD*

"Itzhak Beery is a master storyteller who shares his fascinating journey from skeptical nonbeliever to gifted shamanic healer and teacher. *The Gift of Shamanism* is filled with powerful and engaging stories of transformation that inspire us to tap in to our shamanic potential. Brilliant book!"

SANDRA INGERMAN, AUTHOR OF
SOUL RETRIEVAL, WALKING IN LIGHT,
AND COAUTHOR OF *SPEAKING WITH NATURE*

"In this beautiful book Itzhak Beery, a powerful seer and agent of change, illumines through the ancient art of storytelling the mystical worlds coinciding with everyday reality and the inner magic we each carry."

LLYN ROBERTS, AUTHOR OF
SHAPESHIFTING INTO HIGHER CONSCIOUSNESS
AND COAUTHOR OF *SPEAKING WITH NATURE*

"*The Gift of Shamanism* is eloquent and mesmerizing. It offers an utterly fresh perspective that may reveal shamanic wisdom embedded in your own long-neglected life circumstances."

ARIEL ORR JORDAN, PSYCHOTHERAPIST, WRITER/DIRECTOR, AND FILM PRODUCER

"Itzhak gifts us with an eclectic array of healing stories that bridge sacred tradition and present-day living. This wonderful healer teaches us how to connect with spirits and forces that diagnose and heal."

MARGARET DE WYS, AUTHOR OF *BLACK SMOKE* AND *ECSTATIC HEALING*

"The wonderful message of Itzhak Beery's excellent book *The Gift of Shamanism* is that everyone has this gift. It is our birthright. Through personal stories from his own life and the lives of his many clients, Beery's contribution to readers is his deep understanding of what makes a shaman and how a shaman lives in this confusing world. Even better, his story teaches us to trust the visions of the spirit world to ease the burden of uncertainty and empower our personal lives with wholeness and meaning."

TOM COWAN, AUTHOR OF *FIRE IN THE HEAD* AND *YEARNING FOR THE WIND*

"I heartily recommend this book to learn how Itzhak Beery works, including how he facilitates spirit communication and spiritual healing, helping people connect with their shamanic abilities, such as visions, out-of-body experiences, dreams, and his work with ayahuasca. Beery has distilled his years of experience into this marvelous volume."

LEWIS MEHL-MADRONA, M.D., PH.D, AUTHOR OF *REMAPPING YOUR MIND*, *COYOTE MEDICINE*, AND EXECUTIVE DIRECTOR OF THE COYOTE INSTITUTE

THE GIFT OF SHAMANISM

VISIONARY POWER, AYAHUASCA DREAMS, AND JOURNEYS TO OTHER REALMS

ITZHAK BEERY

Destiny Books
Rochester, Vermont • Toronto, Canada

Destiny Books
One Park Street
Rochester, Vermont 05767
www.DestinyBooks.com

Text stock is SFI certified

Destiny Books is a division of Inner Traditions International

Library of Congress Cataloging-in-Publication Data
Beery, Itzhak, 1950–
  The gift of Shamanism : visionary power, Ayahuasca dreams, and journeys to
other realms / Itzhak Beery.
      pages cm
  Summary: "Discover the shamanic powers within each of us" — Provided by
publisher.
  ISBN 978-1-62055-372-5 (paperback) — ISBN 978-1-62055-373-2 (e-book)
  1. Shamanism. 2. Ayahuasca ceremony—Amazon River Region. I. Title.
  BF1611.B44 2015
  201'.44—dc23   2014033368

Printed and bound in the United States by Lake Book Manufacturing, Inc.
The text stock is SFI certified. The Sustainable Forestry Initiative® program
promotes sustainable forest management.

10 9 8 7 6 5 4 3 2 1

Text design by Debbie Glogover and layout by Virginia Scott Bowman
This book was typeset in Garamond Premier Pro with Trajan Pro, Gill Sans, and
Futura used as display typefaces

To send correspondence to the author of this book, mail a first-class letter to the
author c/o Inner Traditions • Bear & Company, One Park Street, Rochester, VT
05767, and we will forward the communication, or contact the author directly at
itzhakbeery.com.

To my parents, Chaim Kolodzianski-Beery and
Sara Margolis-Beery, who gave me a chance at this lifetime,
and to all the spirits who came before me
and those who will come after me

CONTENTS

Foreword by John Perkins   ix

Acknowledgments   xv

INTRODUCTION   From Skeptic to Believer   1

1   How It All Started   12

2   Dreaming   29

3   Past-Life Experiences   44

4   Soul Retrieval   58

5   Plant Medicine   72

6   Shapeshifting   99

7   "Seeing"   106

8 Shamanic Journeying 130

9 Candle Reading 154

10 Psychonavigation 164

11 Holographic Experiences 182

12 House Clearing 198

13 Healing Ceremonies 205

14 Aztec Seeing 224

15 Using Shamanic Vision in Business 227

EPILOGUE We Are All Shamans 235

FOREWORD

꩜ ꩜ ꩜ ꩜

John Perkins

In 1968 I spent time deep in the rain forest of the Ecuadorian Amazon. Beginning then and ever since I have become close to the Shuar, Achuar, Quechua, and other indigenous peoples. At one point while in the Amazon rain forest I grew so violently sick, without the possibility of reaching any hospital or medical care, that I became resigned to my death. An old Shuar shaman using plant medicine his culture knows and has applied for thousands of years saved my life.

"How did that work?" I asked him.

"The spirit of the plants did it," he replied.

A Calvinistic New Englander and recent business-school graduate, I could not comprehend the meaning of his answer but I was grateful nonetheless. I wondered what these people in the jungle knew that we didn't. As payment for his help, the shaman demanded that I become his apprentice. In the months and years that followed I had the opportunity to listen to the stories of the Shuar. One of the things that impressed me the most was learning how difficult it is for the peoples of the rain forest to maintain their ways of life and livelihood at this time. It became obvious to me that they desperately need our help to stop the encroachment of a civilization—mine—that threatens their traditional ways and the vast knowledge of their medicines.

I asked an elder shaman what could we, the people of the technological North, do to help them.

"We do not need your money," he replied. "But if you really want to help, change the dream of your people."

Since then I've devoted most of my time to encouraging a shape-shifting of our culture. I write and teach about the importance of transforming our technological/materialistic dream into one that manifests a sustainable and just world that honors all sentient beings on this magnificent planet we are so fortunate to inhabit.

Changing the dream of our global society is our greatest challenge—and opportunity. It must start with each person awakening from the shackles of the nightmare we have created in our recent past. We need to recognize the innate ability within each of us to enter into a dreamtime where we can connect to the infinite knowledge of the spirit world, where we can access healing knowledge for our bodies, minds, and souls and embrace the wisdom of our ancestors. To do this we must relearn and pay attention to our birthright as spiritual beings while recognizing that every animal, plant, river, mountain, and rock has a unique spirit and teachings that are relevant to our survival as a species.

The spirit world, as people like the Shuar know so well, is continually interacting and communicating with us through our senses, our visions, and our dreams. Being in close contact with the spirit world helps us sustain and preserve humanity's soul, shapeshifting us from fear-based attitudes to a life-affirming and balanced sense of hope.

We live in the most revolutionary time in human history. It is bigger than the Agricultural Revolution, the Industrial Revolution, the American Revolution, or any other revolution. This is a revolution in consciousness, a time for us to wake up to our true potential as human beings. It's a revolution that will free us from our unconscious stories of lack and limitation and release us from the false values, hopes, and expectations that have kept us stuck in dysfunctional patterns, both as individuals and as a global society.

I'm happy to say that this uprising of passionate and committed people is a cross-cultural awakening that will impact all species. In my travels around the world I've felt the power of this historic global awakening. People are becoming conscious of the fact that the old traditions and the status quo are no longer serving their—our—interests or those of life on our planet. Indigenous shamans from cultures everywhere offer us a blueprint for moving forward. They've seen this coming for millennia. Each traditional culture has a storied history of prophecies of the death of one age and the birth of another.

Since 1968 I've lived, studied, and worked with indigenous cultures on every continent (except Antarctica, where there aren't any). All of them have a prophecy that says we've entered a time that has the potential for major transformation. The Maya of Central America, the Quechua of the Andes, the Tibetans of the Himalayas, the Bedouin of the deserts, and many other traditional peoples foretell a shifting of our world and our reality into a sustainable, just, spiritually fulfilling, and thriving future. These prophecies tell us that we have the opportunity to move out of the period of deprivation, lack and limitation, and dysfunctional patterns into a time of understanding that there's great abundance in our world if only we pursue it together, as one.

In 1990, when I first started writing books and teaching workshops on shamanism, my work received attention only from a very limited category of people. For lack of a better term, they were mostly what we might call former hippies and New Agers; there were few businessmen, doctors, or lawyers interested in this message. But now that has changed. I meet people from all walks of life and from all socioeconomic groups who embrace these ideas and are passionate about changing the world.

Indigenous people from many cultures tell us that "the world is as we dream it," and that the dream is realized by the actions we take. The dream of our parents and those before them, along with the decisions they and we have made, has now brought us to the brink of self-destruction. However, across the planet we are shaking ourselves awake; now it is time to dream a new dream. And to act and change accordingly.

I've known Itzhak Beery since 1996, when he participated in a workshop I taught and subsequently joined me on trips to the shamans of the Amazon and the High Andes. He also assisted at the Dream Change Coalition's Gathering of the Shamans in the early 2000s, and was an active member of the NGO I founded, Dream Change. Committed to a vision he had in the Amazon during a plant medicine ceremony, he cofounded the New York Shamanic Circle, an organization that injects shamanic wisdom into the heart of one of the largest capitalistic cities in the world.

Through his straightforward and surprising stories you can witness firsthand his transformation, from a skeptical nonbeliever who was a New York advertising executive, to a full-fledged shamanic practitioner and teacher for others around the world. This is a testament of personal awakening and a lesson to others, but most of all it is an affirmation of the power that shamanic traditions offer us during this time of extreme planetary vulnerability.

The Gift of Shamanism is also a tribute to Itzhak's teachers, many of whom I know personally and have worked with. This book is written in the time-tested shamanic tradition of storytelling and from the perspective that only through personal examples can we learn the secrets of our own existence and achieve the goal of realizing our highest purpose.

Read on. Be amazed and inspired. Above all, be open to your own powers . . .

JOHN PERKINS has traveled and worked with South American indigenous peoples since 1968. He currently arranges expeditions into the Amazon and has developed the POLE (Pollution Offset Lease on Earth) program with the Shuar and Achuar peoples as a means of preserving their culture against the onslaught of modern civilization. He is also the author of *The Stress-Free Habit*, *Psychonavigation*, *Shapeshifting*, and *The World Is As You Dream It*.

Acknowledgments

⚜ ⚜ ⚜ ⚜

This book was predicted many years ago by my friend, a well-known psychic, Frank Andrews, who encouraged me to write my stories even though I protested; I am forever grateful for his vision. This book could not have happened if it wasn't for Joe Kulin, my longtime friend turned my literary agent, who believed in me and held my hand even at times when I lost faith. Gratitude to my client Roberto Guerra, the filmmaker who made me promise at his deathbed to resume my art career by illustrating this book. Huge credit goes to Ehud Sperling and the Inner Traditions team that guided me every step of the way.

I am grateful beyond words to my wife Margalit who was always there for me, listening to my outlandish stories and growing frustrations, and to my children Ariel, Tal, and Shira who tolerated my unexpected excursions into the unknown shamanic territories of the Andes and Amazon and came out to support me.

My thanks to June Balish, Mindy Melemed, Nora Logan, David Rothenberg, and Shira Beery who took their precious time to help me sort it all out and to Thieu Besselink whose firm encouragement and friendship I valued immensely. Huge thank you to my dearest friend, Ariel Orr Jordan, whose loving, guiding hands and generosity of spirit

I tremendously value. His first recognition of the shaman in me pushed me to become who I am today in spite of my inner doubts and protests. Our daily early morning exchanges as we walked around Washington Square Park were a great laboratory for this book. Deep gratitude goes to Samuel Jakob Kirschner who walks the seeker-of-truth path with me. Both Ariel and Samuel play major parts in my life and in this book, and I thank them for the many years of adventures and unwavering sacred brotherhood. And to Barbara Ensor for her loving support, thank you.

I am forever indebted to my teachers and mentors—first and foremost Don José Joaquin Piñeda who initiated me into his family's tradition and Ipupiara (Dr. Bernardo D. Peixoto) and his wife Cleicha—for their trust and their love throughout the years. I am thankful for the generosity of the many incredible shamanic teachers and elders from around the world whom I was fortunate to encounter during this great journey that gifted me with their treasured knowledge. I hope I am worthy of their teachings; their names could fill up a whole chapter in this book.

I want to give special acknowledgment to John Perkins for his inspirational work and for writing the foreword to this book.

My fellow core members of the New York Shamanic Circle are most treasured by my family and me; thank you for your support, challenges, friendship, and invaluable teaching during the past eighteen years. I also want to express my special thanks to my clients and my students around the world who taught me so much more than I taught them.

Most of all, I am in reverence and gratefulness to the Spirits of the unseen worlds and my spirit guides for teaching me and allowing me to interact with them to bring healing for those in need. And for those of you whom I never thanked for their contribution to the book and my life I do so now.

INTRODUCTION

⚡ ⚡ ⚡ ⚡

FROM SKEPTIC
TO BELIEVER

Don José stopped on his heels in the middle of a dark busy avenue of
Corona, Queens. He turned to me, paused, and looked up at me with
his fierce black eyes, "Did you start doing healings?" he asked. Perplexed,
I watched this short, powerful shaman whom I admired, dressed in a
blue llama-wool poncho, white cotton pants, white fabric sandals, and
a gray felt fedora, in total disbelief. I pretended to not understand him.

"So, did you?" he prodded me.

"Oh no, I didn't, was I supposed to?" I finally said and went on
anxiously protesting, "I'm not ready. How can I? I know nothing about
it. I'm not even sure that this is what I want to do with my life."

"You are ready," he declared flatly and with authority. "Vamos, let's
go eat now," he said as he opened the door to a Chinese restaurant.

This was unexpected. My thoughts were racing. *What does he
mean? Do I have to change my life?* I was confused and also frightened
by the weight of the enormous responsibility he put on my shoulders.
Immediately my old self-doubts cropped up like monsters looming
out of their cage. *Is he tricking me? What does he want from me or
see in me? How can he be so sure I have what it takes to do what he
does? Besides, I am a declared skeptic, cynic and atheist. I'm just an
ordinary middle-aged man who was brought up as a communist Jew.*

1

Oh my God, what did I get myself into? Do I have to? Why me? Why now?

Before we start on this fascinating journey I must confess to you that for the longest time I did not allow myself to believe in the mounting evidence of the existence of unseen worlds, nor did I take the time to learn about them. But despite my doubts I was slowly forced to admit their existence and relevance; I found that I just did not have any other choice. At this point I no longer tried to intellectualize or understand these things in a rational way, as the shamanic experience is truly about learning to surrender to the magical and join in the workings of life's mysterious forces. I'm now convinced that we human beings are truly living in multidimensional realities and that as humans we have the ability to perceive knowledge, images, and information otherwise hidden from our ordinary senses by shifting from the earthly plane into a shamanic state of higher vibrational consciousness. I believe that this is the key to humans' survival for hundreds of thousands of years. It is not trickery or self-delusion as many more scientific and logical people might say, as we'll see later.

Like me and perhaps you, there are millions of people who are now awakening every day, like sprouts after a long rain, to the call to embrace this age-old knowledge. Many indigenous societies have continuously lived with this wise worldview from the very beginning of time. We, in the technological, so-called First World, have forgotten it and in many ways have learned to despise it and label it as backward or primitive, rejecting it outright without even examining it. As the ancient Maya and Inca prophecies point out, since 1993 we entered into a new Pachacuti, a time of realignment and correction of the human journey and consciousness. It is time to be awakened and accept our true nature, by living in equilibrium and harmony between the two opposing and complementary forces of feminine and masculine that exist within each of us. It is a time to take the long overdue journey from our minds to meet our hearts. Only then, when the heart and the mind live in harmony, we can resolve war, poverty, and environmental destruction and ensure future generations' survival on this miraculous planet.

I must confess that like many contemporary males I'm truly excited to play with the latest technologies and gadgets, read about new scientific discoveries, and hear about fresh innovations in every field, and I am sure I passed this enthusiasm to my kids. The future fascinates me, ignites my imagination, and sets free my fantasies. Growing up, I admired my dad's constant search for new ways to improve machines to achieve better production and develop processes to make life's tasks more efficient and convenient. I believe inventiveness and curiosity is ingrained in our DNA, as it is essential to our successful survival as a species on Earth. We have truly achieved a lot in the past few hundred years. We are now able to communicate in an instant all across the planet. Distances have become shorter; we travel into space; we predict the weather a year in advance; our homes are becoming digitized and weather insulated; we harvest solar, wind, and water energies; we engineer food to have long shelf lives; we have a DNA map of our bodies, better medical diagnostic tools, and robotic machines; and we all live longer.

No doubt this process is speeding up exponentially, as my friend Ray Kurzweil and other scientists say. And as this process accelerates, we need to rethink what kind of future human beings we are evolving into. We are now paying a huge price for these advances environmentally as a society as well as individually in our own physical, emotional, and spiritual existence. Obesity is at a record high. More people are using anxiety pills. Religious fanaticism is spreading like brush fire. It seems to me there is social disengagement and a disconnection from nature, which leads us to forget the most important aspect of who we truly are. Humans, like all animals, learn about the world through—and are entirely dependent on—their ability to employ their heightened senses for their survival: the ability to smell whether food is good or rotten; the coming rain; smoke from fire; and the subtleties in the fragrances of flowers. Touching, feeling, seeing, telepathically communicating over long distances, and energetically connecting to the wisdom and knowledge of spirits and our ancestors are all part of our human birthright.

This process of digitally shutting down the senses can be illustrated by this example. As a young graphic designer I still witnessed the use of hot type presses, where each character was set individually by pouring molten metal into a tiny mold and once cold it was hand assembled into a word, a sentence, and a story. The press took a group of three people to operate. Today we only have to type on a virtual keyboard and watch it appear on a flat screen. To create a brochure, we used to personally meet with the client, come up with a concept, draw a sketch in pencil, use water colors, colored paper, or markers (I still love that smell) to fill it in, and measure and draw the brochure's size on a board with three different color pens. Once the copywriter's copy was approved, we sent it to a typesetter. Getting back the galleys, we rolled it into a wax machine (which produced a great smell and texture) at a particular temperature. We then glued everything together on a white board, covered it with transparent paper for protection, and sent it by messenger for the client's approval. Only then did it go to the printer, who then did color separations, prepared plates, etc. Today one person, using only his or her eyesight, with a click of a mouse chooses from prepared color palettes, template sizes, stock photography, and illustrations and can complete this entire process in less than a day on a flat computer screen in a virtual reality without leaving his or her chair. The tactile, physical, sensory, communicative, and team elements of the old process are gone.

Modern technology has certainly made our lives much easier and more convenient, but at the same time it has also separated us from nature. And in the process it has isolated and detached us from our own true human nature. This has bred in us a fear of nature and the unseen worlds that we cannot control. As technology progresses we are learning to shut down our own senses. Instead we rely on smartphone apps. We use these apps for everything from weather forecasting and GPS navigation to finding out about star constellations and taking our pulses. We have learned not trust our eyes anymore because we have an app for face recognition. We do not even have to trust our memory because everything's stored on the Internet and it's so easy to use Google. Consequently, there is a universal memory loss; I no longer need to calculate numbers or remember phone numbers and addresses as I used to because all this information is stored in my smartphone. Who needs to learn a new language when you can have an app that translates simultaneously? The danger is that we lose trust in our senses and ourselves. To diagnose our bodies we put our trust in the medical system. To know the truth about the world we trust what our politicians and the corporate media tell us. To know how to dress we trust the fashion gurus. We give our religious leaders the monopoly on the connection to spirit. We are attempting to make logical sense of and, by extension, control nature, not live in harmony with it.

More and more people are plugged into technology 24/7. *Unplugging* and *digital detox* have now become buzzwords among the high number of gadget-users. People yearn for a time out—a break from the constant slavery of being connected—in order to gain a new perspective on life. There are even Internet rehab centers and technology-free vacations and retreats popping up to help us cope with "reality"! At Shaman Portal (www.shamanportal.org), the website I created as a hub for the global shamanic community, statistics show that three quarters of the visitors to the site come from the technologically advanced societies of the United States and Europe.

This sensory shutdown is real. You can tell by looking at the millions of eyes that are constantly glued to the two-dimensional screens of our smartphones, tablets, computers, and TVs. I am concerned human beings are becoming handicapped, dependent, and sometimes purely apathetic as we trade in our birthright sensual gifts and abilities for the gifts of technology. I believe we are in danger of losing our place as a species. Learning to trust and allow all your senses to come alive again can make you fully engage in life around you. The practice of shamanism helps to reestablish the "seeing" (our sixth sense or intuition), which is an important part of our ability to survive. Seeing is not linear or logical. It communicates to us in symbols, through poetry and idioms, and in body language, colors, shapes, smells, and bodily sensations.

WHY A BOOK OF STORIES?

This book started with a vision—somebody else's, though. "Pages, pages, pages—I 'see' white pages flying all around you," Frank Andrews exclaimed, waving his right hand in the air in a large circle around his head. We were sitting in his cozy wood-paneled reading room for my yearly tarot card reading. A large flower arrangement and an antique crystal ball sat in the middle of the round table as my opened cards were spread in formation on the embroidered tablecloth. "You are going to write a book," he proclaimed with unshakable certainty.

"Me? A book? Oh no, Frank, that's totally ridiculous. I don't have anything to write about or say. I am not a writer, I'm a visual artist. English is not even my first language . . . " I went on protesting, finding all the excuses I could think of.

"But you will," he repeated, looking at me through his large eye-glasses with his big, warm brown eyes. He giggled, saying, "You'll see, you will see. Start writing stories about your healing experiences and spirit encounters, a page at a time." I started to feel a certain excitement, but also mixed with a lot of doubt. Frank's five little white Papillon dogs barked in excitement, looking at us with high curiosity from the gated kitchen door. I had met Frank, said to be one of the ten best psychics in the world, whose portrait was painted by Andy Warhol a few years earlier, and we had formed a close friendship. Later on you will read about a dream he starred in. And so it was, despite my disbelief and doubt in his "seeing."

Some years before this it was an unexpected initiation vision I received in the High Andes that started me on an apprenticeship with my teacher and on the shamanic healing path. You will read about this later too.

I am not unique by any means. The truth is that many other shamans, healers, and seekers, as well as ordinary people, have had similar experiences. But I can only fully stand behind my own experiences, and I hope these will prompt you on your own path.

I am aware that writing this book goes against an old shamanic tradition of oral knowledge transmission. There is a reason why you never find books written by indigenous shamans prior to recent years. The concept of writing down wisdom teachings that have been passed down to shamans by their ancestors or from spirits—which they do not "own" to begin with, as they belong to everyone—has been unthinkable for most of history. Shamans believe that knowledge is not static; it is a living thing that changes in every moment in time, like nature herself. There are only a few things that do not change: the direction in which the sun rises and sets; the seven cardinal directions; and birth and death. Shamans believe that putting knowledge and wisdom down on pieces of paper and binding it between two covers freezes its energy and does not allow it or the reader to develop and grow. The Bible, the Holy Book as it is called, was itself a collection of tribal stories that were passed down as teachings from fathers to sons through many generations. You can expect that each person added his own version and interpretation. But once it was inscribed on parchment or animal skin, the religious authorities forbade changing even one period, let alone challenging it. Worse, some believed that God Himself transcribed it and, if so, we must apply every word, written thousands of years ago, to our more pluralistic and advanced technological society. This attitude has led to close-mindedness and fanaticism, as we see now in many societies around the world. Lacking their own direct experience of the Creator and nature, the representatives of the various religions try to impose their teachings on people. There have been many times that I asked my two teachers to write down their teachings, thoughts, and healing techniques for a book, and I always got slippery answers: "Maybe. . . ." "One day. . . ." "We'll see. . . ."

Actually, scientific teachings are not all that different. All around the world, every day, students sit behind their desks to learn and be tested on scientific "facts" that don't keep up with the times. Moreover, these can even prove to be misleading as every day we learn new things about our solar system, the brain, the body, nature, and human history. Our textbooks are mostly outdated and full of assumptions, not facts, and do not challenge students to discover their world. On the other hand, stories that have been passed down orally, requiring us to learn in more holistic and collaborative ways than pure memorization, teach us about ourselves, our morality, and our values as well as the universal laws and the limitless magic of the universe.

And yet I have to contradict myself again, because I acknowledge that books are a powerful and useful way to effect and spark ideas, to move people to action, and to expand consciousness and possibilities. After all, it was Hank Wesselman's book *Spiritwalker* that introduced me to the world of shamanism. And it was a workshop by Michael Harner, who wrote *The Way of the Shaman,* that brought me to another workshop given by John Perkins, who wrote *The World Is as You Dream It,* which in turn guided me to becoming an apprentice of Don José Joaquin Piñeda, who in turn introduced me to the shaman Ipupiara. And it was a book by Olga Kharitidi, *Entering the Circle,* that opened my eyes to the phenomenon of holographic seeing. And it was a book by Sandra Ingerman, *Soul Retrieval,* about that ancient practice that greatly influenced me. I must also say that even before all of that I eagerly devoured all the books by Carlos Castaneda and Lynn Andrews that I could find. Following in this tradition, and without pretending to be an authority on the subject, I chose to write a book of stories that might connect with you emotionally and guide you indirectly into the shamanic ways of "seeing."

THE POWER OF VISION

Deep within each and every one of us, I believe, lie dormant visionary powers waiting to be realized and freed from the confines of our fears, cultural taboos, and old habits. Once in a while we get spontaneous glimpses of them in the forms of dreams, experiences of déjà vue, unplanned visions, out-of-body experiences, and other phenomena. Most people learn to minimize these experiences: "Just a silly coincidence"; "An accident"; "Only a dream." However, I am convinced that once recognized and intentionally applied to our lives, these powerful intuitive experiences can help us become more in tune with life and help us live in harmony with everything around us, and so make us whole.

Being in touch with our "seeing," our visions, can help us also chart new paths not only for our own life, but for society as a whole, hopefully allowing us to create a sustainable world that honors each individual person as magnificent, promotes equality between people, and builds respect for all animals, plants, and the natural elements. That is why shamans the world over believe that each of us can be a shaman possessing the potential to change him- or herself and the world around us. That is what makes the shamanic practice so relevant to our digital modern age. After all, the premise of the practice of shamanism is to foster real, measurable physical, emotional, and mental change.

Going forward you will read actual, true stories that span generations: stories of premonitions and forewarning dreams; stories of people who have long since passed and have returned to inflict pain or to bring objects to their rightful owners; stories of past lives that continue to influence people's lives in the present; stories about remote viewing of illness or emotional or physical problems, of seeing into others' life situations and homes; stories of meeting people in the spirit world and then meeting them again in real life; stories of seeing spirits of animals that are embedded in people's bodies, and of seeing spirits of unborn or aborted children. You will read about visions of gods and other spiritual entities as they come in holograms, and about animal spirits that manifest in our reality. Through these stories I hope you will be guided to unleash your inner modern-day shamanic powers, to ignite your natural intuition, and to become a shamanic warrior, one that learns to face your innermost fears and to act decisively to achieve your goals and dreams in spite of them. These are my experiences; I hope they will inspire you too.

Most of the stories that you are about to read occurred in my life over the past few years.* I initially recorded them in an effort first to convince myself, and maybe others, that there are some universal phenomena whose origins we may not completely understand at this time, but nevertheless can have an incredibly useful and practical value in our daily lives. The common thread in these stories is that they all started in a vision or a dream, sometimes invited and other times not, and ended up manifesting in what we call "reality." Although many different spirits played an important role in each of these events, the stories are not intended to be spiritual; as I said, they were written simply to record facts, and maybe to inspire.

Messages from spirits in the form of power animals, guides, and teachers during shamanic journeys to other worlds, nightly dreams, or meditation allow us to receive useful insights, answers, knowledge, and healing for others or ourselves. But these techniques are not new. Similar techniques have been used since the beginning of human time by healers and shamans in all indigenous cultures all over the world. The word *shaman* is translated as "person who possesses the knowledge" in Tungus, Siberia. Or as a contemporary Tungus shaman claimed when I asked him, "the keeper of fire," which I like better as it widens the shaman role to the whole community. A shaman (a see-er) is a person who journeys to nonordinary realities in an altered state of consciousness, at his or her own will, and brings back knowledge that can effect physical or mental changes in this realm for the purpose of healing or for knowledge. There are various ways shamans reach these realms—by chanting, drumming, dancing, consuming hallucinogenic brews, or eating mushrooms—but their goal is always the same: to tap in to and connect and align with the vast source of knowledge found in the natural

---

*Please note that most of the names and some of the situational details have been altered in order to protect the privacy of my clients.

world, where all knowledge exists. The shamans with whom I have met or worked insist that all humans have the inherent ability to tap in to this source. Throughout our lives we experience this involuntarily and call it *coincidence, intuition, miracle,* or other names.

⦿ In my workshops I like to tell participants that all humans are walking iPhones. We all have bodies—the phone itself. And we all have software—our brain. And like iPhones, we all have transmitters and receivers or antennas, which enable us to broadcast and receive information to and from long distances out of thin air. As with an iPhone, we can't see the waves of information that enter or depart our bodies; they are pure energy, which travels via different vibrations. But nevertheless we know they exist, as we have the direct experience of the phone ringing and Uncle Bob speaking to us from the other end. All we have to do is raise the bars of our intuitive power and embark on the journey that awaits us.

So let's start on this extraordinary adventure together. For me it was triggered, as I said earlier, by a book . . .

1

HOW
IT ALL STARTED

You heal with your heart's intention. No matter what you know or how big a toolbox you've got.

IPUPIARA

It's hard to pinpoint an exact moment or a specific time. It could have begun at the time I emerged from my mother's womb, which I will describe soon, but it was not until a sunny morning in 1995 that a dark green hardcover book with a strange, colorful illustration and strange name would start me on a fast, bizarre, and fascinating path. In this book I discovered a new world of earthly and spiritual belief systems and ancient healing practices, and was confronted with divination capabilities I never suspected I had. And maybe most fascinating of all, it was the beginning of my journey, in which I encountered, learned from, and worked with powerful, mysterious, colorful, and strange men and women—the shamans by many names and from many different cultures who mentored me and whom I grew to love. I will tell you more about this soon.

⚉ A Chance Encounter at a Local Bookstore

Looking back with the benefit of hindsight, it all looks so reasonable and predictable, as if it was planned by an unseen guiding hand. But in the summer of 1995 it wasn't so clear to me—maybe to the Great Creator, but certainly not to me. I was in the middle of a midlife crisis, struggling to make sense of the past and lost in a thick fog of trying to figure out the future. I had already achieved many of my life goals— I had a beautiful family, had created a reasonable art career, and had made a successful life in the capital of the world, New York City. I had relative professional success, having received many design and advertising awards. But then a big, fat question started to haunt me: What next? Where is the next challenge? What is the reason to go forward? An old fear raised its head: When I was eighteen years old, my biggest fear was that I would live a boring life without meaning. I felt I was starting to slip into the dark cloud of depression. But a series of events changed everything for me.

That summer, Leighton Chong, my buddy from the Urban Gorillas, a men's support group I was part of, suggested I join him for a men's retreat at Kalani Retreat Center on the Big Island of Hawaii. Miraculously, the money I needed to attend manifested, as if sent by an angel. An hour before the car was to pick me up to take me to the airport I realized I didn't have a decent book to read on the long, ten-hour flight from New York. So I rushed a few blocks away, to a Barnes & Noble, and "by chance" picked up a book from the new releases shelf, *Spiritwalker: Messages from the Future,* by Hank Wesselman. It seemed like the right mix of Hawaiian culture, mystery, spirituality, and adventure—just the stuff I enjoy reading on a long plane ride.

As the plane took off I pulled out the new book and started reading. I was completely overtaken by the author's intriguing visionary autobiographical story and could not rest until I finished reading it. Many times while reading Hank's story I could not help but find myself identifying with his insights and messages. I had to stop from time to time and take a big breath, as I felt surprised and even grateful that someone else had the kind of thoughts, experiences, and observations that I had had throughout my life. It gave me hope; maybe after all I'm not *that* alone and not all *that* weird . . .

Somewhere close to the end of the book Mr. Wesselman mentioned his participation in a shamanic workshop facilitated by a man named Michael Harner. I didn't pay much attention to it, as even the word *shaman* wasn't yet familiar to me. But that was going to change soon. A few months later, while leafing through an upcoming events catalog for the New York Open Center, I came across a basic shamanic weekend workshop to be given by Michael Harner. Well, that was a "coincidence" I could not pass up, so I decided to join some two hundred other shamanic virgins.

That weekend we all gathered in a large school gymnasium. It was a large and chatty crowd. Michael Harner, white-haired and bearded and wearing heavy glasses, was armed with his drum and sat at the far end of the room. With a tinge of humor as well as seriousness he introduced us to the world of core shamanism, which he had founded based on his own experiences in the 1960s. He taught us how to journey to retrieve our own power animals and teachers in the upper, middle, and lower worlds. We also journeyed to somebody else's body and spirit to heal it. In our last journey we paired off to retrieve knowledge and healing for each other. I still remember vividly the vision and feelings I had when I journeyed for Pat, who happened to be sitting right next to me. I lay down next to her, touching her lightly. I covered my eyes and journeyed down my portal, a Hawaiian lava tunnel, to the lower world. Soon, a giant anaconda appeared in front of me. His big, muscular body was maneuvering forcefully with twists and turns through the muddy Amazonian riverbank, which was covered by dry, tall reeds. Sensing a great danger in the air, I looked all around me. In the far distance, opposite the anaconda on the muddy ground, was a bird's nest made of dry weeds. In the center of it lay three large white eggs. The bird was nowhere to be seen. I turned my attention back to the anaconda, which continued on his way in the direction of the nest. It was obvious to me that it was trying to devour or destroy the eggs. But it was not to be. I could not see the end of it. Michael changed the drumming rhythm, signaling us to come back.

 As we sat across from each other to share our journeys, I apologized, as I was sure my "vision" had no bearing. But after listening to my story, Pat reassured me: "I just returned from an amazing trip to the Amazonian jungle of Ecuador, where I visited different shamans. This anaconda lives in that area and the river you described was similar to what I recall. I am currently working on three different projects; maybe the three eggs symbolize them. The anaconda, I believe, signifies a man I know whom I believe is like a snake, endangering and trying to destroy my projects." *That was impressive,* I thought. She thanked me then for confirming her suspicions about that man.

This vision and those shared by the other participants at that workshop impressed me greatly. It felt like a window had just opened enabling me to "see" into other realities. I wanted more—maybe to join a weekly drumming circle to continue this work. Unfortunately, my initial few attempts to form such a group were not successful. Two years later, I returned from my first trip to Ecuador, led by John Perkins and Joyce Ferranti of the Dream Change Coalition—a similar trip to one Pat had taken a few years back. Following this I took a seven-week workshop, "Practicing Shamanism," at the New York Open Center, with Nan Moss and David Corbin from the Foundation for Shamanic Studies. These experiences led me to help co-found the New York Shamanic Circle, which I'm still a proud member of.

I met John Perkins for the first time at his New York Open Center workshop. His honest enthusiasm, firsthand knowledge of the indigenous Shuar and Quechua cultures and shamanic practices in Ecuador, and his powerful environmental message completely resonated for me. I just knew I had to go to Ecuador. Don't ask me why; it was a pure gut feeling. Moreover, I could not fully explain this decision to my family. I just had to go. So, I enlisted my two great friends, Samuel and Ariel, to join me. It proved to be a very good decision, as we became the trip's Three Musketeers, looking for fun and adventure everywhere we went, some of which I describe later in this book. But this threesome also provided the essential support system we each needed as we challenged ourselves during this life-altering trip.

That March of 1997 I first met the shamans I subsequently worked with, most importantly Don José Joaquin Piñeda, a fifth-generation *yachak* (a shaman or medicine man) from the village of San Juan de Ilumán near Otavalo, who became my teacher. Through many healing ceremonies, workshops, and personal conversations, mostly translated by his daughter Soraya (as my Spanish is very, very limited), who also studied with him, he passed down some of his ancient family healing traditions to me. In 2000, without announcing it, with his loyal wife and my family looking on, he initiated me at nightfall and crowned me into the circle of twenty-four male yachaks at a sacred Magdalena spring, which streams into Lago San Pablo on the slope of the formidable volcanic Imbabura Mountain, and later in his modest healing room in Otavalo. It was an unexpected event, not usually given to gringos like me. Of course, the questions and doubts popped up in my head: "Why me? What does he see in me that I don't recognize?"

I have always been attracted to spiritual phenomena. I had had a few spontaneous experiences too, such as an out-of-body experience, or knowing who was calling before the phone rang. As a teenager, walking in the old city of Jerusalem, I had detailed visions of bloody wars as I touched the large ancient stonewalls, and got a horrible splitting headache. Years later as I arrived in Florence, I knew how to walk to my hotel as if I had lived there before. As a visual artist there have been times when I had spontaneous visions of new paintings to be painted.

Sometime in the early 1980s I had my first encounter with what shamans call "seeing." It happened while taking a palmistry course with

Richard Unger, who later become a good friend, and with whom I later co-led life-purpose workshops in the United States and Europe. As part of my developing clairvoyance we had to touch a specific area in our client's palm and tell the person what we saw in their childhood. The images I saw were vivid and strong. They were also very accurate and detailed, bringing up an incident of my client's abuse as a child, which was very disturbing to both of us. This newfound ability to see profoundly scared me. I suppose I wasn't ready for it yet and didn't know how to protect myself. I remember distinctly how my face turned white, the blood drained out of me, and I was left weak and lethargic. This is known as *energy leakage*. I decided not to continue with these studies, although I did use this gift on a few occasions with similar success. Slowly, with practice, I learned how to sustain my energy. With the help of Don José, the floodgate of visions and other experiences opened. But what should I do with it?

⋏ EARLY EXPERIENCES

In hindsight, my upbringing turned out to be the perfect introduction to the basic principles of shamanism: deep connection to nature, close encounters with death, boundless imagination, a sense of history, and the importance of community and storytelling.

I was born in Kibbutz Beit Alpha on the eastern border of the Yezrael Valley, not very far from the Sea of Galilee, in Israel. The kibbutz had been founded on the slopes of the Mount Gilboa range, to avoid the malaria-bearing mosquitos and wild boars that roamed freely in the nearby vast swamps that had welcomed the first settlers. King David (circa 1010 BCE), as it was written in the Bible, deep in grief, had cursed Mount Gilboa "Ye mountains of Gilboa, let there be no dew, neither let there be rain upon you, nor fields of offerings: for there the shield of the mighty is vilely cast away, the shield of Saul, as though he had not been anointed with oil . . ." (Samuel II, 1:21) as he heard of the death of King Saul and his son Jonathan, whom he loved, in a battle with the Philistines.

Ours was the first kibbutz—a collective farm—of the Zionist Hashomer Hatzair movement, a fact we wore around our necks in pride, like Mayflower descendants. Established in 1922 by young and enthusiastic Jewish Russian and Polish immigrants, the first kibbutzniks dreamed of returning to the biblical Land of Milk and Honey, returning to work our forefather's soil and build a just society of "a new human model," where we is more important than I, where the well-being of the community is more important than that of any single individual. The founders were proud atheists—they did not believe in spirituality or religion per se, except for the beliefs of Marx and Lenin, and they held Stalin as their sun. Jewish holidays were celebrated as festivals of nature and the changing of the seasons with very little reference to any religious meaning—most likely in the same shamanic ways the ancient Hebrews practiced. We did study the Bible, but as pure history, more like an anthropology book of our ancestors.

Many years later I was invited to lead a shamanic workshop in my old kibbutz for a special women's day celebration. I asked the forty mothers and daughters who were participating to connect to the spirit of Mount Gilboa and bring a personal message for them. It was a fascinating realization to hear how each of the women experienced and personified the mountain, all very intimately. He was a powerful protector from the sun, the winds, and the Arabs on the other side. He was a gentle lover, bringing flowers and life. He was to be feared, with his blackness and wild animals. He was an ancient history teacher. An overbearing father. A mighty witness and observer of our lives. All the women had a very personal relationship with the mountain's essence, and it impacted their everyday lives as deeply as it had mine. Could this also be why later in life I felt so at home and at ease in the Andes and with mountain people in general?

My first conscious memory was of the sound of birds. I was not even a year old, lying on my back in a white metal crib that stood on a lawn by the nursery house. Transparent cheesecloth covered my crib to protect me from the unforgiving sun and the buzzing flies. I remember waking up all alone. There was no other crib or human being around me. "It was your daily sunbath, you needed vitamin D, you were sick," my mother told me many years later. Terrified, not knowing if anyone would ever come for me, I listened to the repetitive mourning doves cooing on the tall *Dalbergia* tree (Indian rosewood) nearby: *Greu, greu, greu, greu, greu.* Even now, whenever I hear this mesmerizing cooing sound, it takes me back to those upsetting moments of loneliness and abandonment.

As children of the 50s we grew up intimate with nature. We walked barefoot most of the time. We planted trees on the dry, yellow mountain in an attempt to transform that old biblical curse. Coyotes howled the nights away, deer grazed in the topmost hidden valley of the mountain, and under every stone you could find poisonous yellow and black scorpions, while snakes abounded. We pulled worms out of the heavy, wet, fertile soil. We watched brown fur nutrias swimming in the fishponds, collected porcupine needles, and watched black bats flying and hedgehogs running in a hurry around our houses at night. Lizards crawling on the window screens were a common sight. We took long hikes and trips into the valley, desert, and mountains. We followed excitedly the many kinds of migrating and local nesting birds, turtles, and winter snails leaving their long gooey trail after them. We knew by name every tree, shrub, plant, and flower growing in the fields around us and on the mountain. We danced in excitement as the first raindrops fell from the sky on the summer's dry soil. We'd be terrified during the dark nights that were fueled by a barrage of piercing lightning and exploding thunder. We could hear the heavy rain pulling rocks and mud through the narrow creek, which we named Wadi Cacao, for the brown, muddy water that ran through it, creating a powerful winter waterfall on a rock formation we called King Solomon's Throne, just beyond our children's house, where we lived separately from our parents, or any adults. We picked different kinds of wild mushrooms and colorful assortments of wildflowers after the rains. We raised chickens, peacocks, goats, rabbits, sheep, and cows. We watched them giving birth, watched them grow up, and then watched them be slaughtered or die naturally.

As we grew older we were assigned to daily work in the vegetable garden and fields, harvesting fresh olives, grapes, grapefruits, and carobs. I spent time helping my father as he worked at the Gan Bait, the first organic vegetable garden in the country, with another inventive man, where they developed a new breed of vegetables more suitable for our land, as well as ways to fight insects without the use of chemicals. There were few radios and no televisions, record players, or computers to sedate us. We had one public phone to connect us to the outside world. We pretty much played in our natural habitat with sticks, rocks, and our imagination. And imagination we had aplenty: the storage room by the basketball field turned into a witch's house. The lone tree on the mountaintop became my guardian. We played thieves and robbers and all kinds of inventive outdoor games. As teenagers we joined the Youth Movement. We often spent time sitting in circles, sometimes around a bonfire, much like a shamanic talking circle, and learned to share our thoughts, listen to others, and discuss challenges. Growing up in the small, tight-knit, isolated community of the few hundred people in my kibbutz was a perfect laboratory to learn about the fragility of human nature. But it certainly had its challenges.

For me, growing up on that land was like living in two parallel realities, the present and that of our ancients, who had left their marks and footsteps there. I believe it instilled in me a deep sense of a tribal continuum. This was confirmed literally when not too far behind our children's house members of our kibbutz, while laying water pipes, discovered an ancient synagogue buried under a pile of land, and the remains of a thriving school from a Jewish settlement from the sixth century CE. Its elaborate mosaic floor with Jewish symbols became well-known worldwide; it depicted the zodiac of the twelve Hebrew months, and inscribed in the mosaic floor were the synagogue's protector symbols of the lion, the dove, and the buffalo. At the onset of the winter rains we used to collect Roman coins washed down from the mountain. Old pottery shards and flint arrows of all sizes were all around us, and many of us had an impressive collection of them. We sat in the same caves the ancients used, along the cliff overlooking the valley below, and climbed down ancient grain silos carved deep into the soft chalk rocks. We dipped in the cold spring that bares the name of Gideon, the mighty biblical warrior. Even the names of all sixteen of my class members were biblical names. I truly felt like a son returning to live on his unknown father's ancient land.

My parents raised me to denounce any reference to the Jewish religion, even though my grandmother Rashka, who lived with us, prayed devotedly several times a day, as was expected of her, having come from a rabbinical family. I recently learned through a newly found old article about my great-grandfather Mordechai Zundel Margolis (my mother's grandfather) that he was a well-known Kabalistic rabbi and healer in Kolno, Poland, who devoted his life to the eternal fight between the forces of good and evil in the universe. Since starting my own work as a shamanic healer I became immersed in this aspect as well, without knowing that fact about him.

I was a surprise child, the youngest of four siblings. As a young boy I was skinny, "like a pencil," or as my caretaker would say, "You are blue and transparent." I was highly sensitive and sick most of the time, as my immune system had been compromised by sickness early on. "If it wasn't for your mother you would not be here with us," my father told me one night while holding my hand before he passed on. "You had typhus in the stomach when you were just a few months old. She sat by your side around the clock, feeding you with a dropper, washing you with icy towels to cool your boiling temperature. Everyone gave up on you, but she fought against all odds to save you." Funny—I looked up the word typhus; it derives from the Greek word for "smoke" or "stupor," because of the hallucinations that it induces in the sick person's mind.

At the age of four I had another meeting with death. While learning to swim in the little kidney-shaped children's pool, I was tiptoeing to the deepest part of the pool when I lost my footing and was sucked into the drain. With all my tiny power I flapped my arms and hit the bottom. It was my father who jumped over the pool fence and into the water with his shoes and clothes on to rescue me. I still remember that moment vividly, in horror, shame, and gratitude.

And as if that wasn't enough, I had a third encounter with death. This time it was on a beautiful winter day, right after a night of a heavy rain. Climbing up the mountain with my sister, we picked wildflowers to bring home to our mom. On our way up we picked lots of red anemone. But then we discovered a lone white daffodil with a golden crown in its center standing in the middle of a huge, wet, steep rock. I decided we must have it too. Against my older sister's objections, I took a few sidesteps in my slippery rubber boots, as my father had taught me, and lost my footing. Next thing I knew, I was rolling fast down the smooth, slanted rock at a huge speed. Short of breath and in a panic, I knew I was going to die, when luckily a ledge almost at the very bottom caught my sweater. My poor sister, frightened out of her wits, ran all around that rock to collect me. To this day she can't forget that terrifying moment.

From then on, death was a familiar entity to me and I was fascinated by it throughout my childhood. Somehow I believed I did not belong here; I wished to go "back home," to the other side, as the old Amazonian Umbanda priestess Bibi once told me many years later. Maybe it was why many years later I burst out with a long, uncontrollable sob of longing at the end of the Mayan initiation bodywork session held by my shaman friend Antonio Oxteik, as I saw my soul group floating in a perpetual cosmic dance, many souls eternally moving in harmony through space. I instinctively knew that I was seeing my real home.

Every night at the children's house before bedtime our caretaker who put us to sleep gathered us in one room to read us fables and stories. I loved hearing those stories as they allowed me to enter into the other worlds of magic, and I had a strong need to tell my own stories and share my own ideas too. But the woman who was my daily caretaker did not have the patience and time to listen to everything I had to say. "You are too chatty; you talk nonstop and too much," she used to complain and tried to brush me off. One day when she had had enough she took me aside, bent down, looked at me sternly, and said, "Itzhak, God gave each of us a limited amount of words to use in our lives. If you use them all up, you will die." I knew it was not true, but nevertheless I took what she said to heart. In shamanic language, as I later came to understand, that was a curse. After that I learned to control myself, fearing I would waste my words. I lived in that fear, so whenever I talked in front of groups my stomach churned, my heart palpitated, and I even used to pee in my pants. I came to convince myself that I had nothing worth saying, that what I thought wouldn't matter to anyone. In his hand analysis reading many years later, Richard Unger shared with me, as he deciphered my fingerprint codes, that my life purpose is to be "a man with a message who needs a large stage to express himself." To hear this said with such clarity was a turning point for me, one that literally set me free from that curse and my self-imposed restrictions. As I write my personal stories I realize that it is an act of profound personal healing for me. I have a deep-rooted fear of putting down on paper my innermost thoughts, feelings, and experiences, a fear that my class members, family, or the entire kibbutz will discover the true me. We grew up without even minimal privacy among hundreds of watchful eyes, with nowhere to hide. We had no personal rooms, locked drawers, or cabinets in which to keep a diary, secrets, or our personal belongings. We had no choice but to conform to the expectation of our society, or wear an invisible shield around us for fear of being exposed and ridiculed.

ᛉ CYNICAL AND SUSPICIOUS

I learned the hard way to be cynical and a doubter. I grew up being aware that my peers considered me extremely gullible. It seemed like every day was April Fool's Day. They laughed at me without any hesitation when I fell for their fabricated stories. I just could not understand why anyone would make things up just to trick me and make me feel like a fool, so I always fell into their trap. One incident from my childhood is deeply etched in my memory.

One afternoon when I was in the second or third grade, I came to visit my parents' house from the children's house, as it was common that the children lived separately from the adults. My sister took me aside. "Itzhak I have a big secret, do you swear not to tell anyone?" she whispered, putting her two hands around my ears. "I promise," I said, feeling so grownup and important. "This chewing gum you chew is made from rubber mixed with camel dung." I was shocked. "Camel dung?" I asked in disbelief. "Do you want to see?" She pulled out a pack and showed me the illustration on the yellow wrapping. Sure enough, it had a red camel picture in the center. She went on reading me the ingredients written on the back in English. Because she was already taking English classes I trusted her. A couple of months later I saw my beloved, most trusted sister pulling a stick of gum out of the same package and chewing on it. I was utterly confused and upset. She had tricked me too. I then made a conscious decision to shed my innocence, thinking *No one will ever fool me again. I need to ask for proof.* I didn't want to be hurt again and became suspicious and skeptical no matter what (in the shamanic language this is describe as soul loss). I guess we think of this as "mature" or "grownup." Funny—when I told my sister this story, not so long ago, she didn't remember it at all.

⚹

I have written the stories in this book as factually as possible, knowing full well that some of you might be as skeptical as I was, and rightly so. That is why it's been so hard for me to come to terms with my own shamanic experiences for the longest time. As I struggled to accept my visions I had many unanswered questions. Why and how do these images appear in my mind? Where are they stored? Who is volunteering all this information? Who is talking to spirits, angels, and teachers—my subconscious or me? How can we actually "see" other people's thoughts? From what materials are thoughts made of? Are all those spirits or images following us in our daily lives? Are they guiding us? Which of these alternative worlds is the "real" one—the world of dreams and visions, or this world we think we know so well? How does the body's energy field translate into images in our mind? Do they all exist simultaneously? Can we communicate with the dead? Where do we go after we pass over?

With so many unanswered questions, I turned to my friend, a prominent Israeli brain research scientist. I wanted him to scan my brain to understand where all these new-found images come from and why now. He listened patiently to some of these out-of-this-world stories, which you will be reading soon, and dismissed them. "There is no proof," he said with the glee of a know-it-all expert in his eyes, and summed it up as follows: "You need to repeat these exact experiences three times so the outcome will be the same each time, otherwise it is just coincidence." I challenged him to join my New York Shamanic Circle meeting, which made an exception and agreed to allow him in. At the end of the evening in which we journeyed to find our spirit animal, I had a convert.

"I just can't believe I met this lion; it was so real. I was afraid I would meet a cockroach, the most repulsive animal for me," he said. "Believe me, it was not my choice at all. It was surely a lion, and how did he know the answer to my question?" The scientist was bubbling with excitement. Some time later he confided to me that he subsequently incorporated this experience in his work.

A few years later over a sushi dinner at a local Greenwich Village restaurant as we reminisced about that evening's experience, my friend said, "I believe, as a person who intensively studied how our eyes and brain see light and process that information, that humans are unable to conceptualize the world as it really is. Each animal species sees the world differently according to its eyesight, light receptors, and brain processing capacity. We know that a frog with its limited vision sees the world foggier and with shorter range than an owl, gecko, or a bee. Or, for example, mantis shrimp have sixteen color receptors compared to humans who have only three. Same thing goes for our other senses; we have a limited range of experiencing nature, and that is why we can't fully comprehend it. And even if we do understand the mechanics of it, I believe that the act of seeing is still a mystery. As scientists we have to accept it."

"There is also the shamanic teaching that says the world is as we dream it, not as we see it," I interrupted him. "Many spiritual teachings say that that is the Great Mystery or The Unknown, what we may call God, which has no shape, form, or name."

"That seems to be true, and we may have to operate within this as we do our research," he said as he took a short breath and added, "Most serious scientists are afraid to go public with this understanding for fear of being outcast from the conservative scientific community." I was surprised to hear this coming from his mouth. "Why don't you say it?" I asked him.

"Oh, leave me alone, I'm not going to ruin my career." He waved his hands impatiently to dismiss me. I went looking for what the father of modern science, Albert Einstein, had said about that question in *The Merging of Spirit and Science:* "The most beautiful and most profound experience is the sensation of the mystical. It is the sower of all true science. He to whom this emotion is a stranger, who can no longer wonder and stand rapt in awe, is as good as dead. To know that what is impenetrable to us really exists, manifesting itself as the highest wisdom and the most radiant beauty which our dull faculties can comprehend only in their primitive forms—this knowledge, this feeling is at the center of true religiousness." He also said, "I see a pattern, but my imagination cannot picture the maker of that pattern. I see a clock, but I cannot envision the clockmaker. The human mind is unable to conceive of the four dimensions, so how can it conceive of a God, before whom a thousand years and a thousand dimensions are as one?"

I truly believe, as do many of the shamans I have had the great privilege of working with, that this capacity to bring knowledge and healing from alternative realities and parallel dimensions is a gift that all we humans share and, oddly enough, it is what makes us good survivors on this planet. Throughout the many workshops in which I have participated, taught, and organized, I have seen so-called ordinary people prove it time and time again. All you have to do is open a portal, trust your intuition, trust the spirits to guide you, and of course, practice.

2

⩗ ⩗ ⩗ ⩗

DREAMING

I believe in everything until it's disproved. So I believe in fairies, the myths, dragons. It all exists, even if it's in your mind. Who's to say that dreams and nightmares aren't as real as the here and now?

JOHN LENNON

Everyone, without exception, dreams a few times during the night; you just can't help it. And really, nobody knows why or how. Are dreams messages from the gods or our ancestors? Do they come from our unconscious, subconscious, or from the spirit world? Are all the characters in your dreams an aspect of yourself? Is it the way your mind processes information stored in a memory bank?

There are simple, ordinary dreams, recurring dreams, and foretelling dreams. Many of us also engage in daydreaming. Some people learn to control their awareness and consciously observe their dreams or interact with them to change the outcome, even to dream the same dream again the next night, as one does in lucid dreaming. Scientists have been working for years to locate the area in our brains that is responsible for dreaming, when we dream, and how often. They have even proved that animals dream. But no one knows for sure the "why."

I can remember a dream from early in my childhood quite vividly, even now . . .

⚡ BALLS OF LIGHT

As the wood-framed screen door closed behind our night caretaker, all I could do was watch it with trepidation. Laying my head on the mattress, I looked up at the lightbulb outside, above the door, to comfort myself from the inevitable thick, engulfing darkness, as the sound of coyotes howling on the mountain became stronger. I was maybe two years old, lying in the children's house in a big white crib surrounded by a high metal railing. I shared this room in a one-story building with two other kids, a boy, Danny, and a girl, Tamar. The children's house was a long distance away from my parent's house; that was how they raised us then in the kibbutz. I guess I had just fallen asleep when I saw two glowing balls of light. They were circling and hovering around each other in the dark space above me, one huge and the other smaller. I watched them with fright while they went on buzzing like two jet engines in perpetual circles, becoming faster and faster, making scary swooshing noises. Then, all of the sudden the small ball of light, in a quick, sharp turn, swallowed the larger one and disappeared. I woke up. My body was stiff and frozen. I couldn't figure out how the smaller ball was able to swallow the bigger one, wasn't that against reason and nature? Where did they come from? Were they aliens that came in spaceships?

That scary dream followed me on and off for more than eight years, always ending in the same way. To this day I can recall every detail and sound, and my body's trembling in the aftermath of this dream. For years I wondered at its meaning and where it came from . . .

Since the beginning of time the mystery of dreaming has fascinated humans. Many theories have been proposed that attempt to find reason and meaning in dreams. In certain indigenous societies a family starts each day by sharing their dreams so they can together decide how to proceed with the day's activities. In our family we always shared our dreams over breakfast, even if it felt uncomfortable. In some cultures dreams have been used to predict the future; in this way the Egyptian pharaoh had a special dream interpreter in his court to help him solve the kingdom's problems. American Indians hang dream catchers above their children's beds to "catch" bad dreams and protect youngsters from them.

Nobody knows for sure why we dream, what dreams are made of, where they come from, and what role they play in our mental and physical health. Some of our dreams seem to be important, helping us navigate our lives or warning us of danger. Shamans pay close attention to their clients' dreams. They can analyze and interpret them so the person can get insights into his or her life. In many of my workshops I often ask participants if they have had significant dreams; there are always raised hands, and amazing stories are told.

Since early childhood I have had many amazing dream experiences, a few of which I include here.

∿ ECUADOR CALLING

After signing up for my first trip to Ecuador in March 1997, which was led by John Perkins of Dream Change, I was full of excitement and anticipation. This was to be my first visit to the land of the High Andes, the condors, and the mysterious Inca, Maya, and Aztec peoples. It is part of the world I never imagined I would ever be drawn to visiting. On two separate nights during the two weeks prior to our departure I had detailed travel dreams. I only remember short parts of them, but in retrospect what I do remember seems very significant.

In the first dream I found myself standing in an unfamiliar South American city, feeling very confused. I was not alone; there were three other people with me. It was midday and we were standing in the middle of a big, bustling plaza. A large crowd of colorfully dressed locals were crossing the plaza, hurrying about their everyday chores. I looked around and could see Spanish-style buildings bordering the edge of the plaza, and one large church stood tall on the left side. At our feet, surrounding us on the well-worn cobblestones, were our big travelers' bags and belongings. Flocks of gray pigeons were busy humming excitedly all around, picking up leftover scraps and grains. We were obviously strangers waiting for someone to come to our assistance, feeling lost and restless and not knowing which way to turn. As I raised my head, I saw coming through the crowd in the distance a young local man dressed in plain western clothing. He walked directly toward us with sure steps and a big smile under his mustache, his arms open. "Hello, my name is Carlos," he introduced himself cheerfully in English. He seemed confident and inspired a feeling of trust. As I awakened, I pondered, "Who is Carlos? Perhaps he is one of the shamans who is waiting our arrival, but isn't he rather young?" I turned over on my side. "Naah, it's probably just my imagination." I dismissed that dream. But then a few nights later I had another peculiar, seemingly related dream.

All alone, I was climbing up a steep dirt road in a landscape I did not recognize. I found myself up on a big mountain. It felt like it was early afternoon; fresh, cool air blew around me, and I noticed that it was extremely quiet and a bit eerie. I looked down the hard-pressed dirt road. It was coarse because of the many unruly small stones sticking out from the ground. Tall green grass grew on both sides of the road. As I moved forward toward an unfamiliar village, I raised my eyes from the ground and saw on the right side, on the top of a steep hill, a secluded adobe house painted all in white. A strange knowing thought came to me in the dream: *That house must belong to a shaman.* But then as I awakened from this dream, I thought, *Maybe it was just wishful thinking.* Still, I was intrigued.

Excited and curious from these two dreams, I called Joyce, our bubbly, redheaded trip coleader, and asked her if she knew whether we were going to meet a young shaman by the name of Carlos. "Not as far as I know, but you can never tell," she said, laughing. "Why do you ask?"

I told her about these two odd dreams. "Do you recognize that house on the hill? Do you know if a shaman named Carlos lives in this house?" I asked her eagerly.

"You know," she said, and took a deep breath, "very strange things happen to people who go on these trips. This might be one of them," and she laughed again. Well, I felt a little embarrassed and even silly. But I was fascinated; I guessed I would soon find out.

Two weeks later, late on a Thursday night, Joyce and my two friends Ariel Orr Jordan and Samuel Kirschner and I landed at Quito's airport. We had decided to get a head start and come a few days before the arrival of the rest of the group the following Monday night. It was late and we were tired after the long trip, but also incredibly excited to start our adventure. We dragged our backpacks through customs and pushed them through the exit doors as soldiers with automatic rifles watched us suspiciously. We found ourselves surrounded by a colorfully dressed throng of hundreds of local people waiting impatiently for the arrival of their relatives. Since none of us spoke good Spanish, we arranged with a local travel agent for an English-speaking tour guide and a Jeep.

We finally made our way outside the airport terminal and stood there for what seemed like a long while, waiting for our guide to appear. *Are we in the right place?* I thought. A few moments later, deep within the crowd, I saw a young man dressed casually walking toward our group. "Hola, are you Joyce?" he asked. Joyce gladly accepted his hand with a big sigh of relief. "Bueno, follow me, my car is waiting up the road." We all piled in the Jeep, he slipped behind the wheel, and off we went into the cool Andean night toward our destination, Hosteria Guachala, about fifty miles north of Quito. Joyce proudly sat in the front seat as the three men crammed into the back. I was tired and cold and the high altitude's thin air didn't help my creeping migraine. We started singing, telling jokes, and having fun with our driver. We each introduced ourselves, and then I asked him his name. "Juan Carlos," he said, with his nice Spanish accent, "but please call me Carlos."

"Wow," I responded. Joyce turned her head to look at me with a shriek of hysterical laughter.

After a restful night's sleep and a delicious breakfast in this former sheep ranch turned into the region's oldest and most beautiful *hosteria,* we decided it was time to meet our first shaman. Carlos pulled a piece of paper out of his pocket on which he had scribbled a few names and addresses of the most highly recommended shamans in the Otavalo area. He suggested we start with Don Esteban Tamayo, who lived only a short distance away. We all agreed. We drove off the Pan American Highway, witnessing for the first time in the morning light the beauty of the powerful Andes—the green cornfields, the cows and wooly llamas grazing on the green slopes. We turned left onto a paved road leading to a small village built on low, rolling hills. The small black pigs tied alongside the road were busy feeding on the grass, oblivious to our arrival. We continued on a winding dirt road between small adobe houses, stopped at a local bodega for the shaman's supplies, as it is customary to bring carnations, rum, eggs, and cigarettes for the healing ceremonies, and then drove on to Don Esteban's home. During the drive I kept looking, hoping to recognize the house I had seen in my dream. I was disappointed—nothing. "Okay, it was just a dream after all," I muttered.

Don Esteban, a tiny old man with a powerful presence, a dark, weathered face, shining black eyes, and a long black braid down his back, along with his two sons, José and Jorge, welcomed Joyce with open arms and led us into their dark healing room, which they shared with their cows and chickens. Then we each in turn had our healing sessions. After my ceremony, which was very powerful, and in which I had an emotionally wrenching past-life experience (described later in this book), I sat on the bench along the wall to rest awhile, observing the three shamans, who continued the healings on my friends.

I needed some fresh air. I decided to go outside. I walked slowly to the cornfields behind the outhouse and stood at the hill's edge, integrating the healing visions into my body while admiring the magnificent view of the rich Valley of the Dawn that lay below me. It was picturesque and magical. The tightly cultivated green and brown fields wove an intricate blanket that was shrouded by a mystical veil of clouds that came from over the soaring volcanic mountains, while the setting sun reflected the light in many warm colors. I took it all in and continued to walk farther down the hill into the valley, enjoying the cool breeze, listening to the sounds of children coming from the village below, and absorbing the healing energy I had just received. I stayed there a while longer. Then it was time to go back and join my friends. I turned back, and as I walked up the steep hill, a funny feeling came over me. It was as if I had been there before. Maybe just déjà vu? I tried to search my memory bank. I noticed the embedded stones in the dirt road, the tall grass along its sides, the lone adobe house of the shaman painted white at the village edge, and I remembered— just like in my dream. Was it a coincidence? Why did I need to see it before my arrival? Was it preparation for what was to come or a warning? Engulfed by these thoughts I went back up the hill.

⩘ A WARNING FOR A FRIEND

It was supposed to be just another ordinary night. Nothing had prepared me to be the messenger of a strange warning for a friend. As usual for me I went to bed late, having watched the late news and unwinding after a busy work day. Finally, I put my head down and fell asleep in no time. Suddenly I jerked up from out of my sleep. *Frank,* I thought, breathless from the intense dream I had just had. The big red numbers on the digital alarm clock showed it was 2 a.m. The house was quiet and in almost complete darkness. Next to me my wife slept. I felt confused, disoriented, and totally drained from extreme yelling in my dream: "Frank, Frank, please, I beg you, don't go to Michigan, you have nothing to do there, stay here and don't go. Your place is here in New York."

My wife, who is a light sleeper, turned over and asked me in a sleepy voice, "What's going on?"

"I don't really know," I told her, mystified. "I had this dream that Frank Andrews was telling me he has to go to Michigan to visit someone, and I was trying to convince him not to go. It took all my powers to convince him to stay. I felt he might be in danger, and then I woke up."

She rolled over to her other side and murmured, "I really need to sleep now, call him in the morning."

And so I did. I called him first thing and left a message to call me back. The next day, Frank, who is an extremely busy psychic, called me back. I told him that I had had a strange dream about him. I didn't understand why, but told him the message of the dream was that he should not go to Michigan.

"Funny you should mention that," he said in his humorous way. "Can you believe it? This woman, a client of mine, called me from Michigan at two o'clock in the morning. She's begged me to go there to read for her. She even offered to pay for the trip, but I told her no, I can't do it. She tried hard to persuade me, but I insisted, and finally she gave up. Can you believe the nerve she had calling me at two in the morning?"

To say the least, I was surprised at the confirmation of the dream, and yet we laughed at the "coincidence" of it. "You know, Frank, from now on please keep all your phone conversations to yourself, especially when they are at those strange hours." So far he has kept his promise.

ℵ A Visit with My Sister

"Miri, Miri, don't leave me all alone," I begged as I saw my sister walking away in the distance on a winding dirt road, walking with another woman whom I did not recognize. Her figure was blurred, as if she was in cloud form. Soon I saw them vanishing into a small cluster of trees on the horizon. "Please come back, I don't want to be alone, come, come back to me, don't get lost, you'll disappear. " I called, yelled, begged, and shouted after her many times. Oblivious, the two women continued to walk farther into the distance, clearly not hearing me, which made me feel even more frantic, helpless, and desperate. I felt like my own world was vanishing from under me.

Quietly, in the warmth of my bed I lay for a few more minutes after waking, trying to hold back the streaming tears and brewing panic in my chest. What was the meaning of that dream? I was trying to figure it out, breathless and genuinely sad, my entire body paralyzed from tension. At my wife's suggestion I called my sister, who lives in Israel. She wasn't home. Her daughter said that she had gone to her son's home to organize their family photo albums and papers. I thought that maybe she was looking at our childhood albums and that had triggered the dream. Later that afternoon I finally connected with her. We talked about all the small things of life. As big sisters usually do, she cheerfully assured me that she was doing fine. I decided to be courageous and tell her my dream. As I went on, I could hear the thickening silence on the other end of the line, and then her voice changed. She took a deep breath and shared her story with me.

"I was really having a very rough month," she said. "My very best friend died of cancer about a month ago. I accompanied her through that long and painful process. It was really depressing and it impacted me deeply, maybe because of all the cancer treatments my husband is going through now too. Since then I have had many repeated and horrible dreams. In these dreams I'm constantly finding myself getting lost; I don't know where I am. I lose my pocketbook with all my identification cards, papers, and keys, and I don't know who I am or what to do."

We both were silent, feeling close, though separated by an ocean.

⚏ MISSED PERFORMANCE

A youthful-looking, middle-aged woman was noticeably distressed, walking barefoot from the back of a badly lit room. Her long hands, swimming lightly in the air, were carefully touching unseen walls. She was of an average height; her short, dirty-blond hair hung lifelessly around her round face. She wore a small, cotton, sleeveless dress the color of her hair. *Why is she there? What is she doing in this weird place?* I remember asking myself as I watched her in my dream. She leaned forward and reached toward me with her right hand. Unexpectedly, a long howl-like plea or a scream came out of her opened mouth "Hommmmme, hommmmmme, I want to go hommmmmme . . ." Mesmerized, I watched her as she continued to beg an unknown person—or perhaps it was me—to let her go home. *Who is this person,* I thought. *Is it me wanting to go back home to my family in Isarel?*

A couple of hours later, as my wife and I were having our morning chamomile tea, I shared with her that I had had a very peculiar dream. "Would you like to hear about it?" I asked her cautiously. She assured me she did. I proceeded to tell her what I had dreamed, and as I was demonstrating the cry of "hommmmme," she looked at me, tears in her eyes.

"That was exactly the amazing dance of Claire Porter that you missed last night at the performance. I really wanted you to see it." Then she gave me an odd look and asked, "But how did you know? *Did* you see it?"

"Oh no," I said, "remember, I tried to get to the dance concert on time but I arrived late, just as the doors closed. The house manager asked me to wait outside until the end of the first dance. Luckily I met our friend Amos, and we were happily chatting until they allowed us in, which was right after her dance had finished."

She questioned me, "Did anyone tell you about it?"

"No, I didn't even have the program," I said, reminding her that she didn't want to tell me anything about what I'd missed since she had wanted me to go see another performance by Claire Porter. I never did go but I guess I didn't miss the show after all.

⚡ Oh, and One More Thing . . .

A few months after the passing, in November 2010, of my friend and mentor Ipupiara, a Brazilian shaman with whom I studied and worked for twelve years, I had an unexpected early-morning visit from him. This time he looked like a strong and happy young man and was completely healthy, like I had never seen him before. Ipu was standing in the jungle; maybe he was back in his homeland in the Upper Amazon. He proceeded to get closer to me, and then he said urgently, "*Uru daurwa, uru daurwa*. Remember those words." He kept repeating this phrase a few more times, as if to make me remember it better. "What does *uru daurwa* mean, Ipu?" I asked him desperately in the dream, a bit confused but thrilled to see him again.

"Oh, I forgot to tell you—when you do the candle readings, the uru daurwa is the exact point where the spirits enter into the candle's flame, and you need to know this," he replied.

"Where is it?" I asked him, surprised by his urgent visit. "It is the point where the wick and the blue flame meet. It is the gateway of the spirits." He then pointed his finger to the exact place and faded away.

I woke up in a hurry, repeating these two words over and over again. I ran to my desk, grabbed a pen and paper, and wrote it down quickly before it would dissolve, as many of my other early-morning dreams tend to do.

This dream took me back to another time, to the Amazonian Green Medicine seminar Ipupiara and I had taught together a couple of years before at a charming farm in Baratti, a short distance away from the Mediterranean, in Tuscany. For this seminar we divided our sessions so that our teachings and ceremonies would not overlap. As I was teaching the large group of Italians and other Europeans the technique of "seeing" using diagnostic candle reading, Ipu quietly walked in, sat down, and watched me intently. It was the first time he saw me teaching the technique, and it made me timid. As I was instructing the group on the main points, the things they must pay attention to while reading the candle, he proudly stood up to question me, like a father challenging his son, to make sure I had covered all the basic points correctly. For this reason I was so thankful to receive this last teaching from him, especially as it had come all the way from the other side.

⚡ MEETING A MACHI IN PUCÓN

"I really would like to meet a local shaman on our visit. Do you think you can arrange it?" I asked my college-age daughter a few weeks before we left for Santiago, Chile, where she was studying. She learned that in the Mapuche (the largest local indigenous tribe) culture all *machi* (shamans) are women, and she made an appointment with a known powerful woman in the south on our way to Patagonia.

That cold December night, after my wife and I had prepared everything for our trip, an unknown old man appeared in my dream. "Come and visit me; I am waiting for you," he said. He was about mid-seventies with a full head of white hair, but not long, a face burned by the sun with little narrow, slanted, dark and glowing eyes. He was dressed in simple working clothes and he looked like an indigenous man, but I did not recognize him. "What's your name?" I asked him. "Don Manuel," he said and disappeared.

As we landed in Santiago I told my daughter of my surprising dream. "I already made an appointment for you. Besides, it was just a dream, and even if it is true, how can we find in all of Chile a shaman name Don Manuel?" she countered me. She was right and I accepted that with slight disappointment. That afternoon my right ankle had swollen up to my knee, the result of the long flight. Walking was so excruciatingly painful that I thought of postponing the next part of our trip. I slept with two bags of ice and in the morning the swelling had subsided somewhat. "I need to see a shaman no matter who it is," I said to my wife.

Early in the morning my daughter came back to pick us up. She was visibly excited as she shared this story with us, "Last night the taxi driver who took me home from your hotel turned out to be a young

Mapuche man. He asked me what I was doing here, so I told him of our upcoming trip plans and mentioned that you are interested in meeting a Mapuche shaman. He looked at me through the mirror and said, 'If you go to Pucón you must visit Don Manuel; he is a very good machi.' I was stunned by the coincidence and asked him how we could find Don Manuel. He laughed and said, 'Everyone knows him; he is very famous, just ask people when you get there.'"

I was thrilled to hear the news. "Let's cancel the appointment with the machi woman," I said. "Are you sure?" my daughter asked, concerned. "Yes. I have to trust my dream." So she made the unpleasant call.

A few days later as we walked into the Hosteria in Pucón, I asked the first person I saw if he know of a machi by the name of Don Manuel. Coincidentally, he was a young, energetic tour guide. "Of course I know Don Manuel; I also know where he lives. I can take you to him tomorrow," he said proudly. The next day around noon, close to a beautiful blue lake surrounded by virgin forests in the backdrop of a beautiful snowcapped Villarica Volcano, we met Don Manuel in the healing room of his modest farmhouse. As he greeted us I could not believe my eyes. He looked exactly the same as the man in my dream except for the black color of his hair. I sat in his healing room and watched him as he attended to a young man with a painful dislocated shoulder. And then he called us. "I can't give a treatment today," he announced. "You have to come back tomorrow, Friday." (He worked—as traditionally customary—only on the good days, Tuesdays and Fridays.) I explained that we were traveling and wouldn't be there the next day, so he agreed to see us. Don Manuel showed us around the healing room and talked about his medicines and how he diagnoses people's conditions through visions and by examining their urine. Then he took a look first at my wife and then my daughter and then at my swollen ankle and gave us his diagnostics, accurately. "You should come back and I will prepare you the herbal teas you need. Your blood is too thick for the narrow veins in your legs; it will make your blood circulation flow better," he said assuredly. When I came back to New York, I had a scan made of my ankle and legs, which showed he was spot on.

Later I learned that in the Mapuche tradition, a man could become a machi if he is chosen by his family or community or if hears the call to take that role. However, he must dress as a woman with all the regalia and makeup to perform healing and public ceremonies as they honor Ngünechen, the divine being that governs the world, the Great Spirit. This custom was almost abolished by the influence of the Spanish macho attitude toward feminine men and is unfortunately now practiced in secret.

3

PAST-LIFE EXPERIENCES

[W]ithin myself I discover this:
indeed, I shall never die,
I shall never disappear.
There where there is no death,
there where death is overcome,
let me go there.
Indeed, I shall never die,
indeed, I shall never disappear.

NEZAHUALCOYOTL

Is there life after life? Is our soul immortal and caught in the birth-death-rebirth cycle? What is the role of our physical bodies?

Many indigenous societies hold a deep belief in reincarnation, in the migration of the departed soul into another person, animal, tree, or other life form. Regrettably, no one person can scientifically prove reincarnation, yet many stories have been told about it over the centuries; it is the subject of the books, poetry, songs, and oral traditions of all cultures, including some religions.

As a self-declared rationalist and atheist I used to be awfully cynical about concepts like past lives. It wasn't so rare for me to make fun of people who, after a past-life regression, said things like "Oh, I was Jesus," or "I was Mary Magdalene," "I was a pharaoh," and so on. I believed these stories were just an excuse for not taking responsibility for what the person didn't want to do or be in his or her current life. I tended to look at these kinds of recollections as a bit crazy and disillusioned. But in my grief over the passing of my mother, I found myself hoping and praying that my mother's soul would return in the form of a daughter. So, when I began to experience the reality of past lives, as in the following stories, it totally caught me by surprise and made me a believer.

⚔ TWO KNIGHTS

"Can you 'see' a past lifetime vision I had recently had?" a new client challenged me as we were sitting to do a candle reading. At first I was taken aback by her forthright question as I always wait for the images to come to me and do not like to be forced or challenged this way. So I took a big breath. Scanning and gazing at her softly, suddenly a picture of two English soldiers riding fast, dark horses and wearing heavy armor materialized on the left side behind her head. It was the middle of a massive battle. A large forest surrounded the slanted green hilly battlefield. I recognized my client as the man on the left. His shoulder was terribly wounded. Blood was gushing freely out of his armor and was streaming down. I watched him as he finally fell off his horse bleeding to death. The man on his right, his best friend, looked backward and continued galloping, realizing he could not protect or save him.

As I conveyed this vision to my client she nodded in sadness and confirmed that it was exactly what she saw and experienced herself. "Why couldn't he save me?" she asked with deep mourning. "That is the story of my life. I am always deeply disappointed when people don't come to help me," she sighed.

ॐ Margaret's Story

From high above, watching like a bird gliding in the sky, I followed a tall, slender young woman. She walked all by herself on the edge of what seemed like a large, immaculate square green lawn surrounded by a row of tall, groomed poplar trees on all sides. Her footsteps were unstable, unsure, almost floating, as if afraid to bother the ground she was walking on. She seemed highly sensitive, disturbed, and frightened. Her honey-colored hair was pulled under a wide-brimmed white sun hat, and her long-sleeved white cotton dress hugged her slim figure as it softly brushed the fresh-cut grass. She moved as if in a dream. It was a bright and crisp spring day with an uncanny stillness in the air, like the calm before a brewing storm. A few feathery white clouds floated in the blue skies. Standing in the background was a large modern white building that had two floors with two big glass doors in its center and many windows on both sides, for each of the many rooms that overlooked the grounds. I recognized it as a mental institution, a sanitarium. There seemed to be no other human beings in sight. I hovered closer to get a better view of her. Somehow, in an instant, and without a doubt I recognized the woman. At first I refused to accept it, but then I realized: *She is me.* Chills ran throughout my body.

It was I who was walking dreamlike toward the tall, black wrought-iron gates, as an unseen hand led me to the edge of that grassy lawn in total indifference. She hardly even noticed the two bearded men dressed in black suits with black top hats who were waiting for her at the gate. As she came closer the gate seemed to open silently, all by itself. The two men firmly helped her climb up into a waiting carriage where she settled into the back seat. There were no words exchanged. Instantly the carriage took off, pulled fast by the two black horses. They drove through tree-lined roads, quite a long distance. All she could hear was the sound of the horses' hooves clicking on the road, like Chinese water torture. They arrived in front of her family's townhouse and stopped. She did not wait for them to help her down. Instead she threw open the carriage door in a panic.

As her heart pounded violently, she threw open the black iron gate and dashed into the open door of the house. The two men behind her yelled at her and tried to hold on to her but she did not pay any attention to them. She ran breathlessly upstairs, climbing the narrow, winding staircase, pulling at her dress as it dragged heavily behind her. She entered her bedroom in the small attic on the fourth floor and without any hesitation she held on to the windowsill, looked down to the street below—the trees, the triangular shingle roofs under her—leaned out, and in a last-ditch effort, threw herself out of the window. In midfall she felt the gushing air suffocating her and she couldn't breathe anymore. Floating from above, she could see, as if a witness, her body slowly falling down, weightless, like a falling yellowed leaf, until she reached the sidewalk. She was finally, oh God, in complete peace.

From this vista I noticed that even the familiar busy street looked calm and beautiful now. I could see clearly the beautiful row of trees that grew alongside the cobblestone avenue, the horse-drawn carriages, the small beautiful houses, and most amazingly, every small detail of the clothing worn by the men and women who were strolling leisurely on this weekend afternoon. At once droves of startled people rushed toward her lifeless body that lay face-down on the sidewalk. I noticed their clothes as they were crossing the avenue to reach her—the men with elegant black suits, white shirts, and black top hats, carrying their walking canes, the women in long, heavy gray dresses with tight waists adorned with black buttons and gray hats. Then the ringing sound of emergency bells came closer, and soon a horse-drawn ambulance arrived and stopped by the dead body. Four men in black uniforms picked up her body and carefully placed it on a simple stretcher, lifted it, and laid it inside the ambulance. The ambulance jerked forward, the bells continuing to ring their emergency sounds, and I followed the ambulance as it started to move up the street until it reached the city hospital. I was totally oblivious to the panic other people around me were expressing. I saw them unloading my lifeless body and passing the stretcher to the waiting medical crew, and then watched them carry me into the building.

Then I left, but before I did, I wanted to know who I was and where this had taken place. I called out and asked her. A message came back to me clearly: "My name is Margaret. I was born in the 1890s and lived in a highly respected section of Vienna, Austria."

Slowly I opened my eyes. I was still standing barefoot, clad in my white underwear on the mud floor of a semidark healing room. The strong smell of cow manure, alcohol, and tobacco smoke in the room had brought me back to my surroundings. Jorge Tamayo was still whipping my head with a bunch of dry leaves, chanting an old Quechua prayer. I couldn't breathe. I felt like someone had knocked the air out of me. My eyes filled with salty tears. I felt deep mourning for the dead Margaret, and for myself.

At the end of the session I slowly got dressed and sat on a bench leaning against the white wall, gathering my thoughts and feelings. I couldn't believe what I had witnessed. Was it a past-life experience? How long did it last? A few seconds? Minutes? An hour? How could I see every detail, sound, and emotion so vividly and clearly? Did I make it all up? I sat there contemplating, trying to make sense of it all. Don Esteban, the miniature elder shaman, wearing a colorful feather crown, snored loudly in the other corner of the room, completely drunk and tired from working straight around the clock. I needed space to figure this all out. I excused myself, got up and went outside and made my way through the herd of cows and busy chickens to the cornfields. There behind the outhouse I stood and watched the beautiful valley below. It was still early afternoon and the setting sun painted the fields in magical colors. Everything looked so unusually unreal and at the same time utterly peaceful. I contemplated: Okay, I was a young woman, not a man, with depression. I committed suicide. How and why is this related to my current life? Why was this past life revealed to me now, here in the High Andes of Ecuador? Is it related to my mother's depression or her maiden name, Margalit?

Margaret was from a well-to-do family—is this why I have an aversion to money in this lifetime? Was this is the source of my present-life fear of heights?

Since my early childhood I have always had an inexplicably strong fear of heights, specifically, falling from roofs. My legs stiffen, my breath shortens, and my palms begin to sweat when I am up high. No wonder when I saw a picture of a hanging cable bridge built over a deep river in Dream Change's trip brochure I was terrified. The bridge was relatively narrow and had no railings or ropes to hold on to. Seeing it made me worry that my legs would become paralyzed, as had happened to me when I was at the top of the Duomo in Milan, Italy, many years before. I was sure that I would fall down into the deep, gushing waters. Did Margaret's story and her jumping to her death uncover the source of that deep fear? If so, maybe I don't need to repeat that experience again. Was that experience my healing?

A week later, in Miazal, in the heart of the Shuar jungle territory, while on our way to the sacred twin falls, we had to cross that very bridge. My heart started to pound heavily with anticipation. I took a big breath, remembered Margaret, made a few cautious steps, and lo and behold, my legs were relaxed and my breath flowed easily. I got to the center of the bridge and started dancing, laughing and cheering uncontrollably. But even then I still had this nagging question: Was it really real or did I just made it up? No way to know. I needed proof, but how? Should I go to Vienna to look for historical records? Nah . . . I dismissed it.

A few years later, on a cold September night at the Omega Institute, a group of us sat outside on a bench, some of the same people who had taken that trip to Ecuador with me, as well as a few others who had joined our noisy reunion. We were all sharing memories from our trip, storytelling, with a lot of laughter.

"Hey Itzhak, tell them your Margaret story," my good friend Ariel Orr Jordan encouraged me. Reluctantly, I agreed. When I finished telling my story, a woman said from the darkness, "You know, I'm from

Vienna and I know that sanatarium. And, you know, it's still there." My heart skipped a beat.

"What a confirmation," Ariel said.

Maybe I need to go to Vienna after all, I thought.

Fast-forward nine years. Cramped in my Italian host Alessandra's packed car, Isabel, Maria, and I were heading back to Florence from Baratti, a beautiful resort beach town where I had just finished teaching a shamanic seminar. Isabel was hurrying to take the train back to her home in Vienna for the weekend. The weekend traffic made the trip even longer than expected, and to pass the time I asked Isabel if she knew of this sanatarium. "Can you describe it?" she asked, and so I described it to her. "Why do you want to know?" she asked suspiciously. I then told my companions the Margaret story. "Aha," she said seriously, her eyes concentrating, trying to think of the sanatarium's name, "there are few possibilities, but you know, I'm working at the Vienna Museum; why don't you come there and we will find out if your story is true?"

Isn't that a coincidence? I thought—I was on my way to Vienna to teach.

Vienna had been on my mind for the longest time. My wife's most admired dance teacher, one of the most influential artists in my life, Gertrude Krause, a Dada dancer, was Viennese. It was an excellent opportunity to visit the places she always reminisced about. I wanted to see those artist and intellectuals' cafés and taste the best Viennese coffee and strudels and see the palace where Gertrude brought the house down when she wildly danced at the first Dada Congress.

At 10 a.m. sharp a few days later, I entered the Wien Museum on the famous Karlsplatz. I walked into a modern three-story building that was filled with every item of the city's rich history. I asked the receptionist if I could see Isabel. A few long minutes later, a beautifully dressed woman showed up to greet me, very different-looking from the wild shaman she was in Italy. "Hey, is that you?" I asked laughingly. She giggled and led me to her quarters, where her stern-faced associate interrogated me again and again about the details of my story. There was a short discussion in German, and then a plan of action was formed. For sanatariums we needed to search the Internet. To find out about the ambulances we would have to go downstairs to the transportation department. For street scenes there was another department. And so after three hours of searching flat drawers, deep drawers, and opening old envelopes, we found it all: pictures of the sanatarium, the stretcher, the horse-drawn ambulance, the bells, the hospital, the townhouses, pictures of men and women walking the streets, and even their exact clothing. We made photocopies of it all.

But the most emotional and confirming moment for me happened while looking again at the photo of the sanatarium in Purkersdorf. In the photo it had three floors, not two as I had seen in my vision. I started doubting myself again. Reading the picture's caption we found the explanation: "The famous architect Josef Hoffman designed it in 1906. In 1935, a third floor was added to the original building." That meant Margaret was in her mid-twenties at the time. "Only very well-to-do families used to send their members there, many from the Jewish community. At that time it was built quite far away from the city," Isabel continued reading. It was hard for me to keep cool on the outside. I started to have heart palpitations, fear was growing in my stomach, my palms were sweating, and I was shaking and short of breath. "Do you want to visit the place?" Isabel softly asked. "It is just a few train stops outside the city; I can show you how to get there."

I consulted my spirit. "No, that's enough for me now," I said.

⚕ MY LIFE AS A WITCH

Very thin, with dark, flowing, curly hair, dressed lightly in black top and shorts befitting a hot New York summer's day, Laurie walked into my healing room. Her brown eyes were bright, playful, and curious, hiding a lifetime of deep suffering. "I need to be prepared for my planned trip to Peru, where I am going for the first time to drink ayahuasca. I want to cure my chronic depression, anxiety, and addiction to painkillers."

These were the reasons she gave for coming for this shamanic healing. Little did we know then that this session would reveal a whole other lifetime. I brought to her attention the fact that most of the time when a person takes antidepressants or anxiety medication, shamanic healing may not be as effective, as it needs to combat those spirits too, while the client's spirit is suppressed. She seemed to understand and agreed anyway.

"I have some pain on the right side of my lower back. Could it be an intrusion of bad spirits?" she asked.

I handed her a jaguar bone to hold between her two palms to check for possession. "No you are not possessed, but you had some trembling in your left hand, which signals problems or disturbances with a mother or a feminine energy," I said. She nodded in agreement. As we continued our conversation, a picture—a holographic image—formed above her right shoulder slightly above her head. A short, heavyset, round, and youngish European woman stood in her kitchen mixing with her right hand what seemed like soup in a big cauldron on a wood-burning stove. Her light blond hair was tucked under a light blue cap, and a white apron was tied to her bluish dress, covering her full feminine figure. While continuing our regular conversation, I thought, *Who is this woman? How is she related to my client? She seems to not have any resemblance to my client, so why is she here? Is she is her ancestor?* I needed more information.

"What is your ancestry?" I asked my client, looking into her dark eyes.

"Oh, part French, part German, and part English. Why do you ask?"

It must be France then, I thought. "I do not know why yet, but there is a woman here." I went on, describing to her the scene that was evolving in front of my eyes. "I think she is a healer, a witch making a special brew to heal someone."

"How does the kitchen look?" Laurie asked.

"Let me concentrate. Well, it is small and narrow, with a brick floor and log walls, and a very low ceiling."

"Do they have windows and animals?"

"The windows are very small squares, I guess to keep the heat in. And yes, there are animals outside, I can feel them but I can't see them." I continued and took a deep breath. "Now I can see a young man walking into the kitchen from the right side through an inner door. He is handsome and has a bushy blond mustache and light hair. I guess he is her husband. He is wearing khaki-colored work clothes and a brown vest. He has to bend his head to come in through the door." I took a breath, and another vision came. "But wait—there is a girl walking in from the door on the left side—their daughter. She is maybe sixteen, looking like a younger version of her mother, but without the cap. The woman is thirty-two years old. She is calmly teaching her daughter to make the healing brew. They seem to be so innocent and peaceful, an almost idyllic image of a young farmer's family, but not for long. I can see a few people coming down a road from the fields. I don't know who they are." I concentrated on them. "Suddenly the front door of the kitchen on the right side opens aggressively and three men walk in. They are wearing black hooded robes."

"Who are they? Are they are priests?" Laurie asked.

"Yes, they are, wearing black robes with hoods over their heads; I can't see their faces. I think they came to take them. Yes, they're arresting them. They are going to burn them as witches." I had to stop and take a big breath, as I felt goosebumps spread over my entire body. I continued: "I have the sense that this woman might actually be you a few hundred years ago. I think I'm seeing you in your past life."

"Interesting," Laurie said as she played with her curly black hair. We had a long period of silence. "You know, it makes a lot of sense. I'm a writer, and for the past few years I have been working on a book about women healers from all cultures who fought against society's judgment. I feel very passionate about it. I'm also working for an organization for women's rights."

"Oh, that's fascinating," I said.

"And you know, I have one daughter too."

"How old is she now?" I asked.

"Twenty-five."

"No, I guess it's not her. Wait—were you pregnant when you were sixteen?

"No, but I was when I was seventeen, and it was too frightening, so I had an abortion," she said.

"Are you very protective of your daughter?"

"You bet! I hope not in a bad way, though," she said, laughing.

"Your husband in this lifetime, does he have light hair and a bushy mustache?"

"When I met him he did, a nice big, bushy blond mustache. Yes, strange . . . And you know what? It is so funny, the women from the French side of our family are all short, round, and have huge behinds," Laurie said with a giggle.

I went on to finish the candle reading, and as we were ready for the cleansing ceremony I suggested that Laurie concentrate on that woman and see if she could communicate with her. "I will also dedicate this ceremony to your previous incarnation, because her soul or spirit also needs healing, and with that we will heal your entire female line." Laurie agreed.

La Limpia—the cleansing session (more about this later in this book)—was intense. Laurie's body finally relaxed, tears flowed down her cheeks, her face became peaceful and clear, and she started breathing normally. "Thank you, Laurie," I said at the end of the session. We embraced. Next, she kneeled down and put her face to the floor for a few long minutes.

"I saw her, we spoke, and it was so powerful, thank you," she said quietly.

Later that week of the cleansing, I got a long e-mail from Laurie: "I went that night to bury the eggs and candle as you directed, and as I was walking down the street I thought of how this kind of activity would have had the Inquisition after me in a flash back in those days, and in fact I felt very furtive doing it.

"Of course, I got busy researching the French side of my family (French-Swiss to be precise) to try to locate a likely time and place of witch persecutions in northeastern France and Switzerland, but was soon overwhelmed by all the names, the mass barbecues, the deaths under torture, beheadings, and so forth, a hysteria kicked off by—who else—the Catholic Church. All high-ranking assholes, royal and cleric, signed ridiculous antiwitchcraft pledges or legislation, exactly as the idiots today sign the no-tax, no-abortions, no gay marriage, etc., pledges. Classic mass hysteria, and about as reasonable as no-tax pledges. Prosecution for witchcraft went from one of these nasty little legal maneuvers used when the court has no case (e.g., Anne Boleyn and Jeanne d'Arc) to a universal remedy against political enemies, inconvenient wives, annoying neighbors, and boredom. Like gladiators, guillotines, and lynching, people just looovvve a day out to enjoy someone else's death.

"I digress. I found quite a few mothers and daughters listed. I didn't get a strong sense of any of them, but by this time the personal tragedy I'd felt during the healing had become so horrifically repetitious that I couldn't feel more awful for any one of them over another. One thing kinda' stopped my heart though, that I hadn't thought of when you were telling me about my girl, was what happened before the fire—burning to death would have been a preferable end over the hideous torture to get confessions.

"I realized that there wasn't anything unusual about my past life. For a European peasant woman living between 1240 and 1690, being burned alive for witchcraft seemed to be almost as likely as a European Jew being murdered in the camps in the years of the Third Reich.

"I think my previous incarnation was called Marguerite. I'm finding myself at a loss for how to reconcile the extremes of her suffering. How facile it would be to tell her to forgive herself, or to try to remember the sweet part of her life when the end would have poisoned all those memories; if it had been just her who had to endure it, if they'd taken just her, I think she'd have moved past it, knowing what the world is capable of. But for her to witness and experience firsthand the agonies her daughter had to face must have been a fate worse than her own death. I can see how a mere 800 to 500 years would not be nearly enough time to heal those wounds."

I replied to her e-mail: "Hi Laurie, After our session I realized I did not ask that woman in the session her name. So after you left, I closed my eyes and journeyed to her, where I found her and asked her to tell me her name. She said it was Margarita. I dismissed the coincidence and did not tell you this, as I had another past-life experience with another Margaret in Vienna in 1890s. So I got goosebumps reading your e-mail."

A week later, Laurie was bubbling with excitement about all the research she had been doing.

So many questions ran unanswered in my head, and I'm sure in hers, too. Was it Laurie's real past life? Is this why she is so interested in women's rights and in writing books about women healers? How much of her current life is influenced by that past life and this death incident? Is it a coincidence that she has only one daughter and had an abortion at the same age as her past-life daughter? Why is it that she decided to return in Laurie's body during this lifetime? Are we really free to choose our own destiny or are we players in something bigger? Are our previous incarnations constantly with us even if we do not see them?

A few months later, Laurie and I had a chance to see how her past life influences her in this lifetime. We did a soul retrieval—a subject covered in our next chapter.

4

⚊ ⚊ ⚊ ⚊

SOUL RETRIEVAL

What I have found after a soul retrieval is that one cannot "numb out" anymore. Each and every one of us must make personal and planetary decisions to stop abusing life. Whether a person has to give up an abusive relationship, take a more active political role, or increase awareness of how we continue to abuse our environment, we all now have to be responsible. Being responsible means responding to what is needed. We find a need to wake up and change our reality to a stance of power.

SANDRA INGERMAN

Most indigenous societies believe in the existence of an immortal soul, not only in human beings, but in any created entity in the universe, whether biological or nonbiological, and they believe that the cycle of reincarnation includes humans, animals, trees, and other objects. It is hard to describe exactly what a soul is. You could say it is the pure essence of a person—it is what makes you uniquely you. Your current body is not really you; it is only a container, made mostly of water and minerals, a means for the soul to manifest so that it can allow the soul to achieve its purpose through the teachings of being incarnated. Some

58

believe that the soul is made of collective parts and belongs to a family of souls or a soul group that manifests at different times to work toward the completion of its group's mission.

Soul loss in the shamanic sense is one of the main causes of illnesses, immune-system deficiencies, and all-around dysfunction of the physical, emotional, and mental well-being. Soul loss typically happens when a person, usually early in life, experiences profound trauma in the form of sexual, physical, or verbal abuse, or through accidents, war, or the death of someone close to them. In each case something happens and a decision is made by the child in order to survive and avoid the pain associated with the experience. At that split second the affected person sends away that part of his or her soul that is hurting and releases it out of the body into the ethers. This can result in the closing of the heart and a general memory loss around the incident. What can ensue is an unexplained depression and detachment from the original source of the pain in adulthood. People who have experienced soul loss often feel empty, sleepwalking through life, with no excitement or purpose, or sad or depressed for no apparent reason. As one person said, "as if there is a hole in my heart."

Shamans, through their ability of visioning, journey into other realities to locate the specific source incident that caused that part of the soul to leave. They track down the place where the soul fragment hides and persuade it to reunite with the client's soul energy. Once that soul part agrees and is ready to come back, the shaman holds it in his hands and blows it directly into the client's portals, the heart and the crown of the head. To fully the integrate and unify that lost part the client needs to become the caretaker of that soul fragment and consciously integrate it back into his or her life. This can be done through additional shamanic journeys to meet and welcome it back and find specific ways to heal the old wounds. It also helps to be aware and acknowledge the changes that happen in your life in the aftermath, have a supportive group of people who can be with you as those changes happens, and consult with the shaman about how to make true physical changes in your everyday life that will reflect and honor your newfound part. I ask my clients to adopt a doll for two weeks or more that could remind them of themselves at the age of the soul loss and take care of it around the clock—talk with it, feed it, bathe it, and take it to work—as a constant reminder. It works miraculously.

Time and time again I have found that in the aftermath of a successful soul retrieval ceremony, people feel more grounded, full, happy, content, or, as one of my clients said, "I experienced a second joyful childhood, one that I was never able to know before. I finally experienced a carefree childhood and found the child who is loved."

There are many ways to conduct soul retrieval ceremonies. Each culture or individual shaman finds its own unique way, and no one way is better than another. Some societies perform this healing ceremony during certain times of the day, such as at noontime, while others do it at midnight, when the cosmic portals are open. And sometimes people can even experience soul retrieval spontaneously, without the direct help of a shaman. This happened to me in a sweatlodge ceremony; Spontaneous retrieval could also happen on a mountaintop or in the midst of a remarkable landscape where the soul part feels safe to return. It even happens to some of my clients during the cleansing ceremony.

ᐊᐧ Laurie's Reintegration

Laurie, the woman I mentioned in the previous chapter whose present life uncannily reflected many of the details of her past life as a witch who had been burned at the stake, returned to me after her initial session for a soul retrieval. This time I asked Laurie to journey with me simultaneously. My power animal took me this time up into the skies. Flying high, we went over a large city, crossed a big river, and then I found myself in an apartment. There I saw a wooden baby crib by an open window whose light curtains flew in the breeze. A four-year-old Laurie was stepping on the baby crib, bending deep down into it, and grabbing a newborn blond baby girl. She was trying with all her young might to lift the baby up over the crib railing. Both girls fell backward on the light-colored carpeting. Little Laurie was deeply ashamed. "How come I failed?" There was commotion, and her mother walked into the room and reprimanded her. Her lost soul part became a dark ball of energy and ran to hide under the dresser. I went there and convinced it to come back with me. Once it agreed, I blew it back into Laurie's heart and the crown of her head.

"Yes, it's true," Laurie said after I shared my vision with her. "We lived in a suburb of New York City, in an apartment. The baby crib was by the window of my parents' room. I remember clearly its light green color. My older sisters, who were eleven and seven, used to take care of my baby sister, and I wanted to show that I could too."

In her journey, Laurie's power animal took her to a time when as a five-year-old she was with her older sister. She was swirling a rope with a stone at the end to hear the swishing sound. It came close to her sister and hit her badly. "I guess these two incidences of soul loss can explain why I was afraid to use my full power and felt many times powerless and ashamed to do the things I wanted," Laurie concluded.

☊ THE COLLAPSING FLOOR

"I suffer from deep depression and lack of enthusiasm for life. I spend most of the time alone, at home," and in a whisper she added, "comforting myself with drinking, a lot."

Nervous and sad, Anna, a woman in her mid-sixties who was a retired teacher, shared with me in our first session together. By our third session she reported a new sense of quietude and clarity, that she was feeling more grounded. She had even started to plan her future, she said. I felt she was ready for a soul retrieval. At one of our sessions I asked if she wanted to try it then and there. She agreed.

After explaining the concept behind this practice, I asked her to journey with me so she could also join in helping me find the lost part of her soul. I sat by her side on the floor, lightly touching her as she lay on the Lakota blanket's blue, red, and white patchwork. She covered her eyes and I started drumming lightly. Soon I met my spirit

guide and an image appeared of a group of seven- or eight-year-old girls dressed in celebratory clothing, with below-the-knee blue skirts and nice, pure white shirts. They walked happily in the afternoon out of a big building. *Is it a school?* I wondered. They were laughing and chatting on their way home. One of the girls—my client—ran forward toward a lone townhouse on the left side of the street, passing by a few trees planted along the sidewalk. I saw her climbing up the stoop, reaching for the worn-out wooden door, and just standing there a while. It seemed that by some strange force she could not enter. Then I saw her pushing the heavy door and slipping into the house and soon disappearing. *What does this image mean? Is this Brooklyn? Is she religious? Why this brownstone in particular?* I was confused. I needed help. I called on my other spirit guide. He showed me a big, dark energetic hole, like a black vortex. I was perplexed. *Help me, explain this to me.* Again the same image appeared. I called on my first spirit guide and asked her for help, and again the same group of girls appeared, my client couldn't open the door, then she opened it and disappeared.

At this point I was resigned to disappointing my client, as it seemed there was nothing more I could do. Then I decided to ask the little girl to show me the part of her soul that had left her. Suddenly I heard a young, playful voice calling me from the top of one of the trees by the house. I flew up there and found her sitting comfortably in a bird's nest. I introduced myself and told her why I was there. She laughed wholeheartedly and said that she already knew. I suggested that she come down with me to reunite with my client, so her life could be healed. After a few minutes of prodding she conceded. I stopped the drumming, raised my arms, held her in the palms of my hands, and kneeling over Anna, blew her newfound spirit part back into her heart and later into the crown of her white-haired head.

Afterward, we sat quietly for a while. "Are you ready to share with me what you have just seen," I asked Anna.

"I don't know why, but I was attracted to a huge tree I knew from my past. In the vision I climbed to the canopy and had an amazing fun and loving time. I really felt happy and powerful."

Relieved, I smiled now. "At least I got part of it right." I shared with her my incoherent vision and, as I got to the end, she stopped me, took a big breath, looked in my eyes, and said, "That incident you just witnessed I have never, ever, discussed, not with anyone! Not with my friends, definitely not with my mother or family, and not even with my therapist of twenty-five years. I was so ashamed of it." She went on to tell me the rest of her story.

"That afternoon I went home with a group of my girlfriends. We were I guess either seven or eight years old, and we had just left the syn-agogue service. There was a haunted and dilapidated townhouse that we used to imagine as our witch house. I ran in front of them and pushed on the big entrance door. I took a few steps inside the house, and all of a sudden I disappeared through the cracked wooden floor. It caved in and I fell through a deep hole into a dark basement. I don't know how long I was there but I managed to pull myself up and walked back out in the dark; I don't even remember how. I was in shock. My beautiful clothes were so dirty and, even more frightening, the gold bracelet my mother had given me had slipped off my left hand and I was terrified she would find out. Fortunately, later I went there with a flashlight and found it, so my mother never noticed." Anna took a big breath, and we sat quietly on the multicolored blanket a while longer. "Since then I always felt that every time I get excited about something, the 'floor falls out under me.'"

Anna then shared with me many more examples of events in her life that had the same pattern. "Maybe this door is the wall I always feel blocking me from moving forward." And, as if talking to herself she added, "I never thought of this incident as such an important event in my life."

The last time I saw Anna, a few years later, it was at a crowded event where I spoke on a panel. She plowed her way to see me. I looked at her in surprise, I saw a different person standing in front of me. She was elegantly dressed, her hair was done, and she even wore makeup. She put her hands around my ear and whispered, "I wanted you to know that I stopped drinking," and then she gave me a big beautiful smile.

⚡ SEXUAL OBJECT

What motivates a person to compulsively strive to be at the top of her field and at the same time compulsively strive to destroy herself? That was Paulina's question when she first came to see me to heal her sex, drug, and alcohol addictions. After almost a year as my client her life had changed dramatically. She had much more awareness of the different parts of herself that took control of her actions when she was in distress and this was greatly apparent in her daily life and choices.

She had now been in a loving and monogamous relationship for a few months, was trying to conceive a baby, and no longer did drugs or drank. She was starting to spend long periods of time in nature. No more wild parties in dark city clubs; she controlled her old compulsion of sexting to find a quick partner, and most of the bad-mouthing gossip and attacks she had been suffering in the press subsided.

"I need to understand why," she said one day.

"I think you are ready for a soul retrieval," I answered.

"No problem. I trust you. Let's do it," she said.

She lay down on my carpet with a pillow under her head and closed her eyes. I sat by her side holding my drum and began to beat it. I called my power animal for help. It took me to a house far away. *San Francisco?* I thought. There was a dinner party there. Immediately I saw a group of adults that hovered above a bathtub like vultures. They were laughing, blowing cigarette smoke, and holding glasses of hard liquor. I got closer to see them pointing at a young blond girl, maybe four years old, who was swaying seductively back and forth naked in the water. Her father, a camera in his hand, took pictures of her, laughing. "That's my girl. . . . That's excellent." Her mother on the other side of the bathtub, dressed elegantly, was also laughing as if to impress their guests. There was a big, frozen smile on the girl's face. I could feel the terror of the young sex model as those people were watching her father taking pictures of her, and her desperation for her father's love and approval. I asked my power animal to look for the girl's lost soul part. It took me through the open window to a star hanging in the dark sky. I asked the soul part to come back with me and reunite with the girl. The star was thrilled. "I have been waiting for this invitation for a long time," it said. And so, I stopped the drumming, held it in my palms, and blew it into Paulina's heart and then to the crown of her blond head. I sat quietly. The scene had made me very sad, and I felt so much compassion for Paulina. *How could they humiliate her at such tender age?* I thought to myself.

We sat facing each other and I proceeded to tell her my journey. "I still remember this event, just as you described it. My parents, as you know, were famous artists and bohemians and hosted many dinners at our home. I was the freak show," she said as she brushed her long hair nervously, "and that wasn't the only time. I had many similar experiences like that. My father became famous from these kinds of pictures. He gained power and success, and later in life I wanted it too, no matter how."

"I'm sorry; it must have been a very difficult time for you," I said.

"I am okay. I think now I can be successful in my own way. I don't have to please any of them anymore."

"Let's do another journey now to welcome this part of your soul returning home," I suggested.

"I really feel more compassion for her," Paulina said after. "I will take care of this little Paulina, I promise."

⚡ BADGE OF HONOR

Robert, a professional designer, was in his mid-forties and had difficulties finding a job he liked or a new career. From a very early age he felt as if he had compromised himself to other's wishes; he accepted their power, as if he had no power of his own. The same was true in his personal long-term relationship. After a few sessions we agreed that he was ready for a soul retrieval, so he could find the source of those feelings and behavior. He lay on the floor while I sat by him, touching him lightly, as I started drumming. I called my guide and asked to be led to the time this soul part had left him.

After drumming awhile, a forest emerged in my vision. There I saw Robert wandering as a young boy, camping with a group of children. Behind him was another boy, his friend, whom I saw sneaking into a large tent where all the other kids gathered. I could not see clearly what it was that he did, but I got a message that this close friend did something bad that had shamed Robert to no end. I called my spirit guide and asked it to help me find his lost soul part. He took me to the root of a large nearby tree. There, buried in the earth, I met it. After talking to it the soul part agreed to come out and be brought back to rejoin Robert. I clasped that soul part in my hands and blew it into Robert's heart and crown of his head to be integrated back into his life.

Afterward we sat facing each other and I began to share my vision. Robert's blue eyes looked moist and sad. He shook his head from side to side as if trying to shake a bad memory, and quietly said, "When I was about eleven years old I went to a sleepover camp with my friends. One of my best friends strongly challenged and encouraged me to steal a few scouts' badges from the tent. I did. I took the challenge because I was afraid to look weak. But later I felt such shame, as if I had compromised my integrity and lost my power to him. I felt used by him and decided never to let anyone tell me what to do again. That is probably why I had so many difficulties at my job and had to quit." He took a big breath and after a while he continued. "But how can I feel free, keep my integrity, and still follow what others tell me to do, all at the same time?" he asked, not sure how. "Accept that soul part, forgive him, and love him again," I replied. "Let's do another short journey where you will welcome him and ask him if he needs your help," I suggested, and he agreed.

A few weeks later his long-term girlfriend came for a session. "I don't know what you did, but Robert finally asked me to move in with him. I'm so happy he conquered his fear. What did you do?" she excitedly asked.

⚡ THE CLOSET

Not sure why he was repeatedly failing in his business, I suggested to Valentine that we perform a soul retrieval. I found Valentine, now a successful fashion designer from South America, when he was a young boy, hiding in a large, floor-to-ceiling dark brown wooden closet, on the right side of a weakly-lit bedroom. His small body was cramped in that dark, small space as he held a few colorful fabrics in his hands, concentrating hard with a needle and thread, trying to stitch the pieces together to make a beautiful dress. I could feel he was consumed by passion for what he was doing but also felt his fear of being discovered, and it affected me deeply, too. I felt such deep compassion for that young boy who needed to hide his true passion.

"That's correct, it really happened," he said, surprised, when I shared this vision with him following our soul retrieval session. Tears filled his deep-set black eyes. I handed him a tissue and he wiped his eyes. He sat with his feelings a while, and then Valentine shared with me his painful childhood experience.

"Every afternoon after coming back from school, the house was still quiet as my father, who was a big, tall man, and my older sister were still away. I used to 'borrow' pieces of fabric from my mom's room and hide in the clothes closet. I closed the door, as I used to be frightened my abusive father might find me there when he came home. He used to hit me and shame me badly, as if I was not enough of a man for him. I really just wanted to make beautiful dresses. Thank you. It was very important for me to connect with this boy. I was ashamed of him deep down. I will now appreciate him more and take care of him."

A few weeks later Valentine came back excited, "My father called me. He rarely ever does. He told me how proud he is of my work and me. I'm so surprised . . . it was completely out of the blue!" Most importantly he no longer felt shame or the need to hide his passion and talent. Sure of himself, he went on to create beautiful couture, receiving rave reviews and accepting his success.

⚡ UNDER THE BRIDGE

Michele, a tall and thin woman in her fifties who is an energy healer, said to me in one of our sessions, "I feel that something is missing in me, like a big void in my heart. I don't know what it is. Can you find out what happened to me?" We decided that soul retrieval would be helpful to discover what it was that made her feel so empty. I sat by her side as she lay down on the colorful blanket. I closed my eyes and started to rapidly drum, calling my spirit guide. I relayed Michele's request and a vision emerged.

On a trail in a forest a four- or five-year-old girl dressed in a light dress was walking happily hand-in-hand with her mom. The little girl was holding a small white dog on a leash. It was a beautiful outing, a great day in nature, so it seemed. I followed them as they crossed a small stone bridge over a small stream and then as they continued down to the riverbank. All of a sudden the dog started pulling her into the rushing white water below. Surprised, she let go of the leash as her legs tripped on some rocks and, losing her footing, she fell into the deep rushing water. She found herself drowning, looking up at the skies from below the water, confused, desperate, and unable to breathe. The little white dog started barking loudly, jumping excitedly. Then I saw her mother running in and pulling her out. In a panic and short of breath she collapsed into her mother's arms.

This vision took me back to a similar experience and feelings I myself had had at about the same age when I was pulled out of a pool by my father, who had jumped in with his clothes on and rescued me from drowning. I asked my spirit guide to help me find Michele's lost soul part and immediately we flew under the stone bridge. There, tucked in the corner, I found it. At first she refused to reunite with present-day Michele, saying that she felt safe and protected there. I convinced her that Michele needed her and that she was stronger and wiser now and would be able to take care of her. Reluctantly she agreed. I clasped her in my hands and I brought her back.

"I remember this incident well. I remember the bridge, the river, and my dog, but I did not know it had had such an impact on me," Michele told me afterward. "Let's welcome her back in our next journey," I suggested. "Yes, that would be wonderful." Following the journey she said, "I now understand the fear that has been following me all my life." In the following session we continued to integrate this soul part into her life. With her panic gone the trembling in her hands subsided, too. She became more confident and even started to see more clients.

⚠ THE STONE

Peter, a lanky young man, very thin, with flowing black hair, complained he always felt passive. "I don't know why I have a constant need to wait for other people's instructions." He desperately wanted to find the cause of these feelings. "I want to become a more dynamic person," he said quietly. We decided to do a soul retrieval ceremony.

In the vision I was taken to a forest behind Peter's house. There I saw a boy buried under a big pile of stones—Peter as a five-year-old. He was panicking, unable to breathe or call for help, feeling desperate and powerless. I asked my spirit guide to help me find his lost spirit part, and we found it on top of a nearby tree. At first he refused to come back; he said he felt very comfortable sitting by himself protected by the tree. We then negotiated, as I explained the reason why Peter wanted him back, and he finally agreed to reunite with the present-day Peter. I held his soul part in my palms and blew it back into Peter's heart and crown. Later, I shared my vison with him.

"I remember that incident," Peter said. "At about this age I played alone in the forest around my house. I usually did that because I had no siblings and there were no other kids around. That afternoon I climbed an old, dry, stonewall boundary marker, and as I got to the top it collapsed and buried me. I remember the weight of the stone on my body.

As you said, I felt totally surprised and powerless. I did not trust myself anymore. I really don't remember who saved me, maybe my mother."

"Did you experience other instances in your past in which you felt the same way?" I asked him.

"Yes, I remember vividly how some kids at elementary school jumped and piled on top of me; I was panicky and didn't have control. Again, I don't remember who saved me," he recalled.

"Bringing back your lost soul part is just the beginning," I told him. "Now you need to integrate it into your life."

"But how?" he asked.

"First let's do La Limpia, the cleansing ceremony. While I'm doing it, journey to that child spirit and welcome him back; ask him that question." And so he did.

"I really liked him. I promised I would protect him from now on," he said later.

On our next appointment he was unusually energetic. "I decided to take action. I am going on a trip to Europe by myself," he said with confidence. "I want to learn who I truly am."

5

PLANT MEDICINE

Madre Ayahuasca, here are your children.
Today we have come to be with you.
Madre Ayahuasca, I am asking for healing
for my brothers/sisters that are today with me.
Madre Ayahuasca, show us the paths
painting visions of a good destiny.
Madre Ayahuasca, we are full of gratitude
Blessed medicine that cures the tribe.

DIEGO PALMA

Plant medicine is only one way by which we can enter a state of dreams, trance, and higher consciousness to connect with the cosmos. Drumming, rattling, singing, chanting, and dancing are also powerful tools used the world over with great success. My teacher Don José Joaquin Piñeda commented to me that a powerful shaman does not need the help of plant medicines to fly; he should use his strong faith, concentration, and connection to his spirit helpers.

My experience with the vision of my past life as Margaret, recounted in chapter 3, was provoked by a traditional La Limpia, which is a typical High Andes or Quechua energy-cleansing ceremony that uses only green branches, sugarcane rum, smoke, eggs, flowers, stones, tobacco, and sound, and is accompanied by chanting. I was also fortunate to experience other significant visions while working with Don José, which you will read about in the pages to come. What triggered those visions is hard to pinpoint, which is what makes this nonverbal shamanic healing method so powerful and effective, so much so that many people consider it a form of magical or miracle healing.

The plant kingdom provides us with many plants, mushrooms, barks, roots, and flowers that allow shamans to fly and connect with spirits and tap into sources of information not readily available to us in our regular state of consciousness. In the Andes, shamans traditionally use the sacred San Pedro (Huachuma), which are thorny buttons from the cactus that goes by that name, and which induce visions. San Pedro is mostly consumed once a year on a specific day in a special ceremony. Similarly, Native Americans consume peyote, a small, round, spineless cactus. In Africa, shamans use iboga shrub bark and roots. In Siberia and other places throughout the world, shamans use various sacred mushrooms.

Shamans of the Amazonian region discovered thousands of years ago that after drinking a thick, brown, bitter brew made of a combination of barks and plants they could have powerful visions enabling them to communicate directly with the plants' spirits and to acquire otherwise unattainable knowledge about the universe. But the brew also has a healing purpose. It induces strong purging for body cleansing. The bitter properties eliminate parasites and bad bacteria, alkalizing and purifying the digestive system, where many diseases begin.

The brew is primarily made of the bark of a vine called *natém* in the Shuar language—more commonly known to us by its Quechua name, *ayahuasca* or *yage*. It is cooked with the fresh green leaves of *chacruna*, a green-leafed shrub that contains DMT, and sometimes with other potent plants or herbs such as wild tobacco. *Aya* (spirit) *waska* (vine) roughly translates as "vine of the soul" or "vine of the dead (ancestors)." Some of my experiences with this brew throughout the years dramatically changed my life perspective and allowed me to enter in to a new understanding of the universe's working forces.

⚡ Visions from the Vine of the Dead

It was March 1997, my first trip to the Amazon. The sweltering equatorial sun was already high in the cloudless sky when we bid our farewells to Don Alberto Taxo, his wife, Alba, and their kids at their simple home in Quilajalo, a small village nestled in a valley south of Ecuador's capital, Quito. It was hard to believe we had spent only two short days with them, as they made us feel so much at home. Our group, which was led by John Perkins and Joyce Ferranti, were a bunch of curious healers, artists, and psychologists gathered from all over the United States. Don Alberto, a charismatic shaman with long, black hair and a long beard, dubbed by some as "Jesus of the Andes," inspired us with his sacred knowledge, ancient prophecies, stories, and music. We were especially in awe of his powerful personal healing ceremonies, as we stood naked around the smoky fire pit in the large, circular healing room he had built himself, and in the sacred spring a few miles away from his home.

We were ready for our next big adventure: meeting with the Shuar shamans of the Amazon. We drove east to Baños, a small, vibrant town surrounded by volcanic mountains. Baños is famous for its ancient thermal baths, towering waterfalls, and sugarcane stands. It is situated at the edge of the Oriente, in eastern Ecuador, the lowland area of the Amazon rain forest, by the Pastaza River; therefore many young people stop at this small, colorful town to get information and last-minute supplies before heading into the jungle. We spent the night and most of the next day in a small hotel opposite the thermal bath known as La Virgen, which is next to a waterfall, and enjoyed the tasty restaurant fare, dancing to Latino music in the local disco, and shopping for that last essential gift.

Finally, at sundown we received military clearing to start moving in a long caravan down the Pastaza River's steep and dangerous gorges to Shell, a poor oil town on the edge of the Amazon basin with a small military airport, from which we would fly to the Shuar's Miazal community. Our expert local bus driver, heading the caravan, navigated slowly and carefully, now in total darkness through streams made by small waterfalls, which dug deep furrows in the rich soil of the winding, narrow, slippery road. It literally took our breath away every time the bus had to make a sharp turn as we looked down, sometimes 200 feet, into a canyon and heard the roaring, gushing water straight below us. I was utterly relieved and grateful to our driver as we approached Shell at sunset.

After buying additional supplies and rubber boots at a local bodega, we boarded a small Cessna plane and flew to the Shuar community of Miazal. The Shuar, who used to inhabit the entire jungle area, fled to this location as western civilization slowly crept deeper and deeper into their once-vast territory. The absence of roads across the Cutucú mountain range and jungle has given them the protection they need to preserve their autonomy and traditional way of life. "The headhunters of the Amazon," as the Shuar are known, are fierce warriors famous for their independence and the head-shrinking practice they sustained until the mid-1960s. The European Christian missionaries who arrived there in the 1950s tried to "save" their souls by forcing them to end this and many other old Shuar traditions.

After a thirty-minute turbulent flight over the most amazing sea of diverse shades of green that included magical waterfalls, snaking rivers, and tall mountains, the Shuar community warmly received us on a grassy landing strip. We were led to a nearby river and put into dugout canoes that took us to our campground, which had been built in the 1990s by Juan Arcos, an Italian missionary who had married Amelia, a Shuar woman. Excitedly, we settled down in our open bamboo cabins and made our first introduction to the jungle fire ants and butterflies, the unbearable muggy heat, and the coolness of the water. The next night, after a day of fasting and a grueling walk to the sacred waterfall, we started our healing ceremonies.

The Shuar healing ceremonies are assisted by the natém, the hallucinatory concoction that only an *uwishin* (shaman) is allowed to prepare and that is also even given to young children.

The preparation is long and arduous. The shaman cuts, slits, and peels the vine bark, adds twenty-four chacruna leaves—freshly cut, usually before dawn to maintain their potency—and sometime adds other herbs depending on the type of healing and the results he is intending. He then boils the mixture slowly for many hours until it becomes a thick brown drink. Throughout this process the shaman chants a special *anent,* a prayer chant for the god Ayumpum, who they believe taught the Shuar how to prepare the sacred vine, and for his ancestors, the jungle, the sacred jaguar, and the anaconda spirits, to help and protect him during the healing ceremony. It is necessary to fast a full day before the ceremony as a way of clearing the digestive system, purifying the thoughts, and concentrating on the healing intention. In addition a vigorous day of physical activities is traditionally done to reduce the body's resistance and intensify the natém's effect.

The natém (ayahuasca) ceremony is performed in complete darkness, around a three-log fire in which only a small cinder is left to burn, after drinking ayahuasca as one's senses become extremely alert, sensitive, and open. It enlarges the pupils, and many people experience full night vision. Being exposed to any light source can potentially hurt one's eyes.

As he prepares for the ceremony, the shaman himself drinks the ayahuasca to have access to his spirit helpers and to be able to journey with his patient. To clear his mind and enhance his visions the shaman may also sniff wild tobacco water through his nostrils and drink *trago,* a pure sugarcane rum.

There are two traditional methods of ayahuasca healing. In the first, the shaman simply hands the patient the drink after a short chant, and the patient goes on to have his own teaching experiences. In the second method, called "blown ayahuasca," the patient tells the shaman what healing is needed, and then the shaman literally blows his personal power, spirit, and soul into the cup of ayahuasca in his hands. He then passes the cup and asks the patient to drink it.

As night finally fell we gathered in the round community lodge. In the middle of the packed dirt floor the three-log fire burned, reflecting light on the surrounding bamboo walls and the thatched roof. I could feel the tension building in the warm, heavy air. We sat quietly on benches made of dugout canoes that had been placed along the walls. We looked at one another for reassurance, whispering and making small talk. We were truly nervous in anticipation of the unknown. Even the jungle's night creatures' cacophony began to sound sharper and more alarming than it had earlier. We were tired and hungry after the all-day hike through the jungle, crossing the gushing waters, climbing up rough boulders of sacred twin waterfalls and, of course because of the fasting we had done in preparation for this event.

Daniel Guachapa, the shaman, jet-black hair, barefoot and bare-chested, wearing only his shorts, sat by his wife, who was assisting, near the entrance. Juan Gabriel, our local English-speaking guide, sat next to them. By now the fire was almost out, and Juan began to describe the ceremony protocol and what we should expect while under the influence of the ayahuasca. Then Daniel poured himself a glass, drank it down, folded his arms on his chest, held his head down, and, concentrating, began chanting an anent as if to himself. When at last he was ready he stopped and motioned to those who had decided to take the nonblown ayahuasca to come for their portions. He started chanting a long and beautiful monotonous rhythm and then he called us one by one. Each person sat on a curved, turtle-shaped wooden bench in front of him, telling him what he or she wanted healing for. He then performed individual chants to each cup of ayahuasca before handing it to the person.

I quickly tried to form a "significant" question in my mind so I wouldn't waste this once-in-a-lifetime opportunity. I decided to ask, "What does the future hold for me before I reach my fiftieth birthday?" When my turn came up, I asked my question, drank my portion, washed its bitter taste down with trago, sniffed tobacco water, and went back to my place.

Swinging lightly in the hammock for a while, I wondered why I didn't feel anything unusual. I thought that maybe I took too little of it. After about twenty minutes of watching the black bats going in and out of their nest in the thatched roof above me, I felt my body becoming lethargic and heavy. Suddenly I felt an electric buzz going through my head and found myself merging with the entire jungle. I shut my heavy eyelids and started to picture many colorful geometric shapes, forms, and lines appearing in fast sequence. I tried to follow them as I felt an enormous pressure clapping my head. Hundreds of rows of small, transparent nylon bags appeared rapidly; inside each of them I was surprised to see small, toylike replicas of our culture's consumer appliances and products. They hung from the sky in countless rows, layer after layer, filling the whole world and multiplying rapidly with more and more washing machines, blenders, televisions, videocassette players, telephones, sewing machines, microwave ovens, irons, computers, refrigerators, cameras—all made of colorful, unbreakable plastic. It seemed there was no way to escape them. I felt out of breath and suffocated. It reminded me of those tempting candies that hang down from store shelves. I felt my friend Samuel, who was watching me, kneeling next to me and asking quietly how I was doing. I whispered to him in despair through my drying mouth, "The whole world is made out of plastic." An unfamiliar voice told me, "You humans are engaging in total destruction of the planet by using all of those appliances excessively. You must stop consuming so much and you must find a simpler way to live." The voice continued: "Wherever and whenever you can, you must use environmentally friendly materials and natural products."

A deep sense of grief and sadness spread into my heart. I felt another buzz, and my vision drifted away. Then I found myself standing in a jungle clearing, surrounded by large, tall trees. It was a bright sunny day, and standing twenty feet away from me was a large, well-built, glowing, golden Shuar man. He stood there with his open golden wings glittering in the sun's rays. I held my breath with surprise and watched him carefully. My eyes were immediately drawn to a large eye embedded in his chiseled chest, just above his heart. I thought it was odd. I examined it closely and recognized it as the eye of my friend Samuel. In some way I knew that this was Hempé, the Shuar god of balance and harmony, who is usually represented as a hummingbird. Hempé took a few steps closer to me and said, "I'm here to guide and support you in pursuing your path." I asked him my question, what the next step was for me before I turned fifty. He replied softly with kindness, "You are on the right track. Keep going, but you need to be more aware of and connected to Mother Earth and help protect her." And with that, the pressure and the humming in my head started to increase and my mouth got dryer. Turning in my hammock, I decided not to fight the feelings and fleeting images that were now pouring through me.

Soon a new vision emerged. I was walking in very slow motion into an exhibition hall. It was housed in a big, low-structured museum surrounded by towering green trees. Somehow it was obvious to me that this exhibition was of my own future artwork. The walls of the gallery's many rooms were hanging with large, square, white, textured canvasses. Hanging in the air in the middle of the room was a colorful pipe about five inches in diameter that sprawled through the space at varied heights, connecting to the center of each painting. The pipe was painted in bright yellows, reds, oranges, and black and white. This reminded me of the coral snake we had seen the other day by the hanging bridge on our way to the mission school. An unknown force led me from room to room deliberately, slowly, so I could carefully observe, study, and remember each of the paintings, every color and pipe curve. As time passed, I felt anxious and unsure that I would ever create this exhibition in my present lifetime.

I lay on the hammock a while, feeling my body getting heavier, like a rock, trying to follow more of the outpouring of images. My stomach was beginning to turn upside down. I needed to throw up. Held by my partner Samuel, we crossed the three-log fire in the center of the lodge, passed by the shaman, and went into the bushes in front of the communal lodge. I bent forward toward the bush's large leaves, ready to puke, but instead a huge gas bomb blasted out of my mouth. At that moment I heard the plant asking me to look down deep inside him. I held the leaves in my hands, brought it closer to my eyes, and looked at it intently. To my amazement I started to see the leaf from the inside and witnessed its internal architecture. I zoomed in on every cell and water vein. They were an illuminated golden green with darker shades of green veins running through them. I felt the sun energy being absorbed in it. I was surprised to see all the intricate tubes constructed in the inner plant, to see the water drops flowing inside it feeding every cell. Each cell had thoughts and feelings and eagerly wanted to communicate with me. I started to connect with the plant through my heart. I knew we understood each other on the deepest and most intimate level. The plant said to me, "You humans don't recognize that we are also complete living beings with wisdom, thoughts, and feelings just like you." It added, "We are truly happy to be here on this earth to help and serve humans with all their needs. All humans have to do is to ask us kindly for it. If you want you can always easily communicate with us directly by focusing your eyes with strong intent and attention deep into our essence."

My wide-open eyes were hurting from the intense effort. I felt exhausted. I fell on my knees to the ground, clutching the dry jungle soil in the palms of my hands. I looked down and saw a small moth on the ground an inch away from my nose. I looked at it meticulously. It was muddy, brown, and hairy, with two large gray and black eyes painted on each of its wings. In an instant the moth grew huge and I merged with it, shapeshifting into the moth itself. I grew big wings and found myself ascending higher and higher, carried by the soft wind above the rainforest canopy. I looked down and saw the green trees under me as if it was daylight. The jungle spirits continued to communicate with me, saying that they wanted me to see this view and that I came here to help protect the rain forest and all the infinite life forms it holds. Also, it said with urgency, time is running out and they need all the help I can give them. Flying high above the jungle I promised to do all I could. I felt a huge sense of responsibility, pain, and fear, which brought me back down. I gathered myself, stood up slowly, and went back to lie in my hammock. Many more visions came and went as I drifted in and out, watching color patterns and listening to the constant humming sounds.

Someone came over to my hammock and asked me to go to the healing bench across the hut. The ayahuasca visions were continually flooding through my head at a rapid pace, so walking in the dark was not such an easy task, even with the help of Samuel. I took off my t-shirt and lay on my back. Daniel, the shaman, holding a bunch of fresh jungle branches, immediately began pounding them all over my body while chanting a rapid rhythm tenderly in his soft voice, "Bee, bee, bee, bee, dee, bee, dee, dee, bee, bee, bee . . ." The geometric shapes that I was now seeing, accompanied by the magical chant, fascinated me. He stopped and started to throw invisible darts, *tsansak,* at different parts of my body, parts that needed to be cleansed. Then he put his mouth over them and forcefully sucked out the bad energy, spitting it out onto the dirt floor to be released into the jungle with big growling sounds. My body seemed to respond by pulling itself up every time. Suddenly I felt a big anaconda snake enter my body through my anus and crawl slowly all the way up through my intestines. My body was turning and twisting involuntarily with smooth snakelike movements. As it reached my throat I stopped breathing. I opened my eyes and to my surprise, to the left of my head I saw a jaguar peeking out from behind a green bush. At first it appeared as a cartoon and then it turned into an actual animal. With true amazement I saw him leap over my face and swallow the dark cloud of junk or bad energy the anaconda had pushed through my body that now emerged out of my mouth. I noted how totally at ease I felt with all these strange events. At that time the shaman placed his mouth over mine with amazing gentleness and blew his spirit and breath into me. Then he put his mouth over my chest and strongly sucked all traces of the ayahuasca from my body. Miraculously my head cleared of the ayahuasca's influence instantly, and at the same time I felt tired, energized, and amazed.

Back in my hammock I lay quietly listening to the night's sounds—the cicadas, the croaking frogs, the wind rustling the leaves, the river running below, and my friends, who were throwing up profusely in the nearby bushes. I stared at the trees on the riverbank in front of me and noticed that they had shapeshifted into three huge sculpted Shuar warrior faces, like the presidents' faces carved on Mount Rushmore. They looked straight at me, talking, winking, and having fun among themselves in the early morning wind. I formed a question in my mind and asked them if they had a message for me, and they said, "You can witness that just like humans—trees are very much alive and each of us has an individual face and a different personality."

A few hours later, as the sun came up, after a short sleep and a long-awaited breakfast, I sat in front of Daniel the shaman on the same stool and described to him what I'd seen and experienced during the healing session. I asked him to explain to me what all this meant. His narrow and intent black eyes brightened and he laughed wholeheartedly. He said that he had seen it all too. As a matter of fact, he said he had sent the anaconda and the jaguar, which are his power animal allies, to do their jobs. I thanked him. He instructed me to go to the river to take a dip, submerging my head, and for the next two weeks he forbade me from eating meat or spicy food, drinking coffee, and having sex. I left the lodge and walked into the cold river for a long dip. My mind was full of nagging and troubling questions.

We had only a short time after that to pack our things, say goodbye to our new friends, and head back to the grassy airstrip through the jungle's path for our flight back to Shell. I walked alone, deeply engrossed in my thoughts, trying to recall one by one the experiences of the previous night. At first my brain tried to give them logical explanations but soon I realized that that didn't work or even matter. I was confused by what the manifestation of this shamanic spiritual healing work would be in the material world. I could not deny it. It raised questions: What is real? Who is real? How would I live in a world that had no clear definitions, nothing to hold on to as "reality"? I felt and knew that the anaconda and the jaguar were real, but were they *really*? Could I prove it? I knew that the shaman Daniel Guachapa had sucked the ayahuasca right off my chest; I had felt it as my brain cleared. When I looked at that plant I knew its feelings and was able to communicate with it through my heart but I could not explain it. And I also knew deep down inside that if we don't do everything we can to save the jungle and these incredible possessors of knowledge, we won't be able to explain that either.

When I returned to New York I continued to ask myself all those substantial questions and tried to integrate the experiences I had had in Ecuador into my regular New York lifestyle. But for eight months I was depressed. I wondered what my family and other people were thinking of me. But then one day I had a new vision while I meditated and I knew I had to go back to Ecuador.

⚡ GOLD NECKLACES

Sitting on a cushion, I was meditating in my New York City apartment as I often do in the mornings. Even though I was trying to brush away any images that invaded my mind, a persistent vision kept creeping back in—I kept being taken back to Oriente, the Amazon rainforest area in eastern Ecuador I had visited just six months earlier. In that moment an unexplained desire to see my Shuar friends came over me.

Suddenly a new vision took me to a portion of a river that I had never seen when I was there. It was a shallow river with clear water. Both banks of the river were glowing bright in the sunlight and appeared to be full of many round pebbles. *Strange, what is it?* I wondered. I zoomed in for a closer look: they were numerous tiny glittering gold pebbles lining the banks of the river like two beautiful sparkling necklaces. Surprised, I zoomed even closer and now it seemed that what I saw were real gold nuggets. Gold, in the Amazon? Was it possible, was it for real? I could touch and feel the stones in the palm of my invisible hands. But where was this place? I needed to know. Immediately my vision took me to a curvy bend down the river not far from the encampment where we stayed before. The water there was much deeper and created a beautiful natural pool. Out of the blue I saw a glimpse of a huge anaconda that came swiftly from the riverbank and with a big splash dove into the waters and disappeared. I made a mental note: *This was her home, she must be the river's protector.* I was astonished. I took a deep inhalation. Wow, I thought—if this is real it could be a great way for the Shuar people to be economically independent. They could solve all their problems, have enough to share with their community, and preserve and support their lifestyle and tradition. I got so excited that at that instant I decided I must join the group going to Ecuador in two weeks headed by my friend Christine Parini. I was determined. They must know about this!

"I don't understand, why do you need to go, and why now?" my frustrated wife asked.

"I don't know, but I have to deliver a message."

She finally gave up trying to make sense of what I had told her.

That's how I found myself back in Miazal in October 1998. But before we reached Miazal, on the second day of our trip in the High Andes, I looked for an opportunity to speak privately with my Shuar friend Juan, who was from Miazal and came up to meet us. That day we stayed at the well-manicured 300-year-old Spanish Hacienda Pinsaqui, an hour and a half north of Quito. Early that cold morning, as the roosters were crowing and the dogs were barking back at them, Christine, Juan, and I took an early morning walk into the beautifully cultivated fields behind the hacienda. We passed the central fountain, went through the back gate, and came to a dirt road sided by rows of tall cedar trees. The sun was just rising over the horizon with a breadth of beautiful yellow and orange hues as a few workers carrying their tools passed by, nodding "Dias," good morning, smiling courtesy at us and hurrying to go to their day's work.

We were exhausted but also extremely excited after spending an almost sleepless night in the legendary room number eight, where around 2 a.m., to my utmost surprise I saw something that chilled me. From behind the tall white curtains a white, transparent female figure moved slowly from one side of our bedroom to the other. According to a local story I found out this white ghost belonged to a young woman who was murdered in that very room many years before.

On our way back from the fields we took a short break, taking in the cool, fresh Andean air and laughing as we made small talk and planned our trip. Wondering if this was the right moment, I finally gathered my courage.

"Juan, I need to ask you a very odd question.

"Sure," he gladly answered.

I went on. "Do you know if there is gold in the river near Miazal?" Juan, who couldn't wipe a big smile off his face since we met, stopped joking. He became very quiet and serious for a long while and looked away into the far distance. I felt uncomfortable but continued. "You see, I had this strange vision in New York, which is why I came back again."

I went on to tell him the entire vision. He listened to my story carefully. After a long silence he raised his head and looked me in the eyes and quietly said, "Our people have known about it for a long time but they prefer to keep it a secret, because it brought only tension, rivalry, and jealousy to our community in the past." He went on, "Above the anaconda's pool on that riverbank there is a longhouse that belongs to one family. We know they collect the gold and sell it, and yes, they are rich and they keep an eye on it and protect it from any passersby. People are afraid of the anaconda in that pool." He took another deep breath, shifted his weight from leg to leg, and continued, "If the government and big corporations hear about it they will come in and ruin our jungle and nothing good will come of it for the Shuar."

Obviously I was pleased with that unexpected confirmation but at the same time the affirmation of my vision was mixed with a sense of great responsibility. "So is there anything I should do?" I asked him.

"Speak with my cousin Patricia when you're in Miazal. She will know what to do."

A couple of days later, after lunch, I caught up with Patricia, the daughter of Amelia, a well-known healer and the de facto leader of the community. The two of us stood quietly by a small fruit tree on which two excited green parrots were noisily chatting, and I shared with her my vision. I could feel her become tense and sad. Quietly, in English, she whispered, "Issack, we know about it, we know about the families from the community that are becoming rich selling the gold. We do not know what to do about it yet. I am not very optimistic about our future here either." Her pessimistic view was real and depressing. We said good-bye and went our separate ways. Back in the communal hut, laying on one of the hammocks, I wished that something could be done with all these riches to benefit the Shuar and to preserve the unspoiled jungle that surrounded them.

I have decided that it is time to share this story in full, as in recent years the secret is no longer a secret. Big corporations, with the help of their governments, are now trying to get to the jungle's rich resources and are consequently poisoning the water and threatening its life and those of the native people. And so I'll backtrack a bit to the complete story.

⚡ THE ELEGANCE OF THE UNIVERSE

As mentioned, my second trip to Ecuador, a year and a half after the first one, was a last-minute decision that had been triggered by the strange vision I had in New York, which I urgently wanted to convey to the Shuar. I joined a trip led by my friend Christine Parini, who had planned to visit the Shuar uwishins in the Miazal community in eastern Ecuador and the yachaks of the Andes. I was excited to meet them again and was also curious to find out how it would be different from my first experience with ayahuasca.

That moonless night was unusually hot and dry as it hadn't rained for a few days. The communal lodge was now in total darkness. I could hear the whispers of the river babbling below and the cicadas in their glorious resonance. The jungle awakened for another mysterious night of hunting. Occasional sparks arose from the three-log fire, accenting the faces of our group members who sat in silent anticipation in a circle along the bamboo walls on dugout canoe benches. Black bats were chirping and circling relentlessly above our heads, coming and going from their nests deep within the thatched roof. They paid no attention to what this group of gringos was about to do.

I sat in front of Uneg, a Shuar shaman who was in his mid-seventies with full jet-black hair and a bare chest. It was a miracle that he even availed himself to us as he had just recovered from a bad stroke. The next day we were invited to their longhouse some two hours walking distance, crossing rivers and climbing steep hills, which he did like a young man. That night we were treated to sacred dancing, storytelling, and singing ceremonies performed by a group of warriors and their wives. I woke up the next morning on the mud floor. As I lifted my light blanket I discovered an unusual guest. I had the pleasure of sharing the night with a black, hairy tarantula in my crotch as she looked for warm refuge from the fierce storm that night. Uneg's wife, seeing me so startled, kicked it outside the door with her bare feet. Poor tarantula, a large black bird came flying down from a nearby tree branch and had a nice breakfast.

Uneg sat on a wooden turtle-shaped stool deeply absorbed in his monotonous anent (icaro) as his wife watched closely. He poured the sacred ayahuasca into a small cup and handed it to me. The now-familiar smell of the bitter brown brew awakened an old memory in me. I drank it in one gulp. He then offered me the fiery trago to wash it down and green wild tobacco water to sniff through my nostrils; I gladly accepted it, as I was told it would enhance and clarify my visions. I thanked him and went back to lie in my hammock. My body relaxed and my thoughts drifted freely as I waited for the familiar sensations to begin.

After a short while I started to feel the familiar effects of the ayahuasca as geometric shapes and colorful lines appeared. I watched them for a while when suddenly they told me that it was not an accident that I had chosen advertising as my profession. "Advertising," they said, "is like the shaman's work. It's about changing people's perceptions, inventing and forming new realities, bringing new dreams, and creating magic while communicating with millions of people." I was taken aback—I wasn't expecting that kind of message to be given to me here in the heart of the Amazon rain forest. However, these words seemed to resonate and answered years of deep inner conflict I had had about my profession. After my return from my first trip to the jungle I struggled to understand why I had chosen to work in a job that promotes excessive consumption and materialism and I felt thoroughly guilty about it. The voices continued: "It's important for you, however, to be selective of what products or services you are willing to promote." I kept turning this lesson over in my mind, looking at it from every angle, when suddenly everything around me, the whole universe, became like a canvas on which there were many tiny colorful particles, dots of varying colors and sizes like in the paintings of the French pointillist painter Georges Seurat. They were buzzing and bouncing every which way with varying energies and speeds. I understood that the jungle spirits wanted me to experience firsthand the structure of the universe, what it was made of and how it works. They told me this lesson was called "the elegance of the universe," because, they said, "all the universal laws and its order must consist of an elegant structure." They continued: "The energetic movements of these tiny colorful dots shape our perception of the world as we experience it."

I marveled at this beautiful sight for what seemed like a long time, then I was shown whitish translucent strings that the spirits called "the musical strings of the universe." A web of these strings hung around me and all over me, creating one big, close-knit amalgamation of connections with everything in our universe. They said, "These strings connect us all. Every movement, even the smallest of the smallest affects the rest of the universe." The colorful energy particles bounced back and forth on these elastic translucent strings, creating buzzing sounds like a gigantic harp. I listened to them carefully and began to hear what they called the "the music of the universe." It flowed gracefully and softly in numerous intonations with different vibrations and voices. A beautiful harmony emerged to fill the entire universe. I noticed that I could easily hear each tone independently and at the same time I understood that each one had a distinct voice identifiable on its own, yet in some magical way they were all in absolute harmony.

I was bowled over. I felt that I had been given a rare opportunity to witness the secrets at the heart of creation. I prayed that I would remember every detail of it and wished there was a way to record this in my mind and bring this information back for everyone to hear and understand: the sacred make-up of our universe; how every one of our actions, even the smallest, is essential and can affect the harmonious vibrations of our planet; how we can all be so very different and yet live and weave a magnificent harmony jointly. It was astonishingly magical.

It occurred to me how different this experience was from the "heavenly" church music human composers tried to capture in their work. A few weeks later, while listening with my wife to a Mozart concert at Avery Fisher Hall in New York, I would hear his music in a totally different way. And a few years later in one of my workshops in Israel (and later in other countries as well) I used these teachings. I asked each of the participants to sing their heart song. First each of them sang alone in front of the whole group and then the group sang it together at the same time. What happened next was just breathtaking, unifying harmony—harmony of solid oneness—and at that one moment time stopped.

With these thoughts about vibrational harmony my mind shifted again and I proceeded to encounter many varieties of quick, colorful geometrical visions. But they did not last long. A growing pressure started to invade my stomach. I tried to resist it and hold on to the visions and keep listening to those exceptional sounds. Finally I could hold it no longer. I jumped from the hammock and sure-footedly crossed the now-darkened fire. I walked into the bushes and puked everything that was in me. I bent down and held the bush's large leaves. As I took one of them to wipe my mouth I heard the leaf tell me, "Today is your second lesson from the plant world." It said, "Last time you were to understand how plants are constructed to give you the tools to communicate with them. But today's lesson is about learning and experiencing from them directly through each of your senses—feeling, touching, smelling, tasting, and seeing." I kissed the plant and went back to my hammock.

I perceived amazingly that I could read my thoughts faster or at the same time as they were forming in my mind, and that instantly I was receiving answers from an independent source of wisdom that looked at the world from a totally objective point of view. I continued these questions and answers a while longer. That source of knowledge continued to say, "There is really no difference between good or bad decisions and deeds and you should learn to accept that what is, is. That's all. It's only the influence of the opinions and personal judgments of others that you were raised with that has made things either good or bad." To prove it they took me back to many instances from my life.

Without knowing why, my head turned to the left and my eyes drifted toward Christine, who was lying in a hammock next to me, obviously in the midst of her own intense ayahuasca journey. At first I felt a strong resentment as I didn't want to waste precious vision time on another member of our group. But immediately the spirits reprimanded me, telling me that "Christine and you need to work together. You have a special lifelong connection and purpose and you will cooperate with each other on many projects in the future." To my amazement, the next day Christine would share with me that she had had the same vision and message and also a similar response as mine. Upon hearing this I relaxed and a feeling of total surrender and acceptance came over me.

I tilted my head back and closed my eyes. New sensations started to come over me. "Get ready for your second plant lesson," I was told. I felt tired and argued with the plant spirit that I was not up to it yet and that I needed to continue with my other visions. "I already had my lesson. Give me ten more minutes," I argued.

"That's how you live your life, with excuses and procrastinations," they responded. This made me really angry. "You are going to learn to use the power of plants for healing and we need to teach it to you now," they told me urgently. I argued with them again, "I do not plan to change my career, especially after the confirmation in my first vision that my advertising profession is the right one." The spirits continued to push me. Finally I felt I had no choice. I got up, turned around, and went to the river with Tom, my partner who had been assigned to watch over me on this journey, following closely behind. My eyes were unusually wide open and I noticed I could see almost as if it were daylight. My senses were alert and sensitive to every movement and sound. On my right I saw the tall majestic *chunta,* a big palm tree, with its hard wood that is used to make spears and canoes and its sweet ripe fruits used by the Shuar to celebrate the new year. He stood there quietly with his canopy touching the stars, surrounded by other bushes and plants. I heard those plants calling me to join them. Without fear I entered their circle quickly and sat down with them. "Begin to experience us fully by using all your senses." They said, "Don't think now, just feel us from your heart; the lesson will come." I opened my arms wide and hugged them, I stroked them with my bare hands, with my face, and with my tongue. I inhaled their strong aroma deeply and felt their vibrating presence. They went on to say, "Plants are more powerful and more resilient than you humans. Our strength comes from our exquisite sense of elegance, balance, and graceful structure, as you experienced it before. Plants were here on this earth long before humans were, and they will be here long after humans are gone." A deep sense of kinship with them and with all that surrounded me came over me, as it seemed as if there was no more separation between nature and myself. I was it.

Thankful for this teaching, I wanted more and asked them, "Can you teach me the third lesson now, as I am already here and am not sure if or when I will come back to the jungle?"

"You will come again for sure," they responded.

"But how many lessons are you to teach me?" I asked.

"One for each visit with us." I guessed they were teaching me what I lack: patience.

I was deeply immersed in this conversation with the plants when I felt an eminent presence watching me from behind the bushes on my left. I froze. Turning my head slowly, I instantly knew it was a jaguar. I saw his eyes studying me. I sent him a message from my heart. "I had been looking for you all day and was hoping to finally meet you. I would not harm you in any way and I am not afraid of you either," I assured him. "I'd sit still and wait for you to make the first move to come closer," I told him. A moment later a few branches on the riverbank moved slightly and his dark body softly moved toward me. He came closer until he reached me and brought his large feline face close to mine. I looked deep into his eyes and smelled him. He opened his mouth and gave me a few licks with his warm, raspy tongue all over my face, and then he rested his head on my shoulders. We sat there for a while, immersed in mutual feelings of deep kinship. Without warning he got up, turned around, and disappeared back into the night.

Following him with my eyes I felt a sense of strength and contentment. I knew that now was the right time for the shaman's healing. I got up and asked Tom, who had not drunk the ayahuasca, if he had seen what had happened, too. "The jaguar?" he said, pointing to the same place that I had seen the jaguar coming from. "Yes," I said, surprised. He continued, "I was watching you from behind and all of a sudden my spine froze when I first felt his presence. Then I saw the jaguar coming from that direction toward you." And he pointed to the group of trees by the river.

Energized, I went briskly back to waiting Uneg. Tom was trying to catch up with me but I didn't need help; I was full of a powerful energy and confidence. I came back to the lodge, crossed the dimmed fire, took my shirt off, and lay down on the dugout canoe bench. Uneg started the healing ceremony. He chanted over me while pounding me with a bunch of dry leaves and then he sucked out the invisible darts and bad energy from my body. My vibrating body was anticipating what he would do and responded easily. I started to chant and sing with him. At first I tried to control myself and stop it as I was afraid I was interfering with his work. But after a while I just let go and joined him and enjoyed it. Different visions from the night were coming back to me and I was trying to sort them out. A clear vision of my wife and our three children, who were thousands of miles away, appeared in my mind and a feeling of deep gratitude toward them came over me. I gave thanks for the deep friendship and love we all felt toward one another. I felt so fortunate to have them in my life that warm tears came down my face. I opened my eyes—a bright window appeared in the jungle canopy above my head and in it the jaguar's face emerged. He was looking at me lovingly with amusement in his eyes, and said, "I told you I'd be back, so here I am. You see me again, and it is not important in which reality it is. I'm real, but you are too obsessive and attached, insisting on having things your own way, not realizing you already have the things you want. You saw my footprints on the hiking trail this morning and insisted on finding me in the cave. You saw me earlier in the bushes, I licked your face, and you still didn't give up, even now." I couldn't argue. I knew he was right. My body relaxed. I knew I would not meet him this time in the physical sense and that was truly okay with me.

My healing session ended. I felt alive, full of energy, and focused, like a cloud had lifted from me. Tom and I stayed outside savoring the cool night breeze, looking at the millions of stars above and listening to the symphony of jungle sounds. I shared with him my visions and we compared notes on our meeting with the jaguar.

The next morning, after breaking the fast and dipping in the river, I sat in front of Uneg again. He instructed me on what to eat and what to do after the healing. I thanked him and then curiously asked him if my participation last night in his chants disturbed him. He smiled, looked deeply into my eyes, and told me, "This is my way of passing my powers to you, and you received it through the anents." I was relieved and deeply honored. I thanked him from the bottom of my heart.

After the meeting with Uneg, Tom and I, still enchanted by the jaguar experience of the previous night, decided to check the spot where we had seen him emerge. We both went independently to the same tree. Under it, behind the tall bushes on the river's edge, we found a few fresh footprints matching those we had seen the day before on our hiking trail. Excitedly we called Juan Gabriel, our guide, and told him our story. We asked him to confirm our findings. He looked at the footprints and then at us and smiled mischievously, saying, "I think they belong to a dog." Well, maybe . . .

When I returned from this second trip to Ecuador I shared these visions only with my wife and a few of my closest friends. A few months later, in February 1999, I had an unexpected confirmation of my vision. As I opened *New York Magazine,* I was stunned to see the headline of the lead article, which was about the Columbia University physicist Brian Greene. It was titled "He's Got the World on a String." It talked about his new book, *The Elegant Universe,* in which he explains the "theory of everything." He writes, "The theory rests on a very simple premise: that the smallest building blocks of the universe—muons, photons, gluons, and all those other particles that sound like Santa's reindeer—are generated by the vibrations of tiny, quivering loops of string. The whole universe is made up of them, tied up with them, if you prefer, as if the cosmos were a shimmering aeolian harp."

A few weeks after that, while reading the *New York Times,* I noticed a Barnes and Noble advertisement with a picture of Brian Greene, who was about to have a book signing and lecture at an uptown store. When I arrived I was surprised to see the large room packed with curious people of all ages. Dr. Greene was enthusiastic and well prepared with charts, stories, and videos. Hearing him describe his research findings and seeing the videos made me truly excited; it was like reliving my ayahuasca visions in the jungle all over again. It made me wonder what would happen if Dr. Greene and other scientists would travel to the rain forest, meet the teacher plants, and drink the hallucinogenic ayahuasca brew. Can science alone find answers to more complex questions and phenomena we don't know much about?

⩕ A LESSON ON THE RIO NEGRO

"Come join us," some sweet-looking spirits whispered seductively in my ears as they hovered above my head like a flock of floating classical dancers in space. "Follow us," they said in angelic, sweet, enticing voices as they approached me.

I was not imagining this. It was as clear as the hypnotic ayahuasca icaros, the magical plant spirit songs that were being sung by Barata the ayahuascero from the Araweté Ipixuna tribe of northwestern Brazil, who sat a few feet away from me. By his side stood his assistants, who were rhythmically pounding on bamboo earth drums on the hard-pressed ground. The rest of our group and I were lying down comfortably on reed mats at the last thatched-roofed hut at Reserva Taruma, the home of Ipupiara, on the banks of one of the tributaries of the Rio Negro in Brazil. My head was just a few steps away from the edge of the jungle. The sun was already slowly setting. The early evening wind softly cooled the hot muggy air. "If you follow us and our teachings you will get what you want and you can become who you want to be," the sweet spirits promised me. "Join us. It is so simple to convert to our religious teachings."

Confused at first, I politely refused. Who were they? What did they want from me? I am an atheist, I was brought up in a kibbutz, and I am also Jewish. I reasoned with them but they refused to accept my arguments and kept sweet-talking me. "Join us and we promise you salvation and all of your heart's desires in return." Who were these spirits? I became suspicious as they continued to try to tempt me more and more.

Then I heard a straightforward, clear voice. I recognized it as the ayahuasca spirit: "It's a trap, it's a trap, it's a trap! Don't fall into the hands of evil, just look up and you'll see their real faces," they warned me urgently.

This wasn't going to be as easy a ceremony as I had hoped to have this time around, I thought.

I looked up. This time I clearly saw their dark, contorted faces that revealed their true nature. I was dumbfounded. We began to argue again as I tried to make my point. "Leave me alone!" I demanded. They laughed bitterly and said firmly, "You can try but you can't resist us. We rule millions of people just like you around the world; they follow us blindly!" We continued to wrestle verbally for what seemed like a long while. At last, even though I was totally exhausted by this struggle, a new energy came through me and I found my inner power and declared, "I choose to follow the light! I'd rather give up my life than join you! Go ahead and kill me if you want to." I surprised myself. They snickered at me as if they already had me caught in their web of deceit. I used all the energy I had left in me, gathered the powers of light, and thrust it forcefully toward them as if throwing a powerful spear, thrusting over and over again until they slowly receded and finally disappeared into the void.

I took a few deep breaths, my body slowly starting to unwind from this colossal struggle. A new vision now appeared. Standing far away from me but moving slowly closer was a light being, a man surrounded in golden light. I recognized him as Jesus. "No, call me Yeshua," he said in a peaceful voice. "The evil spirits of the universe hijacked my spiritual teachings of universal love," he said calmly and sadly as he stood in front of me. "They intend to conquer the world by deceit, pretending to be the forces of light." At that moment I felt an extraordinary beam of light and love streaming from my heart toward this humble and loving fellow Hebrew man, and his light encircled me entirely. "I am you; you are part of me," he continued and gently vanished into the darkened jungle behind me. At the same time my mind began to clear from the ayahuasca's impact. Gradually the mixed sounds of the millions of cicadas and frogs, the icaros, and those who were still crying and purging filled the cool night air. At last I let my mind and body rest.

Back in my hammock I swung lightly back and forth for a few more hours. In my mind I went through each of the vision's episodes and messages that had been revealed to me. Was it really true that there are independent evil forces that roam the universe looking for messengers to do their harmful work for them? What do they want? Why do they need control, and over whom? Is the only weapon against them reflecting light and love on them? Would this monumental struggle between the dark and light forces ever be won? Is it necessary? If Yeshua is real, is he now a sad spirit disappointed by his most devoted followers? Did I make all this up?

It was about five years later that I surprisingly discovered that my ancestor, my great grandfather, a Kabbalistic rabbi in Poland, dedicated his life to answering the same questions.

6

✕ ✕ ✕ ✕

SHAPESHIFTING

From a shamanic perspective, shapeshifting begins with intent. You then give it power if you want it to occur in this world as opposed to the other worlds of nonordinary reality. Action follows.

JOHN PERKINS

Can you transform yourself to become another entity or object in a split second? Our collective mythology, folklore, fairy tales, and science fiction are full of stories of gods, animals, and humans shapeshifting into other cellular forms, spiritual entities, the opposite gender, and mystical and real animals. They do this either by their own will using magical artifacts, or unwillingly due to the wishes of another person. Shapeshifting can also occur in the personal and collective consciousness—in politics, in business, and in society at large. I don't expect scientists to embark on a study of the phenomenon as it is usually classified in the realm of magical or wishful thinking, although these days a lot of research has been done in quantum mechanics and physics that allows for the possibility of shapeshifting. I guess you just have to experience it.

Shamans have developed the ability to transform themselves into whatever they need to be and can even make themselves invisible. From their point of view there is no difference between the physical and the spiritual bodies. They understand that everything in our universe is made of pure energy particles. These energy particles are moving in different vibrations and directions at different speeds; they take on different configurations and we can manipulate them in our mind through the power of intention and concentration. My friend John Perkins wrote a beautiful book about this phenomenon and his experiences. The following minor example illustrates what happened to me after working with John.

I had to return two drawers that did not fit in our new refrigerator. As I entered the big appliance store on 14th Street, two security guards stopped me and demanded to know why I was there and to check my box and my receipts. They warned me that on my way back I would have to again show them my exchange receipt before they would let me leave. It was late in the evening and I was too tired and annoyed to deal with them. After I made the exchange I wanted to leave as fast I could carrying these two big, bulky packages. I remembered John's teachings and decided to try it out. I held my intention to be invisible, to turn into thin air, or wear an invisible shield. I can't tell you exactly how it happened—all I know is that the two security guys did not even see me walking by them and out through the revolving store doors. Once outside I turned my head to look back. They looked as if they were in a dream.

The next story is much more significant and memorable.

⚡ MEETING THE JAGUAR

There is nothing more energizing than waking up in the oxygen-filled jungle. We were in Miazal in the Ecuadorean rain forest. Although I hadn't gotten much sleep I was full of oomph, excitement, and anticipation for our hike to the sacred twin waterfalls that morning. The night before, some of our group had chosen to spend the night hanging in hammocks in the open lodge's communal area. There was a lot

of enthusiasm there as we shared personal stories and much laughter. The warm jungle air was filled with the insects' cacophony, and the black bats made chirping noises as they flew in and out of their nests tucked in the thatched roof above us. One by one we dozed off, only to be awakened at around four in the morning by a special wake-up call. A loud and wild growling filled the early morning stillness like a police siren. It startled us out of our wits. No doubt a real live jaguar had made that sound. It sounded so close, as if it was just beyond the narrow riverbank nearby. *It's for real,* I thought, feeling shivers spreading up my spine. My heart pounded. Were we in danger? Could he leap over the river and come get us? I had to admit I was fear-struck as I realized we were really and truly in the rain forest. And then came silence again.

After a quick, light breakfast our small group started out on a hike. We crossed the hanging bridge, continued toward the mission school, passed the wooden church, and turned right to follow the river path. I was amazed at how every scent, turn in the path, rock formation, tree, and flow of water on the narrow trail seemed familiar to me from my first hike here eighteen months earlier. It felt so good—as if they were welcoming me home.

As we continued our hike along the river my thoughts shifted to that amazing roar just a few hours ago. I had an urgent feeling that we could potentially meet this legendary creature right here and now. I turned to Juan Gabriel, our tour guide, who was walking with me at the end of the line, teaching me about the different medicines of each of the jungle's trees and plants.

"Hey Juan, we should try to find the jaguar's footprints here. I have a feeling that he's here," I said.

He laughed this off, saying, "In the eight years that I have led groups here I have never seen a jaguar. Although, some time ago another group saw one lounging in the sun on a rock by the river, but that's all. Jaguars usually stay up in the mountains; they are afraid of humans. But who knows, it could be because it didn't rain for a whole week that one of them came down to the river."

At that instant something really strange happened. The Shuar warrior who was leading us at the front called out excitedly, asking us to come quickly to the front of the line. As we all gathered around him he bent down and showed us fresh jaguar footprints. There were three deep cavities with claw imprints in the muddy trail. We studied them closely; we felt and measured them with our fingers. There was no doubt they belonged to a jaguar. There was an air of excitement in the group. I laughed at the "coincidence" and as the group continued to move forward I said half-jokingly to Juan, "Hey, wait for me, let me journey, maybe I can find him." He agreed. And with my back leaning against a large kapok tree, I closed my eyes.

I called on my power animal and asked for help to find that jaguar. What happened next was just astonishing and will stay with me for the rest of my life. Without any warning a picture instantly appeared in my mind's eye. I was in a jungle, but something bizarre happened to my body. I could feel myself shapeshifting, transforming into and becoming the jaguar. My limbs stretched and changed. My legs and hands became longer, thicker, more powerful, and were now covered with a protective fur. I could even feel my face change and take a feline shape. I found myself launching forward, speed-running on all fours, navigating amazingly quickly between the thick vegetation and the trees. Sharp branches and thick vines were stroking and hitting my furry body as I raced through the jungle with amazing agility and speed. Breathing heavily and deeply I crossed a narrow, fast river until I reached a small cave opening on a muddy, slanted ledge on the left side of the river. Quickly I entered the cave and rested, breathing heavily. I could observe the tall trees above me and the river flowing below me. At that instant I came back to reality.

I opened my eyes and took a big gasp of air. My body was still full with the rush of excitement and my heart still pounding. I did not know how long this vision had lasted—a minute, five minutes, or an hour. Luckily Juan was still there watching me. I described to Juan

Gabriel what I had just experienced. Again he said with a merciful smile that he believed it was only a vision and couldn't be real. I had a hard time believing it myself, but I knew it was true. Could I prove it?

We continued, walking fast, trying to catch up with the rest of the group. Finally, after two more hours of rock climbing, a few river crossings, and constantly emptying water out of our rubber boots, we arrived at the two sacred waterfalls. It was truly a magical place; no wonder the Shuar used it for shaman initiations. One of the waterfalls was icy cold, as it comes from high up in the Andes, while the other was steamy hot, as it comes from deep within the volcanic springs. This one brought with it rich red iron mud deposits. We enjoyed ourselves, swam in the hot and cold pools, had lunch, painted ourselves with the red mud, and took the obligatory pictures. And this is when this story takes another strange turn.

Just as we began to pack up and put our boots and clothes back on to get ready to head back to our lodge, Justin, a young fellow from our group, took off to explore the area by himself. I followed him with my eyes, strolling up the other side of the river until he disappeared behind the river curve. Suddenly I saw him waving his hands at me. "Itzhak, come over here quickly," he shouted. Without any hesitation I crossed the river and joined him. "Look" he said and pointed, to my surprise, at jaguar footprints on that narrow riverbank. "This might be the jaguar we saw earlier," he said. We followed the footprints with excitement for about fifty yards up the river to a small cave on a slanted ledge. I stared at it in disbelief. It was literally identical to the cave shape I'd seen earlier in my "vision." We knelt down by the cave opening, calling and praying for the jaguar to come out. But then Justin noticed that the fresh footprints led down back to the river; "I guess the presence of our group scared him away," he said, disappointed. "Do you want to hear something really unbelievable?" I asked him. I then told him my jaguar shapeshifting story and we started laughing. Unhappy and disappointed not to have met him as some of our group joined us at the scene, I asked Juan if I could stay there to wait for his return. "We must go back quickly before it gets too dark in the jungle," Juan said firmly. I didn't give up. I was still determined to meet him face to face and that night I did, under the guidance of Uneg the shaman and the sacred ayahuasca medicine.

7

"SEEING"

I shut my eyes in order to see truth.

PAUL GAUGUIN

There is no one, as far as I know, who can explain how "seeing"—viewing with the mind's eye—happens or even why. Believe me, I have tried. I once even asked a famous brain scientist from a research institute in Israel to explain this strange ability, and he shrugged his shoulders. We know about the third eye and the primitive lizard brain in the back of our skull. We know that blind people can "see."

My friend Richard Unger showed me a line on the palm of our hands that in the palmistry tradition indicates that ability—a line that Don José, Ipupiara, and I all happen to have. But then I know of many people who do not have it and they can "see" as well as we do. In my classes there are many students who have never "seen" before but are able to "see" through the exercises I facilitate. I believe you can develop this ability just as you can with any skill. Certainly there are people who cannot see visually but they can sense, feel, or know, and that is the way they perceive.

Seeing is quite helpful. In my practice I often use it to diagnose a client's problems, sometimes as soon as she walks in the door, like the possessed woman who showed up surrounded by her ancestors, who were urging her to start practicing her healing work (she surrendered and accepted her calling). Or the woman who tried to get pregnant and whose unborn child's spirit appeared by her side to tell her, through me, that it was not yet the right time for him to materialize (as I described him she realized he looked like her husband). Or the religious woman in her mid-forties whose aborted son's spirit appeared to counsel her (she never told anyone she had had an abortion). Or when the spirit of a great-great-grandmother came through to teach her descendant an ancient Sicilian midnight fire ceremony and encourage her to become a medicine woman herself (which she is now). Or an animal spirit that was very angry with my client for wearing a red fox fur hat and a mink coat (she gave them away, and her life changed for the better). Or the woman who came to consult with me as to whether she should marry a serious lawyer she was dating only to have her other blond, funny lover appear (she never came back after that reading). Or the Orthodox Jewish man who had to admit he worshipped Maria after she appeared above his head, radiating light (wasn't she Jewish, after all?). Or the time the Indian deity Ganesh appeared over the head of a middle-aged man (it turned out he had studied for several years in India in a Ganesh temple).

In my workshops I can say that 96 percent of the participants successfully see one or two true elements about their partner. It's a great start. I ask people to find a partner whom they do not know and give them their first name only. I ask them to stand a few feet away from each other and gaze softly at each other, and at the same time, with a diffused vision, starting from the top of the head down to the feet, to see with their hearts. I ask them to listen to any messages their power animals, guides, angels, or any other spirits they work with send their way and try not to understand it intellectually. I then ask them to close their eyes and do the same with eyes shut. I encourage them to travel inside the person's body, visit each of the organs, and see their health condition or receive messages from them.

There are other ways to attain shamanic seeing: there are shamanic journeys with drumming or rattling as well as getting into a trance through movement, dancing, and singing.

The stories that follow are some examples of shamanic seeing stories I was honored to be part of.

⋏ SOUL FLIGHT

As we made our way back into the "civilized" world I stared out of the small Cessna's windows with deep sadness. Tears welled up in my eyes as I watched the small crowd of Shuar men, women, and children gathered on the grassy airstrip on the river's edge to bid us good-bye. It was so remarkable how quickly and deeply we felt a connection to these people. I already missed their inner strength, their broad smiles, and their warm, open hearts with which they had embraced us during the short week we had spent with them in Miazal.

From high above I could see their palm-covered longhouses dotting the jungle floor and the tributary rivers that crossed that magical, primeval forest and infinite sea of green. As we crossed over the Cutucú mountain range a totally different view emerged, one that took me by surprise. It was of a huge green, flat area that had obviously been cut for timber to become a cattle pasture to accommodate our ever-growing consumption of cheap meat. Straight roads cut through them as far as my eyes could see, leading to small settlements or cattle ranches that were growing rapidly around them. It truly broke my heart to realize that this life-sustaining, delicate rain forest, and with it the ancient tribal way of life and existence, is in grave and immediate danger because of us, the people of the north—and even I was guilty. Spontaneously, I made a decision, right then, to never eat beef again.

Twenty minutes later we landed at the small military airport in the oil town of Shell. We had a quick lunch and shopped for some more gifts—to support their economy, we reasoned—and then hopped onto our waiting bus to take us to meet the Quechua shamans of the High Andes. As we slowly ascended on the twisting roads higher into majestic green volcanic mountains we found ourselves floating in the midst of

thick, rapidly moving white clouds of mist and fog as if in a dreamland. The air became crisper, cooler, and much thinner, making it harder to breathe, which also made me lightheaded. The sun had already set when we passed San Pedro Lake beneath the mammoth mountain Imbabura and finally rolled in to the streets of Otavalo, the largest town in the Ecuadorian Andes, which is nestled in the sacred Valley of the Dawn. Surrounding the town were three large dormant volcanoes: Imbabura, Cotacachi, and Mujanda. You will hear these names uttered frequently in most local shamans' prayers, as they are a source of power and their personal protectors. We were exhausted, hungry, and shivering with cold after the day-long bus trip, but we didn't want to miss the opportunity to work with the shaman Don José Joaquin Piñeda that evening.

After a short stop in one of the bodegas for an improvised dinner we arrived at Don José's newly built modern house on the edge of town. This was my second visit to Don José. With a broad smile he opened his iron gate and graciously agreed to accept our unannounced group. We waited in his small healing room as he went to gather from his garden the plants needed for the healings. Don José was a short but solid man in his late forties with almond-dark, piercing eyes that rested under his tall forehead. His face was smooth and round, darkened by the Andean sun; he had high, chiseled cheekbones, a long braid of raven black hair hanging down his back, a big gold watch on his left wrist, and a few gold rings hugging his fingers. He wore typical Quechua clothing: a black felt fedora and blue llama-wool poncho over a white shirt, white cotton pants, and white fabric sandals. Don José came back in to the room carrying dozens of bundled plants and put them down by his elaborate altar. He quickly changed his clothing. He was now dressed in all white, the traditional healer's attire.

Standing in front of our group he introduced himself. "I'm José Joaquin Diaz Piñeda. I'm a yachak ["birdman" in Quechua—in other words, a wise person who knows how to fly to other worlds]. I am like a doctor and I heal everything with plants and ceremonies. I have practiced healing since I was fourteen years old. I come from a long line of shamans—five generations. I learned the practice from my grandfather and my father since I was a little boy, and some of my brothers are also yachaks. My work is very well known in the Andes; I have healed many people, even government officials. People from Colombia and other shamans come to see me. I walk the El Camino Luminoso, the path of light, which is the yachak path. It is important to follow the light of your heart."

In a fatherly way he proudly displayed and explained to our group, as we sat around the room on simple wooden benches, each and every stone and item on his altar. He told us where and how he found or received them. "I have named each stone with a sacred name. These names came to me in a dream. I have many stones but periodically I let some of them rest. I take good care of them," he proudly said. He then took a look around the room and then turned to me. Looking into my eyes he said in Spanish, "You didn't do what I asked you to last time you were here."

This statement took me by total surprise; I didn't realize he remembered me. "What do you mean?" I asked through our translator, Juan Gabriel.

"You didn't take the flower bath I asked you to take, did you?"

At first I utterly dismissed it but then, embarrassed in front of our group, I had to admit my unforgivable felony. *How did he remember me and even remember what he had prescribed almost a year and half earlier?* I wondered in amazement.

Don José carefully unwrapped a red cloth bundle and pulled out a colorful, tall-feathered headdress. Cautiously he put it on his head, sat by his altar, blew some pure trago and tobacco smoke, and started chanting, preparing himself for his work. One by one we each had a turn to receive his diagnosis and La Limpia cleansing ceremony. I could sense in my heart the deep impact the ceremonies had on each person as one by one the body posture, facial expression, and eyes of each person softened and changed.

Then my turn came. Surrounded by our group I stood clad in my white underwear in the middle of the room on colorful Ecuadorian newspapers scattered on the ground. I looked down and chuckled; I was standing on a big picture of Audrey Hepburn, my childhood hero. The movie star was broadly smiling below me—a good omen, I thought, as I brushed the white candle all over myself. Then I blew on it three times and passed it back to Don José. I listened carefully to his candle reading and nodded my head with approval. Next, I closed my eyes and listened to his enchanting chants and birdlike whistles. Soon my body relaxed and I breathed deeply.

Immediately the memory of the powerful visions from my previous visit with him surfaced in my mind. The pressure that mounted in my forehead and rays of white light caused the opening of my third eye and I "saw" the magnificent valley with its dazzling rainbow that rose over the lush green mountains, the magical waterfalls, and the feeling of true connection and oneness with all that surrounded me. I wondered if I'd be able to come close to any of them this time. But I was certainly not ready for what would come next.

Don José's chants brought me deeper and deeper within myself. All of a sudden I felt cold shockwaves spreading throughout my entire bare body as the trago spray he forcefully blew hit me and took my breath way. Soon I heard his mesmerizing chant, felt the beating of the plants, the eggs rattling over my body, and then unexpectedly my arms moved up by an unexplained force. I felt them stretching longer and longer and becoming stronger and heavier. I realized I was sprouting long wings covered with dark feathers! *What is happening to me?* I remember thinking. I took a deep breath and started to flap them more strongly and powerfully until I ascended up into the waiting blue skies, flying higher and higher to an unknown destination. I realized that I had turned into an eagle and was flying over a fertile green valley toward a commanding mountain that was standing on the horizon. From afar I recognized a bluish body of water on the right side of the mountain and swiftly started to fly toward it. In one big thrust I dove into the freezing water and stood there for a moment. Then my body rose above the water with an unexplained force, which pulled my heart into the sky. I flapped my long wings and force-fully shook off the cold water. The tiny water drops splashed in the air in an explosion of amazing kaleidoscopic rainbow colors. They soared up like multicolored diamonds in the blue sky, glittering with the reflection of the bright sun behind the mountain. It was an astonishing sight of unearthly beauty. Suddenly, a high-pitched and piercing birdlike whistle came from behind my neck (later I realized it had come from Don José's small ceramic whistle) and I bolted from the chilly water and instantly soared high into the heavens. At the same time I felt my breath, my soul, disconnecting from my body, leaving through my windpipe, out of my open mouth, and then reuniting with the Creator.

"You can dress now," I heard Juan Gabriel, our tour guide and trans-lator saying. Slowly I opened my eyes. Audrey Hepburn was still there, with her almond eyes smiling at me mysteriously from the old newspa-per below. I was cold, exhausted, and shaken by the experience. I could not move. I felt a deep grief and a strong yearning to stay up there. I didn't want to stay in my own body. I put on my clothes and sat qui-etly on the wooden bench in the corner. Again, Don José prescribed a few things for me to do when I got home, including—yes—a few more flower baths. I promised him I would follow his instructions this time.

After all the other healings were done I approached Don José and shared with him my vision and experience. I asked him to explain it to me. Don José's eyes sparkled. He nodded, smiled, and said in his soft voice, "I gave you the doctor's and healer's initiation healing." With my hand in the air I drew the shape of the mountain I saw and described the blue spring. "Yes," he said, "this mountain is Imbabura, the power-ful male mountain. There between the two mountaintops is the sacred spring. It is called Eagle Lake, where I take my pupils for their initiations and healings." I looked at him in utter disbelief. I took a big breath, and asked him if he would be willing to take me to this place one day in this reality. *"Oh claro, no problema,"* he smiled as his eyes were glowing with mischief. "So, when are you coming back?" he challenged me. As we left the room I gave him my word that I would see him again before one year had passed. I did not have to keep my word this time. He showed up in New York before one year was up.

After a short visit to the felt hat store at his home we were back on the bus heading toward our hacienda for a welcome good night's sleep. That Saturday after a hearty breakfast, our group went to explore the treasures of the famous Otavalo market. We wandered around looking at the huge array of handmade crafts, musical instruments, and colorful rugs and fabrics. After a while we stopped next to a stand that showcased hundreds of small, brilliant oil paintings. Each painting described different scenes from the Andean life and those of the ancient Inca. One picture in particular drew my friend Christine's attention. She urgently called me over to see it. It portrayed a ritual ceremony on Imbabura. In the center two Inca priests performed a ritual on a bridge over the sacred spring. A group of Inca and llamas carrying their harvest surrounded them. Two other priests were blowing long horns on each bank of the spring. The bright yellow sun was rising behind the green mountains and a beautiful rainbow connected the two summits. Above, a group of eagles circled in the blue sky. I couldn't leave it there. I bought it and later hung this painting in my home to remind me of the vision I had had and the promise I had made to Don José.

Jump ahead to a few weeks before the year was up, when I called Don José in Ecuador. His wife answered. "José is not at home, he is in New York with our daughter Soraya." I asked her to have him call me. That day he did. The next evening, accompanied by Natalie, a Spanish-speaking friend, I walked the unfamiliar dark streets of Corona, Queens, looking for his address. We turned into the street; a group of young kids was hanging out on the stairs, chatting loudly in Spanish. Suddenly I stopped. I felt a presence behind a tree. I turned to the right, and out of the dark shadows Don José emerged laughing, with open arms. We hugged a big hug. He invited us into the house to meet Soraya. As we walked down the street on our way to a Chinese restaurant he stopped sharply, looked me in the eye, and asked in a very serious tone, "Did you start the healings?"

I looked at him in disbelief. I asked Natalie to translate what he said again; maybe I did not understand it correctly. "Oh no," I said, "I'm not ready. I have a lot more to learn. I'm not sure that this is even what I want."

"You are ready," he said flatly.

With his encouragement my apprenticeship began. For almost three months Don José asked me to assist him in the many healings, teachings, house clearings, and ceremonies he performed. We had many long and intimate conversations in which he taught me the sacred knowledge his father and grandfather had passed down to him. He envisioned us working together, placing a sign above the door that said DON JOSÉ AND ITZHAK, YACHAKS. Little by little he gave me more and more to do in the healings. Usually, without prior warning he would signal me with a quick movement of his head and a smile, handing me a bottle of trago or perfume, some eggs, a plant, flowers, stones, a cigarette, or special massage oils. Sometimes he pointed to a specific part of the person's body. Just before Christmas he went back home.

In April 2000, for our children's spring break, my wife and I accepted Don José's invitation to visit them in Ecuador. We spent an unforgettable five days in the Galapagos Islands and then returned to the Andes to spend one day at Termas de Papallacta, a volcanic hot springs retreat, to rejuvenate. The next day in the early afternoon we arrived at Don José's gate. Soraya greeted us warmly and took me to meet him at the mechanic's garage, as he had been sent there to perform a healing ceremony on a broken car. Don José was determined that I must have the initiation ceremony performed that night. He laid out his plan. "We must start in Magdalena, the sacred spring that feeds the San Pablo Lake; it has very powerful female energy," he said. "The next day we'll continue to the male spring, San Juan Pogio, near my village, Iluman." We all came back to the house and met with his family.

An hour later he motioned to us that he was ready. "*Vamos,* let's go," he ordered us. Don José packed his healing bundles; we put on our coats, packed a few towels, and got into the minivan. Juan Carlos, our guide (the same man from my earlier dream), drove us south through the narrow streets for more than an hour, carefully driving around the large, dark lake and maneuvering the bumpy dirt road. We passed by small houses built along the shores where families were hanging out for an evening chat. After a long and tortuous drive up the slopes, we finally made a sharp turn to the right and rolled down the hill toward the dark body of water. There on the right was Magdalena, the sacred spring. To our amusement we found a family busy washing their big tour bus in the same sacred waters. We patiently waited for them to finish their sacred task. It was a chilly and windy night, the moonless sky was filled with the brightest stars, and in the background I could feel the enormous presence of the volcanic mountain Imbabura.

The frigid air sent shivers along my body. I dreaded the thought of entering into the icy water. I wished it could be done at the hot spring near my kibbutz. Don José asked the driver to point the car lights toward the pool of water. Soon, as the tour bus with the satisfied family on board finally left, he signaled to my son Ariel and me (Ariel had asked to join in the ceremony) to take off our clothes and walk into Magdalena with him. With the freezing water up to our bellies the three of us stood on the smooth, cold pebbles where the water emerged from the volcanic rocks. Don José, a crown of feathers on his head, holding a bottle of trago in his right hand, closed his eyes in deep concentration and started whistling and chanting loudly, calling on his ancestors, the mountains, the four elements, and the four directions for help in the ceremony. To appease Magdalena's spirit he proceeded to give her offerings of trago by blowing it onto the water, rocks, and into the air, and finally—as if it wasn't cold enough already—on both of us. He then gave additional offerings of red and white carnations, *agua florida* (floral-scented water), and tobacco. My body shivered nonstop. I could feel the numbness spreading through my legs to the rest of my body. My teeth trembled uncontrollably as Don José went on chanting. He then scrubbed my frozen body with his healing stone. Then he placed his long chunta spear fashioned from the strong Amazonian palm tree on my head, chest, and back. For our protection he then asked us to splash the freezing water on ourselves six times over each shoulder and our heads and to give offerings to the spirit of Magdalena. I tried to control my trembling by remembering the amazing eagle "vision" I had had the previous year at Eagle Lake on the same mountain, and it all felt strangely accurate and incredibly comforting. There was one magical moment I sensed where everything became one, everything around me blended and meshed together. The crisp, cold air of the dark night, the bright glorious stars above, the uncontrollable shaking of my frozen body, the intense presence of Imbabura, my son's induction into the path, the howling wind, the bubbling sounds of the water flowing into the huge dark lake beneath us, the presence of my family watching us from the banks, my appreciation and love for Don José—my spirit was full of gratitude. And then it was over. We stepped out of the water into the waiting warmth of the dry towels my wife was holding. We dried ourselves off, put on our clothes, drank some trago to warm us up, poured some on the ground for Pachamama (Mother Earth), and drove back for a warm late-night dinner in Otavalo.

When we arrived at Don José's home the next day we found the whole family busy in the kitchen preparing their traditional food—*choclo con queso* (Andean corn on the cob and fresh smooth cheese), lima beans, and pork. Being good guests, we ate much too much of the delicious food. When he was sure we had eaten all we could, Don José invited us to visit his ancestral village, his fields, and the felt factory where the hats are made. Iluman is well known for its old yachak tradition. The village sits on the slopes of Imbabura at an altitude of over 10,000 feet. We parked in the village square and strolled through the narrow streets, sightseeing. The passing villagers, wearing their traditional costumes, nodded at Don José with a look of deepest respect and warmly greeted us with smiles. Finally we walked to his old family house, built of pressed mud and straw on a narrow side street down the hill. From there it was only a short walk down the street to his fields, where he had picked the fresh corn and lima beans we had eaten earlier.

The large field stretched across the entire hill overlooking Hacienda Pinsaqui and the Pan America Highway. Patiently and with deep love, like a proud father, he introduced us to each of the plants and herbs he was growing and indicated which ones he uses in his healing. He asked us to smell, touch, and taste each one of them. Don José said their names and explained their healing properties and what problems they help to solve: indigestion, headache, sleeping disorders, relaxation, broken bones, and so on, as if reading from a botanical guide. I wondered if I could remember even some of this knowledge. *I definitely have to come back for another lesson,* I thought. As Don José reached a certain spot in the field he pointed and told me proudly, "This is where I plan to build the healing center." I roared in laughter as I recognized the view surrounding us. This was exactly how I saw it! I then told my family the following story.

A few months earlier, during one of Don José's New York visits one night at the end of a long healing day, Don José felt that I too needed a good cleansing. As he worked on me I had a short but powerful vision. In that vision I saw an eight-sided white cement house with tall, narrow glass windows on each side and a red-shingled roof. It stood in the middle of a field on top of a hill, surrounded by a garden of tall green plants that reached close to the building. *Oh, that is totally ridiculous,* I thought, wondering why I would see something like that. Later, when I shared my vision with him, a wide smile spread across his dark face as it usually did when he saw that I understood something, and then he shared his vision with me: "I have a plan to build a healing center in my field in Iluman, where we can teach and do healing, where people can come from all over the world and a have a place to stay." So here we were a few months later standing on the very spot on which he planned to build it. Some years later this building was built and his dream manifested—and I had a share in it.

We spent some time in the felt hat factory, trying on different hats and, of course, purchasing one for each of us. We then drove down the hill to San Juan Pogio, the sacred male spring, for the second initiation ceremony. As fate would have it the sacred spring was occupied by droves of local women busy washing their families' clothes in its sacred waters, trying to finish their task and return to their homes before sundown. We leisurely sat on the grassy slopes watching this community scene for a while and then decided to go home and wait for another opportunity.

The next day all six of us gathered in Don José's healing room to watch him perform a healing on Ariel, who suffered sharp pain from his two dislocated shoulders. With fresh stinging nettles, pine tree needles, oils, and other remedies, Don José worked his powers to relieve Ariel's pain and instructed him on how to continue the treatment. Ariel started laughing with joy. "I have never felt so happy in my life," he said later.

We were all ready to go out when unexpectedly Don José asked my family to wait outside and motioned for me to stay alone with him in the room. I was unsure of what he was planning but, as always, I learned to never ask questions. He asked me to undress and stand in the middle of the room on the old newspapers. So I did. I closed my eyes and waited. *Maybe he wants to cleanse me again,* I reasoned. I heard him at his altar praying, whistling, and chanting. But soon I felt that the spontaneous ceremony was quite unlike any healing I'd experienced before. With my closed eyes I could sense a strange, powerful masculine energy building around me and in me, and then, as the chunta spears were cutting through the air around me I felt them entering my heart. Soon I heard the sharp *ocarina* (the traditional ceramic flute) sound piercing the silence. "You can open your eyes now," he finally said sternly. And then, to my total surprise, he said, "I decided to perform a special initiation ceremony, inducting you into the Circle of Twenty-Four Male Yachaks."

Surprised and a bit confused I asked for Soraya to be called to translate what he had said; maybe I hadn't understood correctly. "Yes, that's right; my father gave you a Coronation Ceremony," she confirmed with a big smile. "You can now wear the crown of feathers, as my father does; you are a yachak." I felt honored beyond belief and humbled at the same time, and thanked him with deepest gratitude. I put my clothes on and was ready to join my waiting, curious family outside when Don José's wife, Maria Rosario, with many rows of tiny gold necklaces around her neck, entered the room carrying a heavy package under her traditional blue llama-wool skirt. She slowly pulled it out and gave it to Don José, who blessed it. He handed me a large, heavy, smooth black Incan volcanic healing rock. It was an initiation gift, which I often use in my healing and which is a powerful centerpiece on my altar.

☡ Two Guys in the Otavalo Market

It was a beautiful, crisp March Saturday in 1997. Our group had just completed the sumptuous breakfast at the old Spanish Hosteria Guachala and we climbed on the waiting bus to Carabuela, a small community not far from Otavalo, the capital of the Imbabura region, to visit the shaman Don Esteban Tamayo and his two sons. My friend Samuel turned to me and said mischievously, "Why don't we do something different, like shamanic shopping, instead?" Samuel maintained we had both already had our share of healings with the shaman a few days earlier, so we could just skip it and explore the famous Otavalo market. Otavalo's Saturday open market is the largest and most famous in all of Latin America. I readily agreed as I appreciated Samuel's enthusiastic and sharp-eyed shopping skills. Besides, we had both had some heavy-duty experiences, which we needed to digest apart from the group. So we got into a taxi, paid a few cucras, and went looking for special shirts, pants, belts, fabrics, rugs, ponchos, sculptures, gifts, and big, colorful bags in which to put all these marvelous treasures.

After all the hard work of crisscrossing the long cobblestone streets and visiting hundreds of bodegas and small stores on the side streets, we sat down on a sidewalk to rest next to two young guys who were selling their handmade jewelry. After a short time we got involved in a very interesting philosophical and personal conversation. The tall, long-haired, blond guy was a farm boy from Nebraska. He was traveling with his tent, hitchhiking all over South America trying to find a partner and to find himself. Instead he had found an eccentric revolutionary poet, a younger fellow from Venezuela who was traveling to the North by selling his handmade jewelry. They couldn't stand each other, but traveling life had forced them to share what each had to offer: a tent in return for jewelry, security in return for companionship. Since we were talking about his life's direction, I offered to read the Nebraskan's palm. Immediately we drew a small crowd and others suddenly wanted their hands read. We sat there until sundown, talking, eating, and having fun. The two young men said they were planning to continue hitchhiking across the Amazon east through Brazil. Then they would go north to New York. Quite an arduous journey, judging from the travel map they showed us.

As the sun started to go down we needed to go back and join our waiting group at Hacienda Pinsaqui. We exchanged small gifts and promised to meet them one day, maybe in New York. We called a taxi and headed back to our beautiful hacienda. While in the taxi I closed my eyes, called on my power animal, the white dove, and asked her if we would ever meet these guys again. Flying in the blue sky she said, "You'll meet them again, when the sun is in the middle of the sky, in a city square." I turned this image in my mind for a while. It really didn't make sense to me. I opened my eyes and told Samuel the answer I had just received. "Yeah, sure," he said sardonically.

A few days later, after an inspired visit with the shaman Don Alberto Taxo in Quilajalo, we headed southeast toward Baños, the last town before our entry to the jungle. We stayed in a small hotel overlooking the town. Behind us was a tall waterfall and the public mineral hot springs, which we enjoyed. The next morning we had a few hours until our bus was allowed to start on its way down the winding, dangerous dirt road along the deep Pastaza River, which leads to the jungle, so we went shopping again. We walked down the street looking in each of the small stores, trying to find an extra swimsuit.

We arrived at the crowded town square, a typical scene. On one side stood the town's main church and on the three other sides were many bustling shops. As we turned right to enter another shop I had an odd hunch. I turned to Samuel and said, "I have a feeling we're going to meet those guys now. It is noon. The sun is high above us and we are in a city square, exactly like the white dove said." He gave me that look. As I turned my head back toward the town square, whom did I see in front of me, across the street, but the eccentric revolutionary poet from Venezuela? I whispered to Samuel, "Do you see what I see?" We were both stunned. I called to the young poet. Realizing who we were he ran toward us, full of excitement. He was there by himself so he dragged us to a field a few blocks away at the edge of the town, where the two of them had put up their tent for the night, to meet his American companion. Since they hadn't had anything decent to eat for a few days we invited them to a proper restaurant for a hearty hot lunch. We had a great time, exchanging stories and laughing at this "surprise" meeting. "Our plans changed," the Nebraska boy explained. "Spirits work in strange ways," I thought to myself.

⚡ SHUAR SPEARS

I was wondering what gifts from the Shuar headhunter's tribe I could bring back with me for my two sons. After all, you don't go there every day. So, I asked: "Real war spears," my sons suggested gleefully. So naturally, determined not to disappoint them, when we arrived at Miazal I was on a sacred mission to find two spears.

The day before, we had flown back to the Andes, where many of the Shuar people came from their scattered communities, some a few hours' walk and some a few days, bringing their handmade jewelry, crafts, blowguns, and musical instruments to sell to us in a makeshift flea market, which they had set up just off the kitchen. They placed all their merchandise on low tables and stood quietly behind them, waiting for us to make our purchases. Of course I bought more gifts and memorabilia than I needed, but there were no spears to be found. I was disappointed. How could I go back empty-handed? So I asked Patricia, the Shuar woman whose family owns the lodge, to ask if anyone would sell me two of their own spears. A few minutes later she came back. "One of the men has agreed to go back to his hut. It is a few hours away, though, so tomorrow morning he will bring them, just before your flight back out of the jungle to Shell."

As promised, the Shuar warrior came back in the morning carrying two beautiful, six-foot-long spears, one for ceremonials and one for hunting, both made of the sacred and strong chunta palm tree. I was elated. Carefully I wrapped them with layers of newspapers and bound them together to protect them on our long trip home. As we marched to the airstrip on the winding jungle road I felt proud about achieving my mission. As we reached the airstrip we piled our belongings on the tall grass and had some extra time to exchange our rubber boots, hats, and t-shirts for more jewelry. Excitedly we said our farewells to the many Shuar warriors and their families who had become our new friends and who had come to say good-bye. After the plane was loaded we boarded and took off in a hurry to take advantage of the brief window of good weather.

Flying over the mountains, Samuel asked me if I had been able to fit my two long spears into the belly of the small plane. Only then did I realize that I had left them lying on the tall grass. It goes without saying how very upset I was. "What can I do?" I decided to call on my power animal for help. I closed my eyes, breathed deeply, entered a journey state, and asked her to come. When she appeared, I explained to her the situation I was in and begged her to help bring me my spears. Instantly I saw her flying high in the blue sky over the green mountains, flapping her white wings calmly. I looked at her small figure for a while and then I realized that in her legs she was clasping the two spears, which were dangling in the air. I followed this beautiful image until she disappeared into the distance—in the direction we were flying. I heard her say to me, "Don't worry, I'll bring them to you." I exited the journey state, opened my eyes, and shared the experience with my friend, who tried to calm me down. I was still pretty skeptical, though—it is sometimes so hard to have faith in these shamanic visions. *Is it really going to work? Am I only making this up to calm myself down?* I wondered.

We landed at the small army airport in Shell. I asked our pilot to radio the other pilot, who was now on his way back to pick up the last group of tourists, but we couldn't get through. We had over an hour and a half until the next arrival, so I went to the end of the runway and waited nervously. Finally, we heard the buzz of the small Cessna coming over the mountains. The plane touched down right near where I was sitting. I got up and ran after it the full length of the runway as it taxied to the hangar. I arrived just as they were taking my spears out—just as the white dove had promised.

⚆ A Visit with the Ancestors

*Le kol ha shedim ve haruchot,** I thought. *Where am I? Why are they swarming all around me like a group of jellyfish in a dark ocean of anger and frustration? Who are these people . . . ?*

Hundreds of faces came closer to me: men, women, and children, young and old. "Do I know you?" I shouted. I could see their hollow, sad, angry eyes, the rotten facial flesh and the mutilation, their mouths twisted into horrible expressions, and the exposed teeth showing from under their ashen, stretched skin. Their faces reached even closer to me, whispering in my ears in rasping voices like a stormy wind blowing through the cracks of venetian blinds. *Oh, this is terrible,* I thought. My stomach churned and an unexplained dread enveloped me. I yelled at the bodiless faces. Waving my hands in the air I fought the swarm of circling faces, begging them to leave me alone. But they paid no attention to my pleas and kept on with their unwavering motion, surrounding me from all sides. I could hear their voices: "We're not ready to leave just yet! We did not finish what we came here to do. We need more time!" I could tell they were unaware that they were dead and were stuck between the worlds, unable to let go and move on to the

---

*"To all the devils and the spirits"—a Hebrew expression.

other realms, wherever they should be. I wanted to run away from there as fast as I could but my body was frozen and refused to move. Finally I opened my eyes and found myself still sitting on the green wooden bench in front of my parents' graves. I had no idea how much time had passed.

It was a very hot July afternoon, quite typical for that time of year in Kibbutz Beit Alfa, my birthplace and where my parents, Sarah and Chaim, and my grandmother Rashka are buried. I was completely alone in the well-kept kibbutz cemetery, which is called "The Paradise." It was quiet. I could hear only the pine trees blowing silently in the soft summer wind and a few birds chirping lazily from time to time. I sat facing the Gilboa, watching the dry, yellow mountain and the tall pine trees, looking around at the new and old graves that were holding the remains of those unhappy souls, trying to figure out what had just happened.

It was my custom when visiting Israel to go visit my parents' graves—to water the plants, put a rock on the headstones, and sit in front of them and meditate, trying to connect and talk with them. But this experience was wildly different. I had the feeling I was connecting with all the souls who were buried here in the kibbutz cemetery since 1922, the time the first pioneers had arrived, and many of these souls could not accept the fact that their lives on this earth were over and that they now belong to the world of the dead. I realized how meaningful and important it is for anyone who is passing over to be spiritually prepared and learn to accept his or her own life journey.

⚕ "ARE YOU FOR REAL?"

Jean sat quietly with a straight back, her hands resting heavily on her lap, waiting to hear my candle flame diagnosis. She was restless, sitting beyond my round table, which was set with all my altar objects, healing stones, red and white carnations, a bell, oils, trago, agua florida, and a jaguar bone. Her beautiful face, framed by slick blond hair, was guarded, opaque, masklike. I could sense she was extremely tense, like a coiled spring. I had asked her earlier to brush the unlit white candle all over her body and to blow on it three times to let it absorb her energy. Then she handed it back to me.

I took a few minutes to study the candle's flame. Then I looked up and looked into her brown eyes. "You are having a bad time now. You are sad, you're tired, you have no energy, and there is a lot of negative energy around you as well as much fear. You also have a problem in your heart," I continued, waiting for her acknowledgment, but she was holding back any response so I went on. "One of the valves on the upper left is inflamed and it can't be closed; that is why you feel so tired." I raised my eyes to meet hers and her expressionless, sphinxlike face. "You must go to a heart specialist and tell him you need special antibiotics, not the ones they will offer you at first." She sat there motionless as if testing me. I felt uncomfortable. Usually people react, make comments, or cry. I continued my reading with no further input from her. "Is anything I've said so far ringing true for you?" I asked. She did not answer. Instead I watched her bend over and pull a big manila envelope out of her brown leather purse. "Here, read that," she said in a heavy Brazilian accent, handing me the papers. I glanced at them. They were medical papers: an MRI report from her heart doctor. In it was the exact diagnosis I had just given her. "I wanted to see if you are for real," she said, then she smiled for the first time.

A few weeks later Jean flew to Brazil, where the local doctors treated her successfully with an antibiotic specific to the tropical virus she was afflicted with.

Two weeks later she came back for her next session. This time she was overly friendly—chatty and full of energy. Halfway through our session she quieted down and in a serious voice she said that she had a secret, and a serious business proposition for me. She went on to tell me the following story:

"My great-grandmother's family, who came from Germany, lived in a small jungle settlement. Before she died, as the story goes, she buried a box full of gold jewelry next to her house. Naturally we all tried to find it, as we are not rich and need the money. With your talent I want you to help me find it. I want you to come with me to Brazil. I will pay for your trip and your expenses. If you find it we will share the money fifty-fifty." She looked with anticipation into my eyes for my answer. Well, it's not every day someone offers to take you to Brazil for free.

"Thank you for the offer," I answered, choosing my words carefully. "Where is it? How far is it? How long would it take us?"

"Well, we would have to fly to São Paulo, and from there we would have to take a bus for a day or even two. Then we would have to take a small boat, which takes two to three days. I believe altogether it will take about two weeks."

"Let me sleep on it," I told her, hoping to gain some time.

Two weeks later at our next session, she immediately raised the question again.

"You know what? Before we start, let me try to 'see' if it is still there, and we will see."

I closed my eyes and started to describe a vision that started to form in my mind to her.

"Is the house built of wood? Does it have two floors?"

"Yes, that's it!" she exclaimed with joy.

"As you walk in from the front door you enter in to the kitchen, right?

"Yes, that's the house."

"There are rooms on either side of the house, and then upstairs are the bedrooms. It was built on the curve of a small tributary, surrounded by large trees. From the kitchen window I can see a large tree close to the house, a short distance to the river."

"Yes, yes. It is true! I remember it from my visits as a little girl," she exclaimed.

"I think she buried it next to this tree," I told her.

"Can you draw me a map of what you've seen?" she asked.

I took a sheet of plain white paper and pencil and drew it. There was no end to her joy.

"So, when are you coming?"

"I don't think I have the time to go right now," I said politely.

We agreed she would send the map to her brother in São Paulo, who would go there with a metal detector and see what happened.

A few weeks later she arrived noticeably upset. "My brother went there and could not find it. I ordered him to go back with a stronger detector, and again he could not find it." She said disappointed. "Can you take a look inside the box to see if it was worth all the trouble?" she asked.

Why didn't I think of it before? I thought to myself.

She rubbed the candle over her entire body then handed it back to me and sat down. I lit the wick and concentrated on the flame. "I see that the earth has shifted, as is often the case in the jungle. The river is now flowing through the tree's roots. The treasure box has probably been washed down river," I told her. I took a "look" in the box and saw only a few bracelets, earrings, and necklaces.

"That's all? Are you sure?" she asked.

"Yes. Not much more," I replied. "I guess your family legend was much more powerful than the reality."

8

⚶ ⚶ ⚶ ⚶

SHAMANIC JOURNEYING

*All of nature has a hidden nonordinary reality. That is
something one learns to see in following the shaman's way.*

MICHAEL HARNER

Shamanic journeying into nonordinary realities and other spiritual
dimensions is a primordial practice common in the traditions of indigenous cultures around the world. It is to these places that shamans travel
to bring back knowledge, wisdom, and healing for individuals and their
communities. Shamans access these realities by entering into a trancelike state of mind, using the mind and tools such as rattles, musical
instruments, chants, dancing, and various psychoactive plants.

Today, most neoshamans use a technique that was fashioned by
Michael Harner of the Foundation for Shamanic Studies. It is called
core shamanism. It uses very rapid 160 to 180 drumbeats per minute on
a frame drum made of animal skin or synthetic materials. The rapid
drumming "carries you" and helps you to shift your consciousness to
enter that trancelike state. This enables you to lower your brain activity
from the beta state, the normal awake state, to an alpha state, an in-
between zone that occurs between sleeping and waking. You experience
this state naturally when you first put your head on a pillow and start

dozing off; you know you are awake but you feel yourself going deep into the sleep state. This is the same state that meditators consistently experience after twenty or more minutes, when they are suspended in time. It is our shamanic portal—all shamanic work is done in these liminal, in-between times, during sunrise, sunset, at midnight or midday, when the sun is in the center of the sky.

Shamans journey to the three main spiritual worlds. The middle world, which is what we call our everyday reality, contains the spirits of what surrounds us: trees, stones, homes, rivers, plants, screwdrivers, etc. We can journey to the lower world, the depths of the Earth, where we can meet our power animal allies. These allies are a manifestation of our anima—our life force, passion, and creativity. We can also travel to the upper world, where we can meet our spirit guides, who often appear in human form; they are wise elders, angels, as well as our ancestors.

Journeying, as you will see from the following stories, is a very effective tool for gaining knowledge and integrating parts of our life force that we have lost touch with, allowing us to balance and increase our natural power.

꩜ FINDING HELENA

This story began on a typically hot and muggy August night in New York City but it took another two years for it to be wholly revealed. That Friday night we were jammed into the narrow Parish House on West 4th Street; there were more than thirty excited people who had come for the monthly open house of the New York Shamanic Circle. The last journey of the evening was to be a partner journey. "I'll journey for you and you'll journey for me at the same time." I had paired up with Beth, a big beautiful woman in her mid-forties with a charming smile, who was conveniently sitting right next to me and whom I had just met for the first time. We quickly shared our first names and told each other our personal questions, what it was we wanted our partner to journey for.

We lay on our backs on the red, beaten-up wall-to-wall carpeting, shoulders and hips touching, and covered our eyes. Someone turned the lights off in the back. The big fan was now moving the hot air, cooling us off. After we took a big breath, the rapid drumming began.

I found myself going through my usual portal, the hidden Hawaiian lava tunnel by the Red Road on the Big Island, a place I know and love. It led me to an open jungle in the lower world. I wandered around for a while and finally called out for my power animals. My white dove came flying in and settled on a tree branch just above my head. After a short greeting I told her the reason for my visit and got her permission to ask Beth's question: "What do I need to do to advance on my healing path?"

Instantly I found myself riding on the dove's back and flying over an ocean. We strangely seemed to be traveling from the direction of the Middle East. *Is this the Mediterranean?* I wondered. Then we curved right. "Where are we going?" I asked.

"We are flying over Europe," the white dove answered.

I looked down at the fertile agricultural country, which I could see was studded with clumps of green forests, blue lakes, small farms, and single red-roofed houses. *This must be France,* I thought. We continued flying, this time diagonally, crossing over to a very different landscape. The land became utterly flat, gloomy, and gray, and as we continued I somehow knew that we were flying over Germany. We flew northeast, passing a big industrial city. Clouds of ashen smoke rose above several factory smokestacks in the distance. They were all built on the right side of a wide and twisting polluted river. I felt a deep sadness for this place and for the people who live there. *Where am I?* The name of this city instantly popped up in my mind: Düsseldorf.

We proceeded to fly left across the river to a greener, more residential neighborhood not too far from the sad river. We turned in to a quiet street and over a low apartment building, then flew directly to the next apartment building and entered an open window on the third floor. There I saw a woman with short, straight blond hair wearing a light blue dress. She was standing in the center of a sparse living room; it was almost empty with only a gray rug on the floor. Behind her was a large window draped with white curtains. Strong daylight came through the window. The woman seemed to be waiting for me. Her face was round and serious; her bluish eyes radiated calmness and wisdom. She must have been in her early fifties. I entered the room, stood by her side, and asked her for her name. *Lena* popped into my mind. Oh, no, "Helena," she corrected me. Without an introduction or hesitation I repeated Beth's question.

"I'm Beth's teacher and a shaman and I need to work with Beth and teach her some very important things," she said calmly but firmly. I asked her what she needed to teach her. "I need to teach her to say no, to teach her about her own self-worth, to teach her to accept and love herself."

From what seemed like another world I heard a new drumbeat calling us back. "Thank you," I said, promising to give Beth the message. I returned to the room by retracing my footsteps, trying to remember every detail of this unexpected meeting and vision.

The drumming ended. The lights were on again. We sat up and looked at each other in anticipation. "Well," I said, "I think I got something really strange. It probably won't make any sense to you at all but let me try to tell it to you as I saw it." As I mentioned Helena's name, I could see Beth was dumbfounded. Her eyes opened wide and her jaw dropped in disbelief. She let me finish my account of the journey, took a deep breath, and told me the following story.

"Last year I participated in a workshop at the New York Open Center. One of the participants was a therapist and healer from Germany who now lives here. Her name is Helena. She said that she had left Germany because her industrial town was a very depressing and boring place for her to work and live in. Helena had definitely invited me to work with her and gave me her calling card, but I never took her up on her offer. I think the card is buried under a mountain of papers on my desk. Helena kept in touch with me for a while. She sent me a few notices about her workshops but I didn't have the courage to call her or meet with her."

Now my jaw dropped.

Four months later I got an e-mail from Beth: "Dear Itzhak, I FOUND HELENA!!! I have been excavating boxes and boxes of papers in my apartment and her card surfaced on Saturday. I called and we had a wonderful long talk. I shall begin working with her at the start of the New Year. Thank you for encouraging me to continue in the search and to follow through with her. I am very much looking forward to working with her. She is a Gestalt therapist with specialized training in art therapy. B."

In the next e-mail Beth told me: "When I called her I told her the story re. the drumming circle, your journeying for me, your retrieving her for me. She thought it was a most amazing tale, especially as it was the first time you and I had met. So I am sure you will have the opportunity to meet her and see how well nonordinary and ordinary reality match! Blessings, B."

Two years after our joint journey, on another hot and muggy August night in New York a few blocks from my home, Beth and I knocked on Helena's office door. Suddenly I felt somebody walking up behind us. "Hi Beth," said a woman's voice with a heavy German accent. I turned my head to see a tall, thin, beautiful woman with short brown hair.

"Helena, this is Itzhak," Beth introduced me enthusiastically. We shook hands and walked into her small, sparse office. I looked at her, trying unsuccessfully to match my vision of her with the woman sitting in front of me. Helena seemed somehow confused, both about her role in all of it and by our obvious excitement. She asked us many questions about the circumstances under which we had met and how she had gotten involved in it. Beth patiently recounted the course of events that had led to us sitting there. I asked Beth to read her this account, which I had written down shortly after the experience. "Amazing, amazing," she said, shaking her head. Then Helena leaned forward and handed me a drawing pad and a pencil. "Can you draw for me what you saw?" Somewhat self-consciously I drew the twisting river, the location of the factories, the direction of my flight, the neighborhood she lived in, her building, and the inside of her apartment. I described the feelings I had had while flying over France and how they then transformed when I flew over Germany. I described her small but neat apartment, the curtains, the beautiful light, the location of her bedroom, the kitchen. We laughed at the accuracy of the details and then she said, "You know, I was a young child at the end of the war. I lived for a few years in France, probably in one of the houses you saw. I liked living there. I went back to live in Germany but felt I needed a change and decided to move to New York. The river you saw is the Rhine. It is a brownish gray and polluted by all the industries around it. I lived close to the river, on the third floor, and my window faced south toward a graveyard, which is why I had beautiful daylight coming in. You are right—the living room was very clean, with almost no furniture. But no, I never wear blue. And, oh yes, I was a blond then."

I felt vindicated.

☊ FISH RESTAURANT

Jim, a big burly guy, came to our Friday Shamanic Open Circle for the first time. I partnered with him for our last journey of the night. "What should be my next business move?" he wanted to know.

We lay next to each other, shoulder to shoulder, hips touching. As the drumbeat began, I was immediately transported to a relaxing scene on a beautiful beach. The ocean was extremely calm, the water dark blue, and fresh, salty air filled my nostrils. Small waves washed over the white sandy shore, which was spotted with a great variety of seashells. Barefoot, I walked north. To my left, built on the sand dunes and surrounded by tall beach grass, I saw an old, beaten-up gray wooden beach house. Somehow I had a strong feeling that this place was on Long Island. Walking toward the house I carefully climbed the creaking stairs, which led me to a large deck; from there I entered the empty house and proceeded to inspect it. The house was truly in very bad shape. I called my power animal, and from the direction of the ocean the white dove flew toward me and landed elegantly on the roof. After she settled down I greeted her and repeated Jim's question.

"Jim will meet a very nice and helpful woman named Dina, and she will offer to open up a fish restaurant with him in that old house," the dove said. In a split second my vision changed. Now instead of the crumbling house I saw an elegant fish restaurant. It looked totally renovated, furnished with new wooden floors, green planters everywhere, and elegant light fixtures. On the deck and inside I could see a well-dressed staff serving the vacationing diners. The white dove said, "Dina will want to work with him because he has invented a whole new concept of frying fish. He has discovered a new way to deep fry them in a special oil." She added, "Jim and Dina's partnership will be very successful."

The fast drumbeat signaled the end of the journey. We sat up and faced each other to share our visions. Here is what I learned from Jim:

"I am a real estate agent now. I lived and worked on Long Island. Earlier this very day I met with a woman who wanted to buy a house and open a restaurant on the beach near the ocean. Her name, like you said, is Dina. Before becoming a real estate agent, I sold restaurant and kitchen supplies. We are planning to meet again soon."

Unfortunately, I didn't hear back from Jim to know how the story ended. I hope this venture was as successful as it appeared in my vision.

⚤ GINA'S BEHEADING

At a "Beheading" Shamanic Celtic workshop taught by Tom Cowan I had this hard-to-believe experience. I paired up with Gina and we alternated our role as shamans. Face-down, I lay on the floor as she proceeded with our exercise. As instructed, she held a thick branch in her hand and symbolically swiftly cut off my head from the back of my neck with three sharp strokes. A vision unfolded. Through my neck, which was now wide open, I could see and feel my body clearing the black liquid tar I had absorbed earlier while performing another healing on her. The black gummy stuff was flowing out of me, disappearing into the distance. I asked my power animal, the white dove, whom I was riding, to help me find the source of Gina's condition.

Suddenly, I stood in an old-fashioned classroom. On a small platform below the blackboard near the teacher's desk stood a third-grade girl wearing her best dress and shoes. I recognized her as Gina. She had just finished her show-and-tell in front of the whole class, about what seemed to be a small dark frog that she held in the palm of her hand. The girl was ready to take a step down from the platform and go back to her seat. Her eyes were cemented to the floor and she was noticeably distraught. She felt as if she had failed terribly and swore never to expose herself or make a fool of herself like this again. I felt deep sorrow for her and wanted to hold her in my arms.

The drumming stopped and the vision ended. I turned over onto my back. Gina tenderly washed my face with cold water from the bucket waiting by her side. It brought me back to the room. She slowly helped me rise and we sat facing each other. I was silent for a minute and then shared with her the experience I had just gone through.

"What you have seen is true," she sighed. "When I was in the third grade I was assigned to do a story about a water turtle that I had in my home. He was so small, the size of a frog." I could see tears in her eyes. "I was so excited about it and really prepared, but my mother ridiculed me and it made me very upset. So when I went in front of the class I felt that I was a failure and swore never to speak up again. I also learned not to express my enthusiasm in front of people I know." She looked at me and said, "This is what I asked you to help me with earlier in your healing, so thank you."

⚴ MEETING WITH AN ANCESTOR

At a "Beheading" Shamanic Celtic workshop I performed a healing journey for my red-headed partner Lisa, who was a healer as well. During that vision unexpectedly a large flock of black bats entered into my body. During the second part of the exercise I turned to lie down on my stomach. As instructed, Lisa proceeded to cut my head off with three quick blows of a thick branch to the back of my neck. With that the flock swarmed and cleared out of my bleeding, open neck in big waves, disappearing into the thin air and into the distance. Astounded, I asked my spirit guide, with whom I was still immersed, to help me find the source of Lisa's depression and loneliness.

I immediately found myself standing in a semi-dark, old farmhouse. I looked around, observing the humble home. The flooring was made of wide pieces of lumber. In the middle of the room stood a rough wooden table and two heavy chairs. An elderly woman quickly turned her back on me. Bending over the oven she busied herself with her cooking in the kitchen, which was on the left side of the room. She was heavyset and of medium height. The woman wore a long, heavy brown wool skirt, a blue sweater, a wool hat, and an apron. She seemed to live there all by herself; there were no signs of other people. Through the small window on the wall to the right, framed by light cotton curtains, I noticed a beautiful, bright sunny sky over open, grassy fields and an old barn. I tried to guess where I was. Names of different countries in Europe went through my mind—Switzerland, France, England, but none seemed to be correct. I moved my attention back to the elderly woman, unsuccessfully attempting to see her face, as she would skillfully turn her back on me every time. Finally I asked for her name. "Martha," she said in a strange accent.

Suddenly a flock of black bats flew with a gushing noise from the kitchen and disappeared into the blue sky above through a large hole in the roof. Remembering the bats I had absorbed earlier, I wondered if she worked with bats, if they were her medicine power animals. *She must be a medicine woman, a healer, a shaman,* I thought. *Is she Lisa's grandmother?* Perhaps she had passed on to Lisa the condition she is now suffering from. I turned to lie on my back. Lisa gently washed my face with cold water from the bucket near her and it brought me back to the room. I sat up in front of her and shared with her my experience.

"No," Lisa said carefully. "My grandmother didn't live alone and her name wasn't Martha. Actually, I was named after her. But my great aunt Marge, for whom I had a special affinity, lived alone in a rural area in Wales. She never married. She loved to cook, and people thought of her as strange because of her bulging eyes and the fact that she was very shy and rarely showed her face in public. As a child I remember the black bats that inhabited the barn that stood by her house. Who knows, she might have been a medicine woman, too. Do I continue to live out her fate?" she wondered.

✵ THE DOLPHIN

I returned to Hawaii for another men's gathering at Kalani. I had arrived a few days earlier so I could participate in a three-day basic shamanic workshop led by Bea Joy Borden on the North Shore of Oahu, in a YMCA compound overlooking a most majestic and beautiful Hawaiian bay. Our small group consisted of seven women and myself, which made it quite intimate. One of our last exercises was a partner journey in which I paired with Sofia, a young Spanish-speaking woman whom I knew nothing about. She asked me to ask my spirit guide "What do I need to do about my career?"

We all lay down on the cold floor of the dark gymnasium, shoulders and hips touching, covered our eyes, and listened to Bea's fast, monotonous drumming. My breath became quieter and deeper and I found myself walking through a dark, wet lava tunnel, moving forward carefully so as not to fall on the sharp lava spikes. I went toward the light at the end of the tunnel and came into a clearing in a Hawaiian rain forest. It was a bright, hot day. I looked up at the clear sky and called out for one of my power animals. I spotted the white dove sitting on a large tree branch. Greeting her warmly I asked her to please help Sofia, who truly needed an answer to her question, which I repeated.

In a flash I was taken to a freestanding house with a yard surrounded by a white wooden fence in a small village in Hawaii. The house was made of white painted wood and had an open wrap-around porch all along the second floor. Intuitively I knew it was Sofia's house. It was roomy and airy, almost without any furniture, but it also felt very lonely. *She must live there alone,* I thought. A huge eucalyptus tree stood in front of the house. The large branches were leaning heavily on the house and the porch. Suddenly I heard a *whoosh* behind me; I turned around and saw a beautiful, slick gray dolphin flying through the air. He circled the house a few times and then dove forcefully between two large V-shaped tree branches and got stuck there. Unable to move or speak, the dolphin looked desperate. I felt confused by the peculiar image, so I turned to my white dove and asked her to clarify.

The white dove asked me to hop on her back. For a long while we flew east through the dark blue skies over endless oceans, then reddish deserts. *Is that Morocco?* I thought. At last we made a U-turn back. After a while we turned north and flew above a large, fertile, forested area. We flew closer to some lush mountains and high cliffs that rolled toward the ocean. On the mountain slopes I saw a beautiful white city. Its clean, well-planned architecture caught my eye, and I asked my white dove for its name. "Seattle," came the answer. I was completely surprised, since I had neither seen nor visited Seattle before in real life.

As we continued flying toward the city a new vision emerged in my mind of a blurry man spinning around rapidly. He wore an all-white dress that looked like a costume. I tried to see his face but he did not stop his fast rotating motion. "Who is this person?" I asked my white dove. She said, "This is a very important person in Sofia's life; he comes from the desert." *Maybe he's Arab,* I thought. I asked for his name. "Joe," came the answer. The drumbeat went faster and faster, and he continued to twirl faster and faster until Bea signaled to us with her drumming to end our journey and return to our bodies and this reality.

I took off my eye cover and sat in front of Sofia to share. I asked her to share first, because I was a little embarrassed to tell her about my strange journey. After she shared her journey with me I took a big breath and told her mine. I was surprised that she was as overwhelmed as I was. Sofia, it turned out, was a dancer. She had moved from Mexico to Hawaii. She lived in a house that looked just like the one I had described. There was indeed a eucalyptus tree right in front of her house. She said the dolphin was a symbol for her current situation of being stuck. Although she is by nature like the dolphin, playful and

loves movement, she felt trapped, out of her element, unable to make a decision or move. Most interestingly, Sofia had studied with a Moroccan Dervish dancer, a form of dance that is based on fast and perpetual circling that allows the dancer to enter a state of trance. I guessed that was the reason I couldn't see his face. His real name was Joseph, and he had recently moved to Seattle to open a school there. "I feel there is a message for you here—why don't you move to Seattle, too, and continue your dance studies with Joseph?" I suggested.

"Yes, I think that is what I need to do," Sofia agreed.

ᴧᴠ WATER LILIES

I took a look back and noticed a woman with curly black hair. She was sitting cross-legged on the carpet behind me. I approached her, smiled, and asked if she would be willing to partner with me for the next exercise John Perkins had suggested. The main hall at the Omega Institute was packed with more than 300 people who had come to participate in the Third Shamanic Gathering. John Perkins stood on the stage, drum in hand, and asked us to choose a person we didn't know.

"Sit in front of your partner with your eyes closed, stretch your hands forward, and feel the energy field that surrounds your partner's body, their aura," John instructed the participants. "Then journey and bring them relevant information that could be important to their life or, if you feel it is needed, perform an energy healing."

With a noticeable foreign accent, Aileen introduced herself. With her beautiful, piercing blue eyes, a red dot on her third eye, and mane of black hair, I thought she was quite an impressive lady. We sat facing each other and when the rapid rhythm of the drumbeat began in the background a mesmerizing image started to emerge in my mind.

I found myself in an unfamiliar place viewing flat, green, fertile land that stretched for miles, as far as my eyes could see. The air was crisp yet foggy, like in a dream. A shallow blue river ran slowly, feeding many small ponds that were covered with water lilies. In the distance I could see green forests on both sides. It reminded me of a colorful illustration from a book of old fairy tales. Looking at the center of a pond close to me, I saw Aileen sitting on a large lotus, meditating. She seemed comfortable, as if she owned the area. A soft movement in the blue skies above her caught my eye. I looked up in surprise at the sight. There was an old man hanging upside down in the sky, wearing an orange garment, his white hair and long white beard blowing in the breeze. *This must be her Indian teacher,* I thought.

Suddenly he moved closer, almost reaching down to her with his head, and whispered something in her ear, then moved swiftly and gently away. I followed him for a while. "Who are you?" I asked him. "I am Aileen's teacher and guardian; I am always with her, helping her throughout her life," he answered. I thanked him. I focused my attention back on Aileen, feeling that she might need a healing. I sent her many large waves of water from the pond to cleanse her. Then I called on the power of fire to consume all the negative energy that surrounded her. Afterward I noticed that the lotus flower shone brightly in the middle of that pond. My hands continued to move slowly around her, sensing changes in her body temperature. I felt a void around her pelvic and sexual area, which usually indicates a sexual trauma, so I performed a healing there, pulling a dark mass out of her a few times.

The faster drumbeat signaled the end of this exercise. We opened our eyes and I shared with her my vision. Her response surprised me.

"The lotus is my favorite flower and the place you saw was a place I know, about an hour outside Dublin, Ireland, where I am from. You were right; I was sexually abused as a child and I am still not able to come to terms with it. I do not know who the teacher you saw was but I regularly meditate and always feel the presence of a spiritual helper around me," she said.

The next day, while I was assisting in ceremonial healings performed by the Tamayos, a family of shamans from the High Andes of Ecuador, another Irishwoman approached me. She introduced herself as Aileen's assistant at their healing center in Dublin. Excitedly she said that Aileen had told her about our encounter and that I was the only person who had ever been able to read for her. "She doesn't let people know her," she said. I learned that Aileen is a well-known healer who runs a healing center in Dublin and was now considering a move outside that city. They had been looking at different places but seemed to settle on the place that I had so accurately described in our session together.

⚕ FAMILIAL HEALINGS

Tara, a married woman in her thirties with flowing blond hair, requested in one of our sessions, "Can you journey for my mother, Tanya? She is fighting a battle with cancer. Can you see what she needs and what ways the spirits instruct you to heal her?" I agreed and we set off to journey together.

In the tunnel's darkness, a short, barefoot woman appeared. Her face was full of pain. She wore a torn, dirty dress and had long, straight brown hair. She started running faster and faster, desperately trying to escape, looking extremely frightened. Behind her was a herd of dark sweaty horses galloping relentlessly after her. She finally came out of the long tunnel and emerged on an open sandy beach where she reached the ocean. As she plunged into the water the ocean waves became huge and dangerous and she was tossed around like a piece of driftwood for some time. Then a new image appeared. Searching in the jungle bushes I saw my power animal, a small green frog. "Would you take pity on Tanya and tell me what she needs to do to be healed?" I repeated Tara's question to her. The frog looked happy to see me and said, "She needs to rid herself of everything she owned in life to become clean again. It would do her good and make her feel more comfortable to be in or around bodies of water."

"Can you show me where the illness is manifesting in Tanya's body?" I asked. Immediately I saw a few dark brown spots, one on the right side of her lower stomach, in her colon, and the others in the glands near her ovaries and bladder. The image shifted once more. We were now in her home. The frog repeated her message, "Tanya must get rid of everything she owns." I promised to relay this message to her daughter. We were now back in the jungle on the edge of the Amazon. I saw a big anaconda splashing in the mud and it said, "Tanya's insides needed to be scraped totally clean; they are all decayed." Then, as if in a classic movie finale, I saw Tanya sitting in a wooden canoe with a few other people, slowly floating down the calm river, and after a short while they disappeared into the misty distance. It felt so sad and at the same time I had a sense of relief seeing her peaceful departure to the other dimensions. A new image emerged of a beautiful, multicolored stained-glass church rosette. It sparkled from the sunlight behind it and a message came: "Now all you can do is pray for her and believe she is going to where she needs to be."

Later Tara shared this with me:

"My mother's cancer developed in those two spots you saw, first in her glands, and then it spread up into her colon. She was very frightened, but in the end she stopped fighting and really chose to leave this world peacefully and get rid of everything she owned. She loved water, oceans and rivers—it was an ongoing theme throughout her life; she chose to live most of her life in a small town on the Saddle River."

A few months after her mom's death Tara asked for another journey, with this request: "Can you ask the spirits how I can deal with her death, the grief I am feeling, and maybe even retrieve a message from my mom?"

Again I reached the lower world through the lava tunnel, exiting at the side of a mountain. An unknown man was waiting there for me. He grabbed my hand and we ran naked and barefoot on the sharp lava stones to the beach. While swimming we started making circles with our hands in the water. These movements attracted a large group of dolphins that joyfully played with us. Suddenly I was alone in a forest and noticed dark shadows moving from all directions, chasing me, surrounding me, peeking from behind the trees, and teasing me. I got really frightened; I sensed death all around me. I asked my power animal Tara's question. I was immediately transported to a frame house in a village, in the kitchen; the walls were painted green and oil paintings hung all around. The one that attracted me the most was of large white flowers, similar to one of Georgia O'Keeffe's paintings. The house was disorganized, full of books on bookcases and scattered around, and a few African sculptures stood on shelves. Then the image changed again and I was back on the beach. My power animal relayed a message for Tara: "Every time you want to talk to your mom, go to the edge of a river, lake, or ocean, stand on a cliff or a rock, and the wind will bring her to you. It is time for you now to uncover your roots. Finish the movie project on your ancestors and start to organize your mom's house." And with that the journey ended.

Tara confirmed the vision: "My mother loved to spend time alone with me on the Saddle River, and we had a special rock we used to go to. Her house was full of paintings and books that were unorganized on bookcases and thrown all over the place. And yes, the kitchen walls were painted green," she said with a chuckle.

A few months after this journey Tara's father, Bernard, who had separated from her mother many years ago, needed emergency heart bypass surgery. Tara asked to do a long-distance healing for him. As I started to drum I walked through my Hawaiian lava tunnel again and got out at the Amazonian jungle. There between the trees I saw the Shuar shaman Daniel Guachapa. He was very energetic and busy, which is not very typical of him. He signaled to me that I should not stay in the lower world but rather should go to the upper world this time. I felt wistful at having to leave him but continued on my way. I went up through the huge kapok tree trunk to the canopy and on the first level I met my teacher G. K. She was already waiting for me; she said that she knew I was coming for Tara's dad. She pulled me by the hand and we flew to the upper planes. There, in the middle of the beautiful blue sky, wearing a light blue dress, was Tanya, with her long brown hair and round face and figure, chain-smoking nervously and full of buzzing energy. She didn't waste a minute. She said, "I am aware of Tara's dad's health. It's his heart, which was broken after I died. After Tara's wedding her father realized he had made a big mistake in leaving our four children and me so many years ago. He is full of regret. He has a pain in his groin on both sides and it is very hard for him to walk."

She grabbed me strongly by the arm and we flew into her frame house. "Is there anything you wanted me to convey to your daughter?" I asked her. She showed me that she had left a jar of the berry jam that Tara loved on the kitchen's green windowsill. I looked through the kitchen window above the sink; I could see the grassy backyard framed by tall trees and the wooden deck. The old white refrigerator was on the right next to a small hallway. Urgently she pulled me to her bedroom; the head of the double bed was against the window, which was covered by white curtains. As she bent down she showed me the many cardboard boxes brimming with pictures, documents, and old news clippings about her life's work. Then she said, "Tell Tara to organize these boxes and put them all into books, as I always wanted to do. I want to apologize because I never had time to do it myself. She doesn't, however, have to rush; first she needs to take care of the house. She should do it for the sake of her children, a boy and a girl." As she said this, an image of Tara's husband holding their two-year-old son's hand and walking outside the house appeared in my mind. Tanya went on: "Bernard is going to wait around for Tara's first son to be born. I will take care of him from now on." I was surprised to hear her say it without any bitterness.

Later Tara told me, "Just as you saw in your journey, my mother used to be a chain smoker, and the kitchen was painted green. And yes, through the window you can see the trees and the deck. Under her double bed we found a trove of cardboard boxes full of aging pictures, documents, and news clippings from her long career. And yes, I do love berry jam."

A few months later, Tara and her husband cleaned and painted the house and took before and after pictures. She brought the pictures to show me. I was amazed at how accurate the pictures were to the images in my journey. The bed stood facing the same direction against the window, covered with the same fabrics and colors I had seen. The kitchen layout and colors were the same and, although the refrigerator wasn't in the pictures I could tell where it had once been.

Right before Bernard's operation Tara called and asked us to journey and send healing energy for her father's recovery. Through the kapok tree trunk I flew to the upper world just above the canopy where I met one of my teachers, G. K., who flew me to see Tara's dad. He was lying on a hospital bed covered with a white sheet. He was cold; it seemed as if his soul had just left him. I tried forcefully to shove it back through his mouth with my hand, but Bernard said he didn't want to come back. I felt frustrated, disappointed, and sad. Then G. K, who was still hovering around me, said we had to move away. Suddenly, new images filled my vision. It was spring, the sky was sunny and blue, and flowers bloomed in many colors. Rabbits hopped around happily and there were signs of rebirth and new life.

Later Tara reported, "After the operation my dad's heart stopped. They rushed him back to the operating room and successfully revived him. His recovery was incredibly fast for his old age and gave him a whole new life." A few months later Tara got pregnant with her first child.

꩜ LIFE IN THE PUEBLO

"I have a friend who is very scared right now. Can you journey to see what she needs to do to be safe?" One night a client made this request. She didn't reveal any other details about her friend except for her first name, Louise.

As I started the rapid, monotonous drumbeat, I found myself entering my portal, the dark Hawaiian lava tunnel. For a while I wandered there, and as I exited the tunnel I entered a lush, sunny jungle clearing. High up on a tree branch was one of my power animals, overlooking a small pond—the kingfisher was waiting for me. He invited me to fly with him over the jungle canopy. After a while we landed on the jungle floor and met a few of my other power animals in a truly joyous gathering. Then instantly I felt myself shapeshifting into a jet-black raven.

I stretched my wings, flapped them strongly, and flew high into the windy sky, soaring up higher with the help of the strong current. As I coasted higher my whole field of vision changed; I was engulfed by bloody red scenery. For a moment I thought I was inside a strange tree but it turned out to be an open red mouth of some unknown entity, oozing with blood. I flew through it and found myself flying over a Native American pueblo. I recognized the terrain as that of New Mexico, somewhere around Santa Fe. There I saw a large group of Native American men, women, and children in the village square rhythmically dancing in a circle around a blazing fire in a sacred ceremony. Just above them an eagle was silently circling in the blue sky. At the center of the circle I saw people falling into the big fire, one after the other, as if in a self-sacrifice ritual. Not knowing why, my attention was drawn to my left, where I saw sitting on a stone well a young, dark-skinned teenage girl, whom I recognized as Louise's daughter. I watched her round young face and her long raven-colored hair; she was sad and worried, actually frozen with fear. A message came in: "An underground spring feeds that well, which supplies drinking water to the entire pueblo." I looked at the water as it turned as red as blood. My power animal warned me, "Louise mustn't drink the village water; she is in grave danger here; she needs to dig her own well and grow her own vegetables behind her second house in the valley, away from the village, next to the mountains." Immediately a vision of that simple lone house appeared. Behind it I saw a small patch of vegetables and an herb garden. Then my vision shifted back to the village square. Now a heavyset, strong man with black wavy hair was standing in the center speaking rudely to the large local crowd. He seemed to frighten them greatly. I noticed Louise's young daughter; she seemed to be scared of him, too. I had a strong feeling that this man had something personal against Louise and her family, but what it was all about I could not clearly understand. I stopped drumming and I sat to share my vision with her.

My client wrote it all down and later sent the descriptions to Louise. I had no idea how accurate and relevant I was, because my client did not get a response from her. However, a year later, Louise and her husband arrived at my client's wedding ceremony, to which I was also invited. As they approached my table I had a chance to find out what had happened. I introduced myself and asked her, "How is your daughter doing? Did you start to grow your own vegetables behind your other home, by the mountains?"

Louise looked at me with great surprise and confused eyes. "How did you know all that?" she asked. We laughed when I told her that I had visited her in the journey she had asked me to perform for her through her friend. She sat down and shared with me about her difficult life being a white woman married to a Native American. They lived in a traditional Native American pueblo, and she told me about her need to build that second house, which she often used in order to get away from the harassment she had suffered in recent years. She also talked about her vegetable garden and the village water supply.

"But who is that heavyset, cruel man?" I asked.

"He used to be the head of the village council. He was corrupt and was finally removed from power only two months ago," she sighed deeply.

About six months later, through my client again, Louise asked me to journey for her again. She had certain problems, which she did not disclose, and wanted to know how to resolve them. Once more my vision took me to her village in New Mexico. This time I met my white dove and asked her about Louise's problems. Immediately I had a vision of her with a Native American chief who was tall, dark, and very angry. The dove said, "She was having many disagreements and problems with him. She needed to write a book about her life experiences in the pueblo with the Native Americans and about the healing wisdom of this culture as she experienced it. To do so she needed to leave her home and stay in a male friend's apartment in a building near a hospital in Albuquerque." I remembered once passing through that city in a hurry and had no recollection of its hospital. With that she flew me to see that building. It was painted an adobe color, with a small apartment on one of the higher floors. "This was where she could write her book in privacy. She is also having difficulties with her daughter," the white dove said.

Again my client sent her my visions. This time I got her response: "Yes, I am having big trouble with my teenage daughter. I started to write my book in secret. It's about my difficult experiences as a white woman living with the American Indian tribal society, and the healing techniques I have learned. The village chief you saw is actually my husband, who strongly objects to my writing the book out of fear of retaliation by our community. You were right—I moved to a male friend's apartment on the top floor of a large building by the Albuquerque hospital, which just so happens to be painted an adobe color. Thank you."

☇ SARAFINA

"Okay, let's journey to Sarafina and ask her if she has any message for each of you." In a mysterious and mischievous voice, Cathy made this suggestion to our NY Shamanic Circle's core circle members' meeting as we were trying to agree on the next journey for the night. There were no other big issues pending, so it seemed to be an interesting challenge. We all agreed.

"But can you give us a clue as to who Sarafina is? Is she the big woman La Saraghina from Fellini's movie?" I asked.

Cathy smiled mysteriously. "Journey and see," she politely answered.

We lay down, covered our eyes, and the drumbeat began. I was ready to meet Fellini's huge mythological seductive woman coming out of the cave by the sea, just as in one of his movies. I began going down the lava tunnel, negotiating carefully in the darkness. Without warning, out of the darkness, on the right the ghost of a blond woman appeared. Her transparent figure moved straight into the pink mouth of a huge snake. I could clearly see its sharp teeth and long tongue twisting in every direction. Following her, we continued walking inside the snake's cavernous pink mouth and through its twisted body until we got to the other side and into a thick jungle. It was a bright and sunny day with soft light filtering graciously down through the green canopy. The blond woman's ghost now stood next to me. *Is this Sarafina?* I immediately thought. Apparently it wasn't her. I felt disappointed.

Then I called one of my power animals for help. Through the dense shrubs my jaguar came into sight. Gently he moved closer, licked my face as was his habit, and we had a playful time together. With my back leaning on one of the big trees I explained to the jaguar the reason I had called on him and asked him to take pity on me and help me find Sarafina. When I turned my head I realized that I was leaning on a female anaconda, not a tree. The huge snake was curled around the tree trunk. The anaconda successfully camouflaged herself with brown and yellowish spots that covered her entire body. I jumped forward in surprise. It occurred to me that anacondas don't climb trees; as relatives of the boa constrictor, they prefer living in and around water. *Perhaps it was a boa,* I thought. A message formed in my head: this snake holds the energy of the entire world in its powerful body.

I followed the snake for a while and then I remembered my mission—to look for Sarafina, but I still couldn't find her. As I stared at the water in the river below, the huge snake crawled down and started swimming. I found myself following her into the river and swimming with a large group of brownish fish. I noticed that I was seeing the world through their eyes and gaining insight into their thoughts. It was very serene under the water. A feeling of weightlessness and peacefulness came over me. My body twisted and turned quietly as I swam forward with the rest of the fish. As I looked up I saw the blue sky and the sunlight through the water. It was like looking through a heavy clear glass ceiling. And with that I heard the drumbeat calling us back. I said good-bye to my power animal and tracked my footsteps back to this reality.

The fast drumbeat stopped. We took out our notebooks to write down our journeys and share them later. We eagerly waited to hear from Cathy, who was the last to share about the mysterious Sarafina.

She said, "Well, last week, as some of you know, I participated in a Spirit of Nature workshop," Cathy said. "As part of the training, we were introduced to a few live animals. One of them was a huge female boa constrictor. When we visited her she was curled in her cage. Her name was Sarafina." And she burst out laughing.

9

⚶ ⚶ ⚶ ⚶

CANDLE READING

We can feel the vibration that comes from the candle flame, burning it [sic] way into our innermind, no blurry images, clear as crystal, we enter into the highest consciousness, on our journey back home, we possess the eagle's eye, the eye that can see the invisible.

MICHAEL BASSEY JOHNSON

Since the ancient pre-Incan times shamans of the High Andes and other cultures of South and Central America such as the Maya, Aztec, Huichol, and Quechua have used Grandfather Fire's flame reading as a diagnostic and divination tool in order to "see" and communicate with the spirit world. The practice is used by the yachaks, the shamans of Ecuador, to this day as part of La Limpia ceremony (energy cleansing), except a simple white candle replaces the traditional fire pit. The use of candles most likely took hold in the wake of the overarching influence of the Catholic Church in the Americas following the Spanish conquest.

To fully grasp and understand this technique we need to accept its core belief, which is that around each person's physical body there is an invisible energetic body or illuminated body, sometimes called the *aura*, which houses our memories, emotions, traumas, and the spirits of our

ancestors and the living. This egg-shaped energy orb, like that of an elliptical balloon, is shielded by an unseen electromagnetic membrane that originates from two energy centers. One is located just above the head and is the source of positive ions, and the other is just below the feet and is the source of negative ions. These two polar opposite energy sources constantly stream their energies up and down and all around us, in all directions, thus enveloping the physical body like an egg. You can also imagine it as being similar to the Earth's North and South poles, surrounded and protected by the layer of the stratosphere.

According to this worldview all illnesses, either physical or mental, are caused by the intrusion of negative or heavy energies into this encapsulated energy field. They can enter by the force of those who send them intentionally to harm another person, in the form of curses such as the evil eye or in the form of jealousy. Or they can enter unintentionally, by themselves, as negative energy can exist in natural places that hold negative energies—in places where violence or sickness is widespread. At first these energies stay within our energy field, causing imbalance, stress, depression, and unsettled feelings. Soon, however, they begin to penetrate deeper into the physical body—first through the layers of the skin, then moving down into the tissues, muscles, organs, and bones, creating physical imbalances. This affects all the systems of the body: nervous, immune, digestive, hormonal, circulatory, and reproductive. Once the affected area becomes contaminated it is weakened and therefore open to more intrusions, like a domino effect. This is when people often get sicker.

By watching the candle's wax texture—how runny it is, the wick's formation, the flame's color areas, its movement and shape—shamans learn to interpret their client's state of well-being. I teach this technique around the world, and most laypeople who never thought they could read or "see" anything are pretty successful at it; some even incorporate it into their own practices.

I learned this technique the hard way. Through hundreds of healing sessions over more than three years, my teacher, Don José Joaquin

Piñeda, did not teach me in the traditional sense. "Sit down behind me, watch, and concentrate," he would sternly repeat when I asked him over and over to explain after a session how he nailed yet another reading. I was becoming so frustrated that I started doubting myself, wondering if I would ever be able to do what he did. "I just don't have it in me," I said at one point, sadly resigned to my inadequacy.

Then one day a woman of medium build in her late forties came in for a session. She rubbed her candle over herself and handed it to Don José. He lit it up, whistled his tune, and started reading. Again sitting behind him, I carefully watched the flame. I noticed the dark knot at the bottom of the wick and the heavy black cloud surrounding it. Then I interrupted him excitedly: "José, José, she has big digestive problems and a lot of fear," I whispered from behind his colorful feather crown. "*Shooosh*," is all he said, impatiently.

I finally understood it from my gut. Later on while assisting my Brazilian mentor, Ipupiara, he taught me some more about candle reading. He had a different reading style and incorporated a whole thematic color system and a more Western understanding and communication sensibility into his readings, as he had already been living in the United States for a few years.

So now I want to share with you some of my own candle-reading stories, to validate the effectiveness of this technique.

⚡ HER ALLY

Katarina, a tall, blond, impressive woman in her mid-forties, with a noticeable German accent, was an executive secretary at a financial institution. Somehow she found out her boss was inappropriately charging personal expenses to the company and so there was growing tension between them. She feared she would be fired. She felt very vulnerable and tense and asked to have a candle reading to see what she could do. As I watched the flame two people appeared in the left field of the wick. "There are two men on your floor. One short, heavy man who likes to wear brown suits, whose office is closer to you, and the other, who is tall and slim with dark hair and likes to wear black suits, whose office is at the end of the corridor to the right. Is that so. Do you recognize them?" I asked.

"Yes, it is true," she said. "They are both the heads of other bank departments, but what does this have to do with me?"

"Be careful of the tall black-suited guy—he is probably friends with your boss, but the brown-suit guy likes you very much and can become your protector. Go talk to him. Ask him to move you to his department to be his assistant."

"Oh, no, I can't do that," Katarina said, "my boss would be upset."

"Let the brown-suit guy arrange it," I suggested.

Two weeks later, Katarina was sitting across from me, smiling broadly. "I spoke to the brown-suit guy in confidence. He was very nice to me and offered to help me. A few days later he arranged for me to work for both him and my boss. And by the way, you were right about the man in the black suit."

☇ RELEASING A FIXATION

I opened the door and there she was. Tall, over six feet, with beautiful honey blonde, straight hair, perfect high cheekbones, and the perfect figure. But her almond-shaped eyes were red—sad and distraught. I did not know it yet but she was a European supermodel. She needed to see me *now,* she had insisted. "It is an emergency," she cried. "I can't go on living like this."

I asked her to rub the candle all over her body, blow three times, and hand it back to me. I lit it and took a few minutes to see.

"Natasha, is this the man you are crying over? He is short, fat, and balding," I said.

"But I love him, I want him back, I can't live without him," she wailed.

"Let me see again," I said, and concentrated on this man who dominated her candle. "Is he French? Wait—is he an alcoholic and drug user? Do you know about that?"

"Yes, but I love him, I want him back, I can't live without him," she cried as I handed her more tissues.

"You know, he is not waiting for you; he already has another woman or even more than one."

"I know, I know, I don't care—he only loves me, he is mine, I can't live without him, see how much weight I've lost? I can't sleep, *ooohhhhh* . . . ," and she started another round of tears.

I must tell you the happy ending of this story, which is a testament to the good that shamanic healing work can do. I saw her a few more times and each time we had a long consultation. We talked about events in her childhood and her relationship with her abusive father, which shaped her belief system and behavior. I finished each session with La Limpia ceremony and a special cutting of the invisible cords technique using wooden chunta spears. This method severed the ties attaching her physical body to the man she was fixated on. Lastly I created a protection shield around her with volcanic healing stones. When she was ready to let the man go she did a cutting of the cords journey with the help of her newfound power animal in which she herself severed the remaining invisible cords that were still attached to both of them.

On her last visit, a few months later, she had a mysterious smile on her beautiful, chiseled face. "I met this guy at a party. He is my height, maybe even taller, very handsome, blond, blue eyes, smart, and funny; he is a TV personality here for a New York station. Wherever we go, people are looking at us. I'm so, so happy!"

ॐ SHAMAN IN DISGUISE

The big, heavyset man who was sitting in front of me was crying, a deep, heart-wrenching cry. It was as if he was connecting to the deepest core of his pain. Just a few minutes earlier he had walked through my door in a dark Armani suit and fashionable eyeglasses. He radiated an aura of authority and success that contradicted his state of grief.

The candle flame indicated that he was depressed, surrounded with heavy negative energies, and at the end of a very long and difficult period, but also, to my surprise, that he was a shaman, an evolved spiritual being. "What is it that you do for a living?" I asked him carefully.

"It's a long story. I used to be on Wall Street—one of those tough sharks. I had everything—cars, women, and expensive vacations. I could easily afford everything my materialistic wife and daughters wanted. When the financial crisis began, I was one of those who were let go by the firm. Then my wife divorced me. My world collapsed. I started looking deeper and asked myself who I am, why this had happened to me. I lost a hundred pounds—yes, I was over 350 pounds at one point," he said.

"Were you abused as a child?" I asked as an image of that appeared in the candle flame.

"Oh, yes many times, I was too soft and sensitive. My father and two older brothers constantly ridiculed me. They used to tell me I was a sissy and needed to toughen up, so they beat the hell out of me. I had to prove to them that I'm a tough Italian guy. And I did. I became a ruthless son of a bitch. I did whatever was necessary to be successful, including cheating on my clients. I gained so much weight in order to hide and protect my true self," he continued, wiping his tears.

"You know, the candle says you are a shaman, a teacher on a spiritual quest. I bet you see spirits too, is that right?" I asked.

"Yes, I do, but what should I do now?"

"Embrace it. Start now. Take some workshops and learn to heal others."

A few months later at an event I was hosting, I met him again. I found out that slowly but steadily he found his way and became a healer, the man he was meant to be.

⚡ WHAT IS MY SPIRITUAL PATH?

Once again on the second Friday of the month we gathered at our open house shamanic circle. This time there was to be a variation on our traditional drumming journey. Instead we sat face to face with a person we did not know, with a small white candle between us. Gazing intently at the candle flame with open eyes, we journeyed into the flame as we called our power animals for help, asking for an answer to our partner's specific question.

David, my partner, looked like a typical New Age person, with his long blond hair, colorful clothing, and lots of beads and amulets around his neck, wrists, and on his head. He relayed his question: "Will my new career bring me the satisfaction I'm looking for?" I asked him to journey with my question: "How should I proceed on my spiritual path?"

For about ten minutes we sat quietly facing each other, our eyes intently focused on the flame. When the drumbeats ended we raised our heads, looked at each other, smiled in anticipation, and began to share our visions. David said that his spirit guides had told him that I needed to go to an ashram to be alone for a period of time to meditate and not speak with anyone for a few days, which I wholeheartedly agreed with, as to do so had been my longtime wish.

When it was my turn to share, I told him my vision: "I was so surprised to see you working with computers, as it does not match your personality—maybe you're doing computer graphics or web pages? My spirit said that you would not be satisfied with your new career. It suggested that you should go back to your first love. When I asked what it was, they said creating images, maybe with painting or photography."

David then shared with me, "From an early age I dreamed of becoming a photographer, as I really believe I have a special eye for it. But sadly I never materialized this path. In my new career I am working with computers. In fact, I work for a company that builds websites, and I'm also doing some computer graphics now, but I have big doubts about my choice." I hope David found his way to fulfill his dream and that he is now satisfied.

⚡ THE PEARL NECKLACE

"Okay, but before we start I have a surprise for you. I want to show you something special. I am sure you are going to appreciate it," Leah said, giggling happily. She got my attention. She dug into her purse and pulled out a pink silk pouch. She untied the pink ribbons at the top and pulled out a beautiful old pearl necklace with an antique silver clasp, which was engraved. "Do you remember this?" she asked mischievously.

"No, should I?" I said, confused, as if she was testing me.

"These are my grandma's pearls you saw during our first session," she said with a broad smile. Immediately the memory of my vision from our first session popped into my mind. I had been reading her candle when the image of her grandmother floating above her head appeared, and I recalled the entire session.

"Were you close to your grandma from your father's side?" I had then asked her carefully.

"Yes, she was my favorite grandma," she confirmed.

"She had the same energy as both you and your dad have."

"Yes, I felt that all my life. I loved her—we had a very special relationship."

I took a deep breath and communicated with her grandma again. "She is saying that she left you a pearl necklace. Do you know anything about this?" I continued.

"No, no, no one ever mentioned that in my family." She tried to dig into her memory. "Well, that is her message to you—she wants you to have it."

Having been reminded of that earlier session with Leah, I asked her how she found the necklace. Leah, with a big, victorious smile, told me the following story.

"A few weeks after our session, I was so curious to know if it was true that I went to visit my mother, who is seventy-five. As we were sitting in her room I told her that my grandma came to me in a dream—I could not say a shaman told me so—and told me about the necklace. My mom looked at me puzzled; she then got up from her armchair, went to her bedroom's cabinet drawer, and pulled it out. She came back to the room and without saying a word she handed it to me. I was shocked. None of us in the family ever saw her wearing it or knew about it. She probably got it as an engagement present from my grandma and didn't like it."

As we were admiring the necklace, I wondered aloud how spirits from the other side are able to interact with and intervene in our lives and fulfill their own wishes as well as ours.

"Do you want to see something really strange?" Leah continued with my train of thought. She went on to pull out an old, very striking diamond ring that was hanging on her neck on a thin gold chain.

"What is it, and how is it connected to our story? I asked.

"Well, a few years ago my second-oldest sister gave it to me. She said that this was our grandma's but she really felt it belonged to me. I was so surprised and truly happy. I recognized it, as my grandma wanted me to have it but when she was on her deathbed, sick and delirious, she could not remember my name and instead said my sister's name. So I respected her wish and handed it to my sister, reluctantly. I always felt connected to it and that I was the rightful owner of the ring. My sister agreed and later gave it to me."

On our following session we continued to discuss the pearl necklace story.

"I wonder how many pearls there are in this necklace," Leah said. She sent me this e-mail after she got home: "I counted the pearls this morning. There are 54. I was born in 1954. Is it a coincidence? Thought you might find it interesting."

10

PSYCHONAVIGATION

The most beautiful thing we can experience is the mysterious.
It is the source of all true art and science.

ALBERT EINSTEIN

Psychonavigation—long-distance viewing—is different from traditional meditation, which encourages the person to clear the mind of any passing thoughts or images and concentrate instead on breathing or a specific mantra. In psychonavigation we are encouraged to do the opposite. This technique is intentional and engaging and sometimes may feel like hard work. You need to sit in a quiet place, undisturbed and totally focused, sitting with purpose. At the same time you must be relaxed and passive, as if watching an unfolding movie. In shamanic terms it is an intentional journey to the middle world.

Usually I start with a simple, basic short breathing meditation. I count my breaths backward, from ten to one, for as long as I can. There are times that I will feel a growing pressure in the area of the third eye and soon an opening will emerge. It's as if a portal opens in a white cloud's center. I will then send my intention through it and direct it toward the person or location I'm interested in learning about. This technique, which is self-taught, enables me to scan people's bodies, diagnose diseases or physical conditions, locate missing persons, and follow the whereabouts of other people. For example, in the case of my teacher Don José, many times I am able to see where he is in Ecuador, how many bags he has at the airport, and the date he is arriving in the United States.

One time a dear friend marveled to me that I always call her when she opens her apartment door after arriving back in the country. "How is it that every time I fly back and open my door, you call me?" she finally asked. I laughed and then shared with her my secret. She did not laugh. "You need to get my permission," she said sternly. And it's true, as sometime it can be a bit invasive to another person. So ask permission.

☈ THE MAN IN THE WHITE CLOUD

Just before sunrise my friend Brian sat on the edge of his bed in meditation, his back straight. His face was dark, as only a few faint rays of the rising sun shone on him from the open window. At the same time I was meditating a few miles away in my house. With his full permission I scanned his body up and down, checking on his health and his mood. It all looked quite normal and uneventful and I was ready to move on when unexpectedly, a few seconds later, a thick white cloud formed just above the top of his head and grew fast to surround it entirely. Surprised, as I had never seen such a sight before, I concentrated on the center of this white cloud and noticed the face of a middle-aged man start to emerge. *He must be about fifty-four years old,* I made a mental note to myself. Thick, black eyebrows surrounded his piercing, coal black eyes, but his hair was pure silky white, blending perfectly with the fluffy, cottony cloud forming above his head. *Is it some kind of god or angel that I'm seeing above his head?* I wondered as I continued observing this apparition. I was most of all startled by the severe look of anger in his eyes. *What is this vision all about? Who is this man? And what does he want from my friend Brian?* I pondered for a long time, and then continued with my meditation, concentrating on my breath, and soon started drifting to other images. But the memory of this vision continued to trouble me.

A few hours later I called Brian from my office. I had to cancel our scheduled lunch for that Friday. Brian sounded really sick. "I wanted to call you, too. Sometime in the middle of the night I started to feel a sharp pain in my throat, which now has become full-blown strep throat. I had better rest and see you next week," he painfully whispered on the other side.

During the next three days I visited Brian again in my morning meditations and noticed that the man in the white cloud was still there, although every day his size was diminished somewhat. On the fourth day the cloud disappeared and a bright rainbow appeared around Brian's head. I knew my friend was feeling well, but I called him to confirm.

"Oh, I'm good. I woke up this morning and knew I was healthy, like something had lifted off me," he said happily.

I wondered if I should tell him my strange visions. We continued with our small talk for a while, about my upcoming trip to Israel, as I was leaving the next day. I finally had the courage to tell him. "Listen, I want to tell you what I have been seeing around you during the past few days. It might sound crazy, but hey, you already know me."

"Oh, sure, go ahead, I can accept anything," Brian laughed.

I shared with him every detail of the man in the white cloud visions and my concern that this had something to do with him getting so sick. "It's just too much of a coincidence. Who was that man?" I asked curiously.

"Well, you won't believe what I'm going to tell you now," he said, and he proceeded to tell me this incredible story. "My friend Richard just called me. He wanted to let me know that his partner had died on Thursday night just before midnight. It was just about the time I started to feel my throat acting up. It all sounded so odd. Apparently they had a very romantic anniversary dinner, and at the end of the evening they went home and made love. He said that according to his boyfriend it was the most passionate lovemaking they have ever had. Happy, they both went to sleep. Merely an hour later his boyfriend was dead in their bed. He had had a massive heart attack."

"Oh, I'm so sorry to hear that. Was he fifty-four?" I asked.

"No, he was fifty-two," Brian replied.

"Did he have white silky hair, dark eyes, and dark eyebrows?" I continued.

"Yes, exactly," he confirmed.

"What was your relationship with Richard's friend?" I asked.

"Well, he took some of my classes a few times. We knew each other more as me being Richard's teacher."

"Do you think it's possible that this man, surprised by his own untimely and sudden death, was desperately seeking an explanation for what had happened to him through you, Richard's spiritual teacher? Maybe that's the reason you got strep throat," I suggested.

"Wow, that's a possibility," Brian responded.

We both took a big long breath, and there was a thick silence on the line for a long while. "Maybe," he said.

☿ MORE SAMUEL VISITATIONS

Samuel was sitting on the edge of his bed. It was early and a soft morning light came into the dim room through the large window. I could see that my friend's face was stricken with unbearable pain. Suddenly a huge bright yellow light burst from inside his head. The sight alarmed me and I was wondering what had happened to him. A few hours later I called him to see how he was doing. Samuel told me that since the night before he had had an unusual and enormous headache clamping his head.

The next morning while meditating I saw him again. This time the burst of light, although decreased in size, was still quite big around his head. The day after that I visited him yet again and it was smaller and one day later it was completely gone. Each day I called him to confirm what I had seen and his condition.

On another occasion I saw Samuel sitting on his bed at home with a large white light coming out of his head—it looked like a long light bulb. He seemed to be more excited and happy than usual. I had a feeling he had discovered something new and significant that could change his life. I called him later that day, curious to learn about his discovery. He laughed and told me that last night he had finally figured out the right phrase to describe what he was doing as a healer. This was a most important task for him, as it made it so much easier to explain to others the complexity of his healing work. He had been engaged in this task for months, even enlisting the help of a few copywriters.

Another day I saw Samuel sitting in the corner of his room. He was pensive and withdrawn. I received a message for him. "It's not a day to make any rash decisions. It is a wait-and-see day." We talked on the phone and he confirmed that he felt pushed to make a decision he wasn't ready to make.

When I saw Samuel another morning, his neck, shoulders, and hands were hurting and he was twisting in pain. Had he had an accident? I wanted to warn him not to take his bike out. I called him. He told me that two days earlier he had had a biking accident—he had fallen off his bicycle and while attempting to block his fall with his hand he had hurt his whole upper body and even had to go to the hospital for a few stitches.

ᴁ WOLF

It was a cold and foggy morning. In the forest a lone gray wolf unexpectedly emerged from the snow-covered trees to my right. The wolf was running frantically in all directions, searching for something unknown to me, sniffing in the fresh snow, his tail tucked between his legs. The wind was harsh, blowing hard, and the snow fell heavily, covering the naked branches and putting a fresh white blanket on the forest floor. Curious, I followed him, observing from high above the trees. At last the troubled wolf seemed to find the shelter he was looking for in a hollow under a large tree. The exhausted animal dug himself into the hollow and disappeared under the fresh snow. I kept watching, waiting for him to reemerge, but after a while I lost my concentration and my mind drifted. Other visions passed through as I sat on my bed during that morning meditation.

That initial vision troubled me. The wolf appeared many more times in my meditations. I couldn't understand why. What message was I to learn from meeting him? If he is one of my power animals, why is he not creating a connection with me?

And then one day Wolf sat right in front of me, drinking a cup of herbal tea.

It was on an unbearably hot and muggy day in the middle of June in New York City. I was riding my bike back from a meeting with a printer down on Seventh Avenue. As I crossed 23rd Street, I saw a Salvation Army store where my friend Lou had once bought a beautiful suit. Because I needed a new jacket for an important business meeting the next day I decided to stop and have a look. I locked my bike and walked into the crowded, air-conditioned store. I spotted the suit rack and started to browse. It took me only a few minutes to realize that I didn't even know my size, so I searched for a salesman to measure me. I went to the front of the store and asked a young guy for help. "Oh no, I don't work here, but let me try to help you anyway," he laughed whole-heartedly. *What do I have to lose,* I thought. I tried on a few jackets and we started to talk. Soon we both realized that neither of us could find anything appropriate, so he invited me to continue our cheerful conversation over tea at a busy coffee shop next door. Over tea I introduced myself and asked him his name. "Well, my real name is Jejomar Impoc Gumato, but everybody calls me Wolf," he said. I sat back in my seat, stunned. Here in front of me sat my wolf.

Wolf returned to his wife and children in North Carolina, but I often saw him in my morning meditations. To my utter astonishment I realized that I could tell by the wolf in my vision, by its body language and movement, what Wolf the person was experiencing. I knew what his moods were and what was happening in his life. I saw his sadness, fears, depressions, arguments, happiness, and victories. Sometimes I called him to confirm what I saw and we talked about the situations. Two of these stories are worth telling here.

In a snowy forest I saw two male wolves facing each other. One was slightly larger and older. They were engaged in a brutal battle, thrusting forcefully toward each other with their front legs, trying to outmaneuver each other. Angry, ferocious, and unforgiving, they were biting and slashing each other's throats with loud growls and screams. I was mesmerized by the sight and at the same time sad to witness such a hopeless fight. I called Wolf an hour later and asked him how he was doing.

"Oh, great. Everything is really fine," he said cheerfully.

"Don't lie to me," I replied, "I saw you this morning. You can tell me the truth."

"Okay," he said reluctantly. "I had a huge fight with my teenage son. It's already been a few days. I really don't know what to do, but this time I'm not going to give up and I'm not going to talk to him until he gives in." He went on to tell me the details of their rivalry and fights. I felt that he was dead serious and I encouraged him to look at it in a different way.

"Can you see it as your son's fight for your love, attention, and approval?" I asked.

"Maybe," he said, followed by a long period of silence.

I made Wolf promise me to have a good dad-and-son conversation that night. A week later, he called me: they were buddies again.

During one of our telephone conversations Wolf raved about an out-of-body book he had just read. He wanted me to read it, too, and promised to send it to me. I shared an experience with him that I had had many years earlier that had a strong impact on me and that was quite terrifying:

"I was maybe twenty-one and visiting with a friend in Tel Aviv. We were talking until the wee hours of the morning. It was early morning when I finally went to bed. I wasn't sure if I was dreaming or if it was really happening, but suddenly I observed my physical body from above lying on the bed below. Without warning my legs started to float higher, toward the window, and I started to levitate. I flew legs first through the open window and into the dark sky. I was soaring above a beautiful green valley for a long while. The current of the wind held me gently. It was strangely soundless and mesmerizing but at the same time I was aware that my earthly body was in a total panic. In an effort to return quickly to safety in my physical body on the bed, I held my breath and forcefully tightened my muscles to make my body heavier to force it down. I came back as I left, through the window, head-first. As I merged with my body on the bed I was shaken. The next few days my entire body was in pain. I never wished to experience whatever had happened that night again."

A few weeks later Wolf called to say that he couldn't find the book he had wanted to send me and he apologized. I was sitting at my office desk and unexpectedly I felt a rush of energy flowing to my brain. A picture appeared in my mind.

"Are you in your bedroom?" I asked.

"Yes, how did you know?"

"Well, do you sleep on the left side of your bed?"

"Yes, How do you know that?"

"Look to your left—there is a blue carpet next to your bed, isn't there?

"Yes, a blue carpet," he said, intrigued.

"What is it?"

"It's actually an extra bed with a blue cover," he said.

"Move it. The book is behind it, next to the wall."

"You're too weird," he said, and hung up. He never sent me the book.

⚡ THE MONEY BASKET

It's not every day that I receive a phone call from my friend Sandy, who lives in Israel.

"Do you have a few minutes?" she asked hesitantly.

"Sure, what's going on?"

"I need your professional services. You wouldn't believe what happened to me. I went to the bank to exchange money to bring with me on my trip to the United States. I remember putting it in a regular white envelope. I was tired and absentminded and had a headache. I crossed the street toward my car, and just then my cell phone rang. I got into the car, talked to my friend on the phone, and then drove home, not paying attention to the money or anything else. At home, I looked for the white envelope and couldn't find it anywhere—not in my purse and not in my bag. I'm really going crazy! Can you try to find it for me?"

"Okay, let me see," I said. "Did you have a straw basket with you?"

"No," Sandy said.

"I don't know, but I see a straw basket, artificial straw, made from plastic."

"No, I don't have such a basket."

"Did you look in all your bag pockets, in the car, under the seats, in the glove compartment?"

"Oh yes, yes, of course, I did all of that. This is what everyone told me to do. I just can't remember what I did with the envelope. It's like I had a blackout."

"Sandy, I don't know but all I can see is that straw basket sitting in the back seat of your car. Why do I see that?" I asked her.

"Oh my God, you're right! I did have a basket there. It was full of blocks of wood. I brought it to the place where I teach the children, and after I emptied it I saw at the bottom there were a bunch of old papers. I dumped them in the garbage cans near my home. I remember seeing one bright white envelope and wanted to check what was inside but was too tired."

"Sandy, run down and see if it's still there in the trash," I told her.

"It won't help, it was last week and the trash has been picked up, but I'll try," and she let out a big sigh.

My Brother-in-Law

As I was sitting doing my meditation one morning I wanted to do some long-distance viewing to check on my sister, but instead my vision drew me toward my brother-in-law. I was a bit confused but continued to scan his body. Starting from the head down I could see his dark lungs, blackened from many years of heavy smoking. His heart was pumping hard and the layer that protected the heart was dark and diseased. I concentrated there some more; it looked like he had a dark ball the size of an orange stuck between his lungs and his heart. "He must go for an immediate check-up if he wants to live a few more years," was the message I clearly heard in my head.

I ran to the phone and called my sister in Israel and asked her to take him in for an immediate check-up. "Oh, he will never do it," she said desperately.

"He must do it," I insisted.

"You don't know him, he won't, especially after he just got a clean bill of health from his doctor," she replied.

A few months later, as they were vacationing in France, they were traveling on a boat through the French wine country when suddenly he was gripped with an enormous pain in his chest and stomach. When they returned home it was discovered he had a big cancerous tumor in his upper stomach, pushing on his lungs and his heart.

I continued to follow up on my sister. One morning I saw her in her car driving at an incredible speed. Her two hands were gripping the wheel. She was so worried, almost in total panic. I stopped what I was doing, ran downstairs, and called her. "Itzhak, I can't talk right now. I'm driving. I'll get a ticket," she tried to say. "What's going on?" I insisted. "I have to buy an ink cartridge for my printer to print my husband's test before we go to see the doctor and I have to get to the store before it closes. Call me later."

☡ A VISIT WITH MY WIFE

While my wife was away in Israel visiting our family with our three kids, I visited with her in my daily morning meditations from our home in New York to check on her health. One morning as I scanned her entire body, her stomach looked quite bloated and she had a large dark spot in it. It looked like she was having constipation, which had created a feeling of anxiety and heaviness.

I picked up the phone and called her.

"Did you see me?" she asked,

"Yes, I did" I said.

"What did you see?"

I told her my vision.

The next day she looked much more relaxed and at ease than she had the first few days after her arrival. I called again.

"Did you see me today?" she asked with a cheerful voice.

"It's the first time in over a week that I started to feel better. I'm no longer having constipation."

ᾼ TRAVELING WITH NAVA

My longtime friend Nava is herself an excellent intuitive healer. Many years ago, as we discussed prosperity and abundance or the lack thereof in our lives, she taught me a special "green table" prosperity process she does each sunrise. Thereafter we did it daily—she in Tel Aviv, and I in New York. Afterward I would always check on her, and in doing so I can sometimes tell whether she is happy, sad, working with people, or other events going on in her life.

On one of these occasions I found Nava in the middle of a healing session, sitting in her dimly lit healing room a short distance from an older man who was lying down on the mattress in front of her. His face was buried in the pillow, his hand held tightly against his body, as if to protect himself. I could see he was frozen, anxious, holding on to his emotions. A few days later when I called her, she confirmed having worked with this man and my diagnosis of his condition.

A few months later when I "visited" Nava again, I saw her sitting in her big armchair cuddling herself. Strangely, she was sitting in a different room of her spacious apartment than she usually does when I "visit" with her. She seemed sad and cold. There was a strange blue light reflecting off her face, and I noticed that she was wearing a long burgundy robe. I wondered what had happened so, later, after our regular chitchat on the phone, I asked her if she was wearing that long, dark red robe.

"That's unbelievable, you saw me!" she said. "I'll tell you what happened—it was very strange. On my way home a thunderstorm broke and I got soaked. As I was running home I fell into a big puddle. I was so miserable. I came home and wrapped myself in that old red robe and sat watching television in my bedroom. I just can't believe you saw me."

Now I understood the blue light reflected on her face in the vision.

A few months later I arrived in Tel Aviv to teach a seminar and I paid her a visit. As I walked into her bedroom, I noticed that very same robe was hanging on the closet hanger. And we laughed again at this story. She was so impressed with how I was able to see her red robe that she asked me to teach her how to practice psychonavigation too. I suggested we try it together right then. We lay on the bed, shoulders and hips touching, and chose our mutual friend Doron as the focus of our exercise. We each closed our eyes and began with some deep breathing. I asked her to concentrate on Doron, who is a successful fashion designer living in New York. We both gave our answers at the same time and added details as we went along.

"Where is he now?" I asked.

We both saw him in his office.

"What does the office look like?"

We both saw the big cutting table in the center of the room with paper patterns on the walls.

"Is he there alone?" No was the answer, as we both saw the three young female assistants around him discussing different fabrics and materials.

"What do they look like?" Two of the women had light brown hair and one was blond.

"What is he wearing?"

He was wearing black pants and a light gray knit shirt. We disagreed on the shade of the gray. Nava said it was bluish gray; I said it was it was light charcoal gray.

"Now, let's see if we were right", I said. "Call him up."

"Now? We'll disturb him," Nava protested.

"Yes, now," I urged her.

Doron was in his New York office. He was surprised to hear from us. Nava told him about our exercise and shared with him the details of what we saw. There was one detail we did not get right though. The blond woman: we learned she was a blond, but she had dyed her hair to a shocking red. Nava was right about the shade of his knit shirt.

Nava was truly excited. "It was so simple," she said, "I have to do it more often myself."

ᘜ A Hawaiian Vision

The sudden downpour woke me early that morning. Big drops of rain were pounding heavily on the glass doors by my bed. I rolled out of bed, opened the doors wide, and took a big breath of fresh air as the first light of the new day emerged. The rain slowly stopped. A soft Hawaiian breeze blew quietly, ruffling the tropical trees surrounding our *hale* (house). I slipped into my sandals, wrapped myself with a flowery green sarong, and went down the dirt road that lead to the ocean. I greeted the small tomato-tree grove, stopped to inhale the strong smell of the plumeria flowers, said hello to the grazing horses, and reached the gate of Kalani Honua, a retreat on the Big Island of Hawaii. I stood on the old, narrow, one lane, sacred Kapoho Kalapana road, or as it is known today, the Red Road, imagining the ancient Hawaiian monarch's convoy passing through from the north side of the Island to the southern tip in the cover of darkness so no ordinary people could have a glimpse of them. I took in the beauty of the mile-long green tunnel formed by the tall old mango trees.

Crossing the Red Road, I made my way along a narrow path to The Point, a secluded lava rock that hangs high above the gushing ocean waters on the easternmost tip of the island. I sat to meditate facing east and made blessings to the rising sun, took in the ocean spray and the blessed sister wind, and watched a sea turtle surf the strong waves. Slowly the sun rose higher and the fog and mist moved out. From the distance I heard a conch shell blowing. It was time for yoga class and breakfast. I skipped the class and went directly to a small mound on the retreat grounds. There, in the background of three tall majestic monarch palm trees, I entered into the skeleton of tree branches that formed the sweat lodge and sat down. Its covers had been removed right after the powerful ceremony of the previous night. There was still a strong smell in the air of the mixture of tobacco and sage that had been burned on the hot stones, along with the salty sweat of more than twenty men who had been sitting in the circle praying, singing, crying, and breaking through their barriers. It was all embedded in the wet soil around the vacant stone pit and in the emerging memory of my own young child soul part, as I understand it now, who spontaneously returned to me and had a desperate need for cuddling, love, and healing in the height of the heat under the sweat lodge covers.

I sat cross-legged, closed my eyes in deep meditation, and breathed deeply, trying to reconnect to those spirits we all shared last night and especially to my own vision from early childhood, an experience that had been unveiled to me so significantly and powerfully. At once I felt an extraordinary pull from the crown of my head. Like a powerful string, a white ray of light was lifting me higher, pulling me farther and farther up into the sky. At the same time I felt another strong force pulling me from my anus in the opposite direction, to the core of the Earth. Soon I sensed that I had become a hollow vessel and this intense energy traveled through me and connected me to the entire universe and to Mother Earth. Then a strange new vision came to me. I actually saw myself from high above sitting in the sweat lodge, a line of light penetrating vertically through me and around the earth. There were hundreds of rings of light surrounding and embracing us all. I had the profound awareness that we are all truly in it together and connected by these energy rings; that we are all really one. That we are much like the trees, birds, stones, and worms, as well as drops of water. I knew it in my body and in my soul that I was not more or less important, not higher or lower in the universal pecking order than anything else. I was in awe. I felt an incredible release and a quiet, peaceful acceptance, a sense of belonging that I had never experienced before. I knew I was a part of the universal whole, no longer a separated entity. And I took comfort in knowing this. I also knew that I'd never have anything to fear, as we are all equal and the same and that whatever happens to me happens for a reason.

The sound of the conch announcing that breakfast was ready shook me out of my reverie. I sat there quietly under the three monarch palm trees, breathing in deeply the smell of the earth for a little while longer, taking in that exquisite experience. Watching the men pass by to the dining hale, I looked at each of them as a reflection of myself, without judgment, as just another part of myself.

There were three other amazing insights and visions during my first visit to Kalani. One night we had an ancient kava-kava ceremony held by a local Kumo Hula (master teacher of the Hula tradition). The ancient kava-kava ceremony was performed at night by the leader's council, men only, as a way to reach decisions and resolve conflicts based entirely on consensus. The properties of the kava-kava root helped them talk from the heart, until a unified decision could be reached.

During that week of men's retreat the Kumo Hula taught us the ancient Hula, a powerful warriorlike dance unlike the more feminized versions of Hula performed today. He taught us to use our body, leg, and hand movements as sign language to tell heroic war and love stories and communicate with the gods and their mortal rulers. The movements were accompanied by vigorous yells and chants in a powerful rhythm.

In a short ceremony in my hale the Kumo Hula bestowed on me a Hawaiian name: Hau'oli Kāna, happy, smiling man. Perhaps he chose this because I told him the meaning of my Hebrew name Itzhak: "he (will) laugh" (originating from Abraham, then one hundred years old, laughing at God who told him he was going to have a son—Itzhak). My new Hawaiian name was not to be confused with the derogatory *haole,* a person who doesn't know how to breathe, as I was told is used to describe white people.

As we sat in a circle, the large bowl of kava-kava was nestling in the center. The bitter drink was prepared a day before by women who chewed the roots and mixed it with their saliva to help it ferment. They then added some cold water, very much in the same way Chicha is prepared from the Manioc root, as I found out many years later as I witnessed the Shuar in the Amazon). The Kumo Hula opened with an old Hawaiian chant and then served the brew to each of us as he swiftly moved in and out of the center on his knees at the eye level of the man he served. Each man drank from the coconut shell and shared something personal from his heart. We went on like this for a few hours as the calming effect of the drink started to take effect on us.

My mouth and tongue were numb but an unfamiliar feeling came over me. One of total relaxation, true love for all the men around me and total acceptance of the world.

As the ceremony ended I walked outside the hale to the hot dark night. There was no moon, the electric generator stopped churning at this late hour, and the stars were big and bright. I realized that every pore of my skin was radiating aliveness I did not know existed. I could feel it connect in magical strings of translucent light to the galaxies and the entire universe. As we said good-bye to each other I embraced one of the guys; it was maybe the first time I felt that there was no separation between us. We were one.

The following night we paid a visit to Madam Pelé, the goddess of volcanoes, "the earth-eating woman" as the Hawaiians calls her. As we walked carefully on the newly formed crust of earth we watched under cover of darkness (the park ranger already left) the streaming rivers of red and orange molten lava spilling slowly from afar into the ocean. We stood on the hot, fragile newly-formed volcanic crust in awe. It was one mesmerizing sight. Huge white steam columns rose out of the churning ocean as the fiery lava spilled down in huge swooshed sounds, sending strong sulfur fumes and bright light into the dark sky. I was bowled over, witnessing nature's destruction and creation cycle. We lay our gifts of flowers and fruits to appease Madam Pelé and made prayers for her and our well-being and safety.

After a sumptuous vegetarian lunch the next day, Daniel, who had visited Madam Pele with me the night before asked me, "Do you want to truly see Mother Earth as a living being?"

"Sure. Of course!" I said excitedly. "Let's go to the steam vents, then," he said. I joined him and two other guys and drove up the road for about twenty minutes. We parked the car by the side of the highway, jumped over the guardrails, and walked in single file through a field of wild vegetation and colorful purple flowering orchids. There were a number of vents of many sizes all spewing white clouds of steam. "I think we should take the big one; we can all fit inside it," Daniel said with the authority of someone who had already been there. It looked like a deep cone-shaped cave. We climbed down a flimsy and slippery wooden ladder, slid deep down, and sat around the edges. We took turns, and one by one, in only our birthday suits, we sat in an embryo position at the dark, narrow mouth of the breathing earth for a few minutes. The hot steam was gushing, inhaling and exhaling strongly in constant flow through the narrow tunnel opening. This was a true healing ceremony as Mother Earth sent wave after wave of hot spray, bathing my skin and my soul to purify me. I could not stop thinking how lucky I was to be in a sacred place where all the four elements—fire, water, air, and earth—interplayed so powerfully, dancing with each other perpetually. It made me feel so energized and awakened.

11

☸ ☸ ☸ ☸

HOLOGRAPHIC
EXPERIENCES

*The best and most beautiful things in the world cannot be
seen or even touched. They must be felt with the heart.*

HELEN KELLER

Olga Kharitidi, a Russian psychologist, wrote a superb autobiographical
book titled *Entering the Circle,* in which she describes her encounter
with an old Siberian woman shaman. She tells the story how in one of
her visits to the old lady's home she witnessed the same spirit the shaman worked with flying in the air. It was the first time I read about
this phenomenon. Reading it, I immediately thought *I would never be
able to experience that phenomenon, it is the act of a real shaman.* But
one day it just happened unexpectedly while I was teaching a workshop
in Tel Aviv. I was perplexed and shocked. But since then it seems I have
been able to harness this newfound ability in my healings and seminars.
I have no idea how one can see holograms; they just somehow appear
with either open or closed eyes. These images could be of deceased or
living people as well as places. They can be of the present or of the past.
Most startling is the fact that these images happen to be accurate and
relevant to the people for whom I see.

What are these holographic images? Are they spirits? Are they energy footprints people leave behind? Curious, I looked up what scientists say about holography. They say it is the creation of a three-dimensional captured light field that is illuminated by two rays of light. One goes through the image and the other is at a certain angle. The image changes as the position and point of reference of the viewing changes, in the same way as if the object were still present, making the image appear three-dimensional. It consists of a random structure of changeable intensity and density.

I definitely see many of these when I do house clearings. In the Quechua tradition it is believed we all have physical and nonphysical bodies. Within this energy-illuminated body we store life impressions of traumas, memories, events, ancestors, and living people. It's all there and we carry it with us wherever we go. That is why the Quechua have energy cleansing ceremonies whenever they feel out of balance.

My own holographic experiences have raised many questions for me: Can thoughts be manifested physically? Would I be able to "see" thoughts in ordinary reality without the influence of a beating drum? Can I influence other people's thoughts? What is it that allows me to perceive thoughts? From what material are thoughts made of and, if it is energy, can we change our thoughts by changing our physical and mental energy?

The following stories will, I hope, shed some light on the phenomena of holographic experience.

⚡ HOLOGRAPHIC POWER ANIMALS

The entire week the skies opened up; heavy rains, sleet, high winds, lightning and thunder filled the winter days and nights with no break. It was the heaviest rainfall in Israeli history—so said the Beer Sheba elders. It also happened to be the week I was visiting. I had promised a few of my friends I would teach them shamanic journeying techniques. Thirteen brave ones showed up at my friend Nava's apartment in the center of Tel Aviv that stormy night. I began the evening with a short introduction about my involvement in shamanism, what shamanism is, and what we would be experiencing that evening. I told a few personal stories to my typical Israeli skeptical audience to explain the phenomena and the powers we would encounter.

We started by purifying each person with sage. Our first journey was to find a power animal or an ally in the lower world and establish a relationship with it. They all lay down on their backs, their eyes closed, and I started to drum in a rapid, monotonous rhythm. After a while, I started to hum a Quechua tune that I had learned from my teacher, the shaman Don José Joaquin Piñeda. This time I held my drum higher, close to my head, and drummed in a circular motion. I started to sense that my body wanted to follow that motion. I felt the drum's vibrations bouncing off the walls, floor, and ceiling, and I slowly entered into a meditative state. I was in a deep trance, floating in space while my hands continued drumming. I could hear the strong rain and winds pounding on the glass windows. The smoky air in the room felt richer and fuller. In my song, I called my power animal, the white dove, to come and help me overcome the flu that I had been fighting all day and also to help the other people meet their own power animals.

All of a sudden, a beautiful white dove flew from within my drum directly above Rama, the woman who was lying in front of me, and disappeared into the darkness of the room. This amazing sight surprised me, and I could swear I wasn't dreaming, as my eyes were wide open. I continued drumming for a while longer and then signaled to the group with another set of drumbeats to conclude the journey and return to our reality.

As people sat in their places I asked them to share their experiences. Some of them described in great detail their remarkable journeys and the meetings they had with different power animals. I was pleased with their effort but also disappointed that no one said they had seen the white dove. I decided to see if that vision had been something I had made up and I asked if anyone had seen her. The woman in front of me raised her hand and said that she had seen a white dove flying from my direction above Rama's head. Satisfying as this confirmation may have been, it nevertheless left me confused. I still wasn't sure if I had made it up or if it had really happened.

We continued on to our second journey, this time asking our newfound allies, the power animals, a meaningful personal question. I asked everyone in the group to lie down, and as I started to drum, I began drifting into a familiar altered state of mind. I scanned the room slowly, and surprisingly a vision formed above Rama again. I saw a muddy lake surrounded by tall water plants. Close to the surface I saw a school of brownish fish swimming slowly in a very tight formation. I looked up and saw the white dove coming from above. When she reached the water, she shapeshifted into a different, larger bird of many pastel colors. As I stared at her, the odd bird started to multiply. Now there were three birds sitting in front of the lake. One was looking to the right, one toward me, and the third one was looking to the left. I stared at them intently, trying to capture every detail of this strange sight. Thinking about what I had just witnessed, it reminded me of a holographic image, a three-dimensional picture in the air.

I decided to move to the other side of the room and for a while I stood there drumming. Suddenly, I was startled as a dark shadow of a large feline jumped from the open door onto another woman. The black panther lay his full body on top of her, warming her body and licking her face fondly. I watched this reunion of spirits in astonishment. I glanced at the clock. Time was up, and I had to signal them to finish their journeys and return to this reality.

This time more people wanted to share their journeys. Rama described hers in detail—how she had seen the dove and how it had turned into a pastel-colored bird. The other woman described how the black panther had jumped on her and licked her face and how exciting and gentle this experience was for her. I felt excited, too. It seemed that I was really able to witness parts of their journeys, but I was curious to find out where the brownish fish were and why Rama had seen only one bird.

After the evening was over some people stayed to talk and enjoy tea and cookies around the kitchen table. Rama was there, too, so I asked if she had also seen the brown fish at the beginning of her journey. "Yes, I did," she said, "but I didn't think much of it so I didn't share." Then I asked her if she had seen only one bird.

"No," she said, "I saw three of them, each looking in different directions." This was quite a validation.

A few weeks later I was back in New York at the drumming circle. I joined the other drummers at the center. More than thirty people were lying on the mats journeying, some of them for the first time. Their first assignment was to look for their power animals in the lower world. I wanted to see if I could see the hologram visions again or if it was only a one-time experience. As I was drumming I raised my drum to my head and looked intently over the heads and bodies of a few people whom I chose as they were journeying. I focused my intention and my eyes above their faces, and different images of animals started to emerge. I could feel that my previous experience in Tel Aviv was not accidental—I could indeed manifest them consciously.

☊ VISION OF HOME

An old friend introduced me to Francisco. He had just arrived from Colombia for a visit in New York and wanted to experience his first shamanic practice at our shamanic circle's open house. I welcomed him warmly and asked him to meet with me afterward to see how he liked it.

During the journeying session, as I walked around the circle beating my drum, I stopped by Francisco. I stood in front of him, drumming and chanting quietly to help him on his first journey. Suddenly, above his slim body, which was dressed all in black, I saw a beautiful green fertile meadow surrounded by low hills. In it I saw a brownish gray horse grazing peacefully. Two more horses came running from the right and joined the first one. As I zoomed out I saw Francisco, this time dressed in plain working clothes, alone, with his back to a simple farmhouse, walking into the vast valley of green fields. He seemed to be looking for these three horses. I could sense the deep connection and belonging this man had with his land. The sunny sky was a deep blue, the air cool and crisp, and there was a beautiful serenity all around. Watching the interaction between him and his horses it seemed as if the first horse I had seen had a very special place in Francisco's heart. I followed these images until it was time to stop drumming.

When the evening came to a close, I asked Francisco if he had met his power animal during the first journey. He looked at me sadly, raised his arms in defeat, and said in a heavy Spanish accent, "I'm sorry, I have failed. I did not see anything." I was disappointed for him and for myself. I thought that perhaps I'd imagined what I had seen. I decided to share with him my vision anyway—why not? I told him about the brown-gray horse behind his house, and that I thought it was his special power animal. I described to him the beautiful scenery, the other two horses, and the farmhouse I had seen. Francisco opened his wide puppy eyes, smiled, and said, "I was so homesick, all I could do was to think about my house, the lush green valley, and my three dogs I left behind and miss so much. I understand why you saw them as horses—my dogs are really big and tall, they look like small horses. One of them is my favorite and a special friend."

⚡ URBAN JOURNEYS

Once again we stood drumming around the candlelit mesa at our open house. After a while I turned my back to the center of the circle to face the people who were lying on their mats around the perimeter of the circle, journeying. It was the first journey of the night, in which novices journeyed to meet with their power animals, a different journey from what the old-timers were doing. In front of me lay Nick, a first-timer. As I watched him with half-open eyes, I could see that above his head and body a heavy white cloud was forming. Two birds of prey were circling in it above his head. They flapped their wings forcefully and nervously. I tried to identify them; one was larger and looked like an eagle; the smaller bird could have been a red-tailed hawk. *Maybe they want to get his attention,* I thought. I looked down at Nick's face: a large wavy ocean was forming there and the two birds were now flapping their wings rapidly above it. At that moment a sharp movement caught my eyes above Kathleen, our core member, who lay next to him. A dog jumped on her body and vigorously licked her face. I remembered her as a tiny puppy when Kathleen brought her to one of our meetings, and now she was covering Kathleen's whole body. A large white mane of long hair with a mix of many gray tones had replaced her grayish puffy hair. What a joyous sight!

As I packed my drum and bags Nick came over to offer to help me.

"How did you like the new experience?" I asked, curious about his first-ever experience.

"Oh, it was great, really interesting."

"You shared with us that you met a dolphin on your first journey," I said. "I was wondering if you also saw above your head two birds of prey?"

He looked at me, somewhat puzzled. "No, they appeared in my second journey. But how did you know about them?"

"Well, I saw them, like I'm seeing you now—they were waiting for you from the very start."

"Unbelievable," he responded.

Then I turned to Kathleen, who was listening nearby. "Kathleen, I'm amazed at how big your dog is now!"

She was laughing. "You saw it?"

I told her about the vision I had with her and the dog.

"You're right, I went to talk to my tree in Central Park, as instructed, and as I was sitting by the tree, I realized my dog was missing so I frantically called her and she surprised me by jumping on me."

☡ A Childhood Vision

The auditorium lights had been dimmed. Only a large circle of candles reflected light on the beautifully decorated altar in the center of the room. The many people who had come to our monthly open house shamanic circle were lying down, ready for our next journey. A group of drummers, myself included, stood in the center and began drumming in a fast, monotonous rhythm. The objective of this journey was to connect to a fun place or memory from childhood and bring it back to the present day.

After drumming for a few minutes, I turned around and stood facing a man who was in the circle for the first time. I stood there for a while drumming and watching the energy above his face. At first a white fog formed, hanging above his head and body. Slowly an image became visible over his head: a young boy, maybe six years old, walked on a dirt road, shirtless and barefoot, toward a pond. He was slim and had dark skin just like the man lying in front of me, who could have been from India, I judged. Tall trees surrounded the pool of water, their big branches bowing down, their leaves touching the flowing water. The boy pulled on the branches and swung happily. Then he stopped and climbed into one of the trees. I could feel the joy and deep connection he had with the tree. A girl with long blond curly hair wearing light cotton clothes, also barefoot, came into view. She crossed the dirt road on the right to play with him. I started doubting myself. If he is from India, I thought, what is a blond girl doing in his native village? I thought I might be imagining things. I even looked for a dark-skinned girl, but none appeared. Watching the two young people interacting, I sensed their deep affinity and friendship. I moved my eyes as some images that drew my attention started to emerge from the thick fog above the man's body. I noticed that just above his solar plexus a dinner table appeared in a dimly lit room with dark wooden walls and floors. Four figures were sitting for dinner. I could not see them clearly. It was perhaps early evening and I could sense who the father figure was as well as the young man sitting opposite him who appeared to be the boy I had seen previously, and there were two other people. I watched them for a short while and felt a quiet sadness. I noticed that there was no conversation around the table. At that moment, my fellow drummer nudged me to come back to the circle. The images evaporated into the space. It was time to bring the journey to a close.

Later, I came over to the man and asked him if he would share his journey with me.

"I didn't see anything," he said in a strange accent that clearly was not Indian, I realized. "I just felt warmth all over my body and saw my dog, whom I love so much, but I probably made it up. It couldn't be my power animal."

"Where are you from?" I asked.

"Brazil," he replied in that beautiful rolling accent.

"Do you live in a village with a river and trees?" I asked.

"No, I live in São Paulo in a regular apartment building, but our family has a big country house that we used to go to on the weekends. It has a natural pool with many trees around it."

"Do you love trees?" I asked.

His eyes brightened. "I love trees, they are my best friends!"

"Did you have a blonde girlfriend when you were young?"

"Yes, and we are still very good friends, we keep in touch quite often."

"Are there four people in your family?"

"Yes, but my parents are divorced, and I was thinking during my journey about my father, who is the most important person in my life."

⚉ MIKE'S GRANDMA

The e-mail read, "Confirmed! See you at noon today at your office for lunch and discussion. Mark Peters."

Mark was now sitting in front of me at our office conference table, a young African American man in his early thirties dressed elegantly in a dark suit. This was the first time I was meeting him and he was excitedly telling us about his public relations agency and his new career. I invited him to discuss the possibility of cooperation between our two agencies. The conversation turned personal when he talked about the honeymoon he and his new wife had just taken to the Caribbean Islands. As he finished telling his story we continued the conversation about our businesses. Unexpectedly a smiling old black woman appeared clearly just above and behind his head. Although I was a bit surprised to say the least, I tried to ignore her and concentrate on the conversation at hand. But the old lady kept on smiling at me in such an openhearted and friendly way I thought I'd mention this to Mark but I held back, reminding myself that at our first business meeting I should be a little cautious and act more professional. I wouldn't want to appear foolish. So I tried to brush her off, telling her to leave us alone, and she disappeared. But a few minutes later she appeared again. This time she was wearing a bright, short-sleeved orange dress. She stood in a vegetable and flower garden in front of her small house on an island and stopped her work to greet us. Her old face was glowing behind Mark's head, looking at him proudly and waving at me.

Finally I could hold back no more and without further ado I heard myself saying, "Mark, what is your relationship with your grandmother?"

He stopped at this break in our conversation and looking puzzled, asked, "What do you mean? Why are you asking?"

I told him that his grandma was here with us hovering above his head. Mark's dark eyes started to fill with tears and then, full of emotion, he went on to tell me his family story:

"Many years ago my grandma encouraged her older son, my father, who was in his early twenties at the time, to leave the island and the family home. She did it despite the strong objections of my grandpa, who was afraid it might break up the family. She wanted my father to make a better life for himself. She encouraged him to have a better education and find a well-paid job in New York. My father left the island and really did quite well. After finishing law school he became a successful and respected lawyer. He married my mother and we all lived in a nice Connecticut neighborhood. Meanwhile, my grandpa passed away and didn't have the chance to enjoy all our success." He smiled and continued. "After my wedding, for our honeymoon I wanted to introduce my wife to my grandma. I also wanted to show her my deep appreciation for her courage, which enabled us to have better opportunities. My wife happily went along with this plan and we spent two wonderful nights in her home."

"I think she wants you to know how proud she is of you and that she is following you with her blessings everywhere you go," I told Mark.

We resumed our meeting after acknowledging the blessing of laughter, enthusiasm, and humor of Mark's grandmother.

⚡ AREYDA'S HEADACHE

This story could not have happened if it wasn't for the encouragement of a healer friend named Areyda, who pushed the limits of what I thought was possible and helped me confront my fear of spontaneous readings.

"I have an incredible headache," Areyda called one day on the phone, "Can I come to visit you?" When she arrived an hour later she was holding her head in both hands. "It hurts," she said.

"Why don't we go outside so you can get some fresh air?" I suggested, as it was a beautiful sunny, cold spring day.

"I think it started right after I finished the healing session this morning," she said.

"Would you like me to see what caused it?"

"Oh sure, go ahead, tell me what you see."

I took a few deep breaths and looked at her colorful Garifuna* attire, her eyes, her forehead, and then I glanced above her head, half-focusing. After a couple of minutes a vision came.

"You know, I see this tall black guy," and I started laughing.

"Oh, go ahead, don't stop, just say what you see," Areyda reprimanded me.

"Okay, Okay," I said and looked at the same place again, concentrating on this man. "I see him now standing in a park. I see trees and grass. He is really good-looking, slim, well-built, maybe about thirty-seven years old. I think he is about six two or three. He is wearing a

---

*The Garifuna are descendants of West African, Central African, Island Carib, and Arawak people who live primarily in Central America along the Caribbean coast in Belize, Guatemala, Nicaragua, and Honduras.

blue windbreaker, white t-shirt, khaki shorts, and sandals—very preppy. I can see that he loves being in nature and being alone, and I think he is very artistic, maybe a painter? And he loves music."

"Wait a moment," Areyda interrupted me. "That's the guy the neurotic woman I had the healing session for was obsessing about."

"Are you sure?" I asked.

"Yes, yes, she showed me his headshot and a letter he had written her. He said that he used to be a model, that he is six-foot-two and a painter who loves the outdoors. He is actually forty-three but really looks much younger, and he now lives in Woodstock."

"But why was she talking about him?" I asked.

"Oh, I can't tell you all the details, but you know, my headache is almost gone, thank you."

"You mean her relentless babblings about her romantic obsession with him caused your headache?" I asked her.

"Yes, I guess . . ." and we laughed. "What else did you see?" Areyda urged me.

"Let me see . . . I have a feeling he doesn't like your client very much, or any other person as a matter of fact. He is a loner and doesn't really trust people."

"She wanted me to tell her where she could find him because she has a crush on him, but he disappeared on her."

"Did they ever meet?" I asked.

"Yes, once, in Central Park, but he never contacted her again after that."

"Wait, you know he already has lots of white hair . . . "

"Oh yes, he cut his hair very short," she said. "But what does he want from me?" Areyda asked.

"Let me ask him," I said. "Hmm . . . I think he wants to get in touch with you, something to do with your creativity and connections in the art world."

A week later Areyda called. "Do you remember the woman whom I did the healing on a week ago? She called me. I wanted you to know that everything you said about him was absolutely correct—his character, his looks, his clothing, his profession, and the fact that he wanted to contact me for an artists' project he is working on."

⚡ NIAGARA FALLS

One early afternoon sitting in my office I got a phone call from a friend, a fellow healer and shaman. I was in the middle of working on a complicated design project but took the call, to hear a desperate request: "I am calling all my shaman friends to journey on behalf of my client whose husband disappeared two weeks ago. She doesn't know why or where he went. He did not leave a note about where he was going. Can you help?"

I took a deep breath and asked her to stay with me on the phone. I then turned my face to the window, closed my eyes, and called one of my spirit guides. We flew to Upstate New York. I found myself flying toward Niagara Falls and then down to the banks of the Niagara River a few miles south of the falls. We got closer to the water and there he was, floating in the foamy waters face down between the reeds. He was now bloated, still dressed in his long khaki pants and light blue shirt. I checked to see if he was still alive but his soul was no longer there. A huge ball of sadness fell on me. I could smell death in the water. I opened my eyes.

"I think I found him," I told my friend.

"Where is he?" she asked with anticipation.

I shared with her my vision. Two weeks later the search party found him there.

⚡ UNIVERSAL LOVE IN THE YUCATÁN

I met Antonio Oxteik, the Mayan elder, some years ago by pure "coincidence" on the last day of one of our trips to the Amazon, in Manaus, Brazil. The planes had been grounded because of a huge storm and so a fellow traveler brought him to our hotel to wait it out. As we each caught the other's eye in the modest Plaza Hotel lobby a huge smile came over our faces, as if we had been destined to meet, and a vibration of joy filled the room. So a few years later we were ecstatic when he invited my wife and me to come and help him clear the land he had purchased in the middle of the Yucatán, where he was building his new home and center. It was a dream he had hoped to turn into a reality for many years. We worked hard and were rewarded by a special visitation of the majestic white eagle sitting in front of us on a high tree, and by the appearance of not just one but three sacred quetzals, one of the rarest of Mayan birds, long-tailed, colorful, and magical.

Antonio is about five feet tall with a round, sunny face, glowing eyes, a long silver ponytail, and a white goatee. He is always dressed in white. He is known worldwide for his Mayan initiation bodywork, a traditional deep tissue massage. I have to tell you, it is not for the faint of heart. On one of the days we were there a small group of European tourists arrived for treatments. Antonio asked us to concentrate and send energy while he was working on a young French guy. He asked him to undress and lie on the carpeted floor and for the four of us to sit in each of the cardinal points around him—east, south, north, and west—to support the healing by directing energy through the palms of our hands. Antonio was digging into the boy's body and the boy was screaming in pain, his body twisting and trembling as tears flowed from his eyes. Antonio prayed as he continued to massage deeply into the boy. I sat there in awe, with total concentration, remembering my own session with Antonio a few years earlier back in the United States. From time to time I opened my eyes to observe his work and the others in the room. And then it happened.

As if the sky opened just above the boy's heart a figure emerged, like a faint cloud of colorful smoke. It rose from his heart. Fascinated, I stared at it trying to understand what it was. A clearer image started to form. To my astonishment I recognized Mary carrying in her arms the Baby Jesus. I was perplexed—after all, I am an atheist Jew who grew up in a communist kibbutz—why was I seeing Christian iconography?

Mary's presence was undeniably full of love and completely graceful.

She held her baby in her arms in such a motherly way, with a faint smile. It was a beautiful symbol of total surrender and pure love. Tears started to roll down my face. And then the image dissolved into his heart.

A few moments later the session ended. We all sat quietly, holding space as the young Frenchman rested. I was quietly praying, not sure what to make of the visitation of Mary and Jesus, and then I heard Antonio's voice.

"Itzhak, Itzhak, did you see her?" he asked softly, with a brotherly smile and a twinkle in his eyes.

"Yes, I did, thank you," I said, wondering how he knew.

"I work with her," Antonio said. "She is the embodiment of the universal love energy."

"But how is it that we both could see the same image at the same time?" I asked him.

A huge smile came onto his round face. We hugged warmly.

12

≈ ≈ ≈ ≈

HOUSE CLEARING

*And while I stood there I saw more than I can tell and I
understood more than I saw; for I was seeing in a sacred
manner the shapes of all things in the spirit, and the shape
of all shapes as they must live together like one being.*

BLACK ELK

Energetic clearing of a house or other space is a very important task
shamans perform for their clients. Just as the shaman attempts to bring
balance, healing, and rejuvenation to a person, so this also needs to be
done to the environment in which the person lives or works.

The premise behind the clearing of a space is that we all leave
energetic footprints wherever we are and wherever we go. We hold
them in both our physical body and our illuminated body, or aura.
If you or people you live with or people who are visiting you carry
negative energy, abusive behavior, or feelings of anger and frustration,
it will show up in your home or office. Sometimes this kind of negative energy is the result of illegal activities, violence, or trapped and
confused entities. It appears as stagnant, toxic, heavy energy. If not
cleared, you can develop depression and lethargy, which can affect your
health, relationships, and business success. The techniques to remove

negative energies vary as different traditions employ different tools.

I follow Don Jose's teachings as we performed many ceremonies together. First you assess the space—feel it, concentrate, allow the space to show you images and give you messages—with either open or closed eyes. Make sure the windows are open. Set up your altar and light a candle. Once this is done, walk through the space as you chant your prayers and blow trago (pure sugarcane rum) to change the electromagnetic field (from positive ions to negative ions). Then smoke the space with sage to lift the negative energy. Then use a rattle or clap with your hands or healing stones to shake the stuck, stagnant energy and release it from every corner. Once the negative energy is lifted, blow agua florida throughout the space, then blow tobacco to appease and bless Spirit. You conclude by ringing a bell to harmonize the space and offering a prayer for the wellbeing of the residents.

The following stories illustrate some of the experiences I've had with cleansing spaces.

☇ THE EX'S FOOTPRINT

"Can you come clear the energy from my apartment soon?" Rasheem was a high-tech executive with a distinctive Indian accent, who called me one day with this urgent request. "I just got divorced. My ex moved out and I want to remove her energy. Can you help?"

His Lower Manhattan apartment was immaculate. It was furnished in a clean modern style, with minimal furniture and one big white wool shag carpet.

"I would like you to do a cleansing for me, too," he said after I had settled in.

Armed with my tools I set up an altar and started the apartment's energy cleansing, first in the living room. "I see your wife. Was she sitting here on this couch with her legs folded under her, watching television?" I asked as her image appeared.

"Yes, that's true. That is what she used to do all day," he said with a bit of sarcasm in his voice.

"Did she have long black hair and like to dress well?"

"Yes, she did," he laughed.

Then I went to the well-kept bedroom. I looked over the bed and their image appeared clearly. "Did she sleep on the right side of the bed?" I asked.

"Yes," he confirmed.

"You did not have a physical relationship, did you? I asked.

"No, that was the problem. I don't think she liked me. It was an arranged marriage."

I cleared the bed above and below and laid a mix of red and white carnation petals on the two sides of the bed to bring new love energy back.

Then I went to the immaculate modern kitchen. There were no signs of her energy there. "Did she ever use the kitchen?" I asked.

"No, she always ordered food in," he sighed. "That was part of the problem; she never really wanted to be my wife."

"Okay. Now that the apartment is cleared let's do the cleansing ceremony for you," I said. He took off his clothes and stood naked in the center of the big white carpet. A few minutes into the ceremony, as my eyes were closed in concentration and I was smoking him with sage, I started to smell a heavy burning fume under my feet. I opened my eyes in a hurry. "Oh my God," I yelped. The white carpet was burning under him. At once he opened his big brown eyes. He looked down. "Don't worry about it—I felt it, too, but I think it's time for it to go, too," he said and chuckled. I put out the fire, he closed his eyes, and we continued the ceremony as if nothing had happened. "Thank you. It was amazing—I feel so much better and lighter," he said when we had finished. "Let's turn the carpet and lay the coffee table on top of the burn mark."

A few weeks later I bumped into him on the street. "I can't thank you enough for the ceremony. My place feels so much different." He went on to say with a laugh, "I am dating a new girl now."

☯ Infertility and Possession

Rama, a Middle Eastern woman, wrote an urgent e-mail: "I would like you to come to the office and house and clear me . . . my not being able to get pregnant is no accident."

It was a few months after I had first gone to her apartment and then a few weeks later her office and warehouse, where she and her workers felt dark negative energies inhabiting the place. At that time, above her desk and in her stock room I saw a dark spirit of a jealous woman that was trying to create havoc and I successful removed it. The office returned to balance. We assumed the spirit was of a previous business partner.

Rama had come to see me earlier for a different reason. She desperately wanted to get pregnant. She was in her early forties and was going through in vitro fertilization, after her husband of twenty years left because she could not get pregnant. In successive sessions I helped her get pregnant using an Amazonian needle technique and other healing ceremonies, but not before our last apartment clearing.

In our first session, before she had her son, as I was reading her candle a beautiful dark-haired and black-eyed five-year-old boy's image appeared in the flame. "Who is this boy?" I asked her in curiosity. "I don't know anyone like that," she said with certainty.

"There is another heavyset woman dressed all in black, maybe a relative; she can't take care of him," I told her. "The boy seems to be related to you somehow—maybe he is a part of your family and you might be able to adopt him in case you don't get pregnant," I suggested.

She shook her head—she couldn't make sense of what I was saying. "No, it's impossible; I know all my family members, and there isn't anyone like this," she claimed.

So I dismissed this vision as a fluke, thinking it can happen to the best of us.

Months later, when I arrived at her apartment after her urgent e-mail, her large green eyes were on fire with anger. Without wasting a moment she burst out, "Do you remember that five-year-old boy and that dark woman you saw in your candle reading?"

"Yes, of course," I said surprised by her welcome.

"I discovered via other channels that behind my back my husband took a second wife in his country a few years ago and she gave him a son. He is now five years old, just as you said. His mother is possessed, many sheikhs were brought to cure her, she speaks in a man's voice, and she is trying to ruin my business and me." She took a deep breath, paced the room fuming, and continued, "I believe she was possessed at the same time I was feeling ill and suffering from the infertility treatment. I need you to clear me and my apartment from her energy and my ex-husband's." And then she burst into a storm of colorful curses that I cannot repeat here. I was shocked by the news. That vision was really true after all.

So here we were in her large apartment. It had a long, decorated couch covered in ornate Arabic patterns. As I was going around the apartment to do the cleansing ceremony, I asked her, "Is this the same place I came to the last time at night more than a year ago?"

"Yes, it is the same place, don't you remember?" She was surprised.

"Just vaguely," I replied. And then an image popped into my mind and I remembered her big, heavyset husband.

"Oh, now I remember. Your husband was here, too. He was sitting on this couch watching TV the whole time, was he not?"

"Oh no, Itzhak," she said laughing hysterically. "I kicked him out way before then. You saw him in your mind. You are mixing realities. And yes, this was his usual sitting place."

I went on to clear the apartment's energy, mostly removing his persistent energy from every room. Three months later she sent me an e-mail: "I am finally pregnant . . . a long story but so far so good, about eleven weeks now! Thanks for all of your help getting me to this point—Insha'Allah. By the way, my husband divorced his second wife and married a third wife . . . guy lost his mind."

♑ CRIME-RIDDEN CARPET STORE

"You must come and clear our new home décor and carpet store. My boyfriend and I are having bad luck; there is something there, I am sure of it." Josephine, a blond Brazilian woman, spoke to me urgently after one of our regular sessions.

We agreed that she and her boyfriend would pick me up in their car and we would travel to their neighborhood deep in Queens. As soon as I walked into the shop I could sense the illegal activities that had been done there. My body shivered. I started to see people arguing, stealing, packing cartons—all in a very sleazy way.

"Did the people who owned this place before deal with stolen merchandise?" I asked.

"You know, the landlord did not tell us exactly in those words but we understood it was a very dark business," Josephine said.

I spent more than two hours going from room to room, clearing and changing the energy from corner to corner. I gave special attention to the back shipping room. I blew trago, spread sage smoke with my feather fan, rattled my rattle, and clicked the black healing stones until I was satisfied. Then I brought out the agua florida and blew it on the entire space. I rang my bell and puffed tobacco and finished with the Tibetan cymbals, all the while chanting and praying for Josephine and her boyfriend and for the place. When it was all over I invited them in and performed the same cleansing ceremony on both of them. While working on her boyfriend I saw in a vision an old childhood incident he was holding on to in fear, and released it away. The boyfriend was still suspicious, "Will this work?" he asked. To which I replied, "We will see soon."

A few weeks later Josephine came back to my office. "How are you doing at the store?" I asked her curiously.

"We are doing great!" she smiled. "We are very busy and we're even thinking about renting the store next to us."

And they did. I went to clear the other store, too.

⚡ THE BRAZILIAN SCAM

My client Hillary, who emigrated from Brazil, opened a healing center in midtown Manhattan. One day she called me urgently, "I want you to come to clear my center's energy as soon as possible, and I'm going to rent a few rooms to a famous Brazilian healer who will be visiting New York soon. This man is a superstar. He was written up in a big international newspaper as one of the ten best healers in the world. I want him to like my center." And so I did a clearing and he liked her space.

A few weeks later she called again. "I want you to come back and clear the energy in the same rooms. And by the way, let me know what you feel when you're clearing them." So I did. This time she followed me around as I was clearing the space. "Tell me what you see," she urged me.

"So here is what I see," I told her. "They used the table in the center of this room. The head of the client was facing north. I can see a blond woman sitting near the client with her back to the window. Who is she, and why is she just sitting there doing nothing? And I don't see the Brazilian man. Oh, now I see—he's in the other room. What is he talking about and with whom? I don't like the energy here. It is heavy; I feel as if this is a scam." I felt slightly inappropriate for seemingly bashing my client's idol but she had requested that I give her my impressions.

"I called you because I felt something was wrong, too," Hillary said. "You are absolutely right. The blond woman, who is his wife and assistant, sat right where you said she sat and did nothing. He then walked into the room, greeted the client, said a few words, and then went into the other room to talk about money, money, money on the phone. What I really did not like was that they pushed their clients to come for a few consecutive sessions in the same week. I believe you when you say it was a scam."

13

ꗁ ꗁ ꗁ ꗁ

HEALING CEREMONIES

Mother Earth is doing fifty percent of the healing, the patient is doing forty percent, and the shaman only ten percent. So how can one take credit for that?

IPUPIARA

Shamans of the Andes believe that all physical and mental health problems are the direct result of an imbalance in our physical and energy bodies. That imbalance can occur by encountering harmful spirits or energy attachments—spirit intrusions, curses, jealousy, and envy sent either unintentionally or intentionally by another person. Sometimes it can happen simply by being in or around locations that hold negative air or wind energy, like a place of murder, battlefields, places where people have had conflicts, or sites of natural disasters. It can also happen as a result of a trauma, shock, or sudden fright, and that is when a soul loss can occur.

Through chants and prayers the shaman prepares to enter into the healing state of mind, evoking and connecting with spirit helpers. During the ceremony shamans aim to awaken and activate all of the client's five senses as well as the sixth sense, by opening the third eye to enable the client to "see." They work to clear the stored negative energies clients hold. By opening the blocked energy channels among all four body areas—the head, which corresponds to air; the chest and digestive system, which correspond to water; the lower abdomen, which corresponds to fire; and the legs, which correspond to earth—and the spirit, they activate and resume the flow of energy. That creates in the patient feelings of emotional and physical well-being and deep connection to the entire universe, which then allows the process of healing to begin. Every object and element used during a healing ceremony—plants, rocks, rum, perfume, eggs, flowers, fire, smoke, sound, and so on—are chosen not by coincidence. They contain profound spiritual meanings and symbolism and also scientific physical reasons that are time tested to bring the needed results.

The unique power of shamans—besides their vast knowledge of herbal properties and the elements and their expertise in human psychology—is their uncanny ability to see, communicate, and interact with energies or spirits on behalf of their clients, the community, and the environment in order to bring these things back into balance.

The following stories are some examples of the power and mystery involved in shamanic healing.

⚡ FATHER'S LAST WORDS

Aaron stood at the center of the healing room breathing silently, ready for the ceremony to begin. I took a step back, closed my eyes to prepare myself, and then opened them again to study him. What I saw was surprising. A thick fog surrounded him. In it I could see an old man, maybe five-foot-seven, wearing a black hat, suit, and thick reading glasses.

I directed a question telepathically to the apparition: "Are you Aaron's father?"

"Yes, I am," he replied. I welcomed him and asked him to help me in the healing of his son and asked him if he had a message for him.

"Not really; he is doing fine," he said.

"Did you want Aaron to become the psychotherapist he became?"

"Oh no, I wanted him to be a writer," his father said. "Being a writer was the most important thing for me." He went on, "But let me tell you that I did not like my wife—actually, I hated her."

Surprised, I did not reply and changed the subject back to Aaron. "Did you take your son to any special places when he was a child?" Immediately an image appeared. I saw him as a younger and taller man holding the hand of a young boy, walking barefoot on a sandy beach in Far Rockaway. Their khaki pants were rolled up and the ocean white-caps broke on their bare feet. The scenery was very calm and peaceful, just father and son. Suddenly an image of Aaron's sister appeared at the top right. She looked older and taller, with black wavy hair and a bright self-confidence, but also arrogance.

"She's a bitch. I did not like her either," his father said.

I was surprised and a bit confused. Why did this man have to convey these messages to me? Why did he want to let his son know this?

As we sat down to talk after the ceremony was over I shared with Aaron some of what I had just experienced.

"You know, it's pretty accurate," Aaron said sadly. "I have one older sister and there was always a competition between us for our father's attention. And yes, she was and still is very tough and our relationship is rocky at best. My father was taller, maybe five-foot-ten when he was younger, and as he got older he shrank to about five seven. He wore heavy reading glasses. He loved the sea; as a young man he had served on a merchant ship for a long period of time. I remember he used to take me to the beach for a long walks. Although he had limited formal education he loved to read. My parents divorced long ago; he really didn't like my mother."

"But why did he come back to tell you all that through me now?" I asked him. Aaron turned over the information in his mind for a minute. "It's hard to know; I can only guess that he wanted me to know the reason why they got divorced and why he had to leave me." He paused. "I guess he could'nt do it while he was alive. Maybe he felt guilty. Or was he implying that the way I felt about my mother and my sister and later about other women was not my fault?" he quietly asked. "I am actually relieved to hear that. It all makes sense now," he continued and smiled.

☊ MEETING THE AKURAS

"I am an actress and a playwright. I had another relationship break up, I lost my creativity and I don't know why. I need help; I don't know what to do."

Felicia, an attractive woman in her late twenties, walked into my healing room for her first shamanic healing. She was depressed, angry, and frustrated. *Hey, nothing out of the ordinary,* I thought.

I proceeded to follow the traditional diagnostic steps. I asked her to brush a candle all over her body; then I lit it and proceeded to read the candle's flame. *Deep fear and childhood trauma,* I made a mental note to myself. Looking at her palm I thought there was still nothing out of the ordinary. I asked her to stand, facing me, to start La Limpia, the cleansing ceremony.

A few days later Felicia sent me an e-mail: "The next morning I felt calm. It was a calm I have not known for a long, long time. A sense of control. I felt rational and clear and just not angry anymore. It was a feeling that almost brought tears to my eyes; I was lucky to finally feel as if I had a new lease on life."

On her third visit to my office, after we did a few shamanic journeys to work on the issues she originally came for, I gave her another cleansing ceremony. I took a deep inhalation and then had the surprise of my life—just as I was closing my eyes and getting ready to blow the energy-cleansing trago, I noticed a wicked-looking black furry creature high above her, descending fast in her direction. I couldn't believe my mind's eye as I watched it attempt to clutch her in its long sharp claws. Its huge monkeylike eyes popped out while it screamed through a black, crooked, eaglelike beak. There was truly an evil intention in the creature's eyes. Although I never believed in the existence of evil I could recognize it at once. My body trembled.

What in the world? I thought, and then, more urgently, *What should I do about it?* My intuition told me I had to find the warrior within me, fight this creature, and remove it, even though my training had never prepared me for such a battle. I doubted myself. Improvising, I called on my spirit guides and my teachers for courage and protection and quickly used all the cleansing techniques in my arsenal: fire, smoke, rum, swords, spears, prayers, and threats. Finally, after what felt like a long time, I was able to kick most of it out through the crack under the door. And then I finished with a longer protection ceremony.

When the ceremony was over, my client's posture had completely changed. She was now calm, relaxed, and grounded—even smiling.

"How do you feel?" I asked.

"Fine—lighter and more energized," she answered happily.

I, on the other hand, was exhausted and a bit in shock. I wondered if I should I tell her what I had seen. Perhaps I should, and so I asked her if she would like to know what just happened. She listened carefully.

"I guess this evil entity is my ex-boyfriend or maybe my father, both of whom I always considered evil." This gave us an opportunity to discuss deeper family issues she had not been willing to discuss earlier. It had to do with her exposure to her father's psychology practice in their home for men who were pedophiles. I asked if she would grant me permission to consult with my mentor shaman about what had happened. She readily agreed and after she closed the door behind her I called Brazil.

Ipupiara's cell phone rang. "Olá," my late mentor answered.

"Ipu, I need your help! Where are you? Can you talk?" I asked desperately.

"Oh, I am on a canoe on the Rio Negro having a good time with Shoré [the master shaman from the Kannamarie tribe]. "What's the matter, Itzhak?"

I described to him all the details of what had just happened.

"Oh, don't you know? That is Akura! Everyone knows that," he said dismissively in his funny Portuguese accent.

"Everyone?" I asked in disbelief. "Akura? You never mentioned that in all the six years we've known each other."

"Well, you were not ready to see it until now," he answered and then paused. "Hold on." I could hear him conversing with Shoré, telling him the story in the background. "Okay," he said with authority, "here is what you have to do. Write this down." And he went on to prescribe me a list of ceremonies to perform. "But—and this is very important— ask her if she likes the color green, wear green clothes, and if she has green plants in her home, because Akura hates anything that is green and alive. They feed on darkness and fear." I thanked him and Shoré and immediately after I hung up, a long stream of doubt-filled thoughts ran through my head. Would it work? Can I do it myself without his direct guidance?

I called my client. She agreed to the treatment and then, just to be sure, I asked her Ipupiara's most important question. In a disgusted and curt voice she said, "I hate the color green. I never wear green clothes and never have plants in my home. They all die anyway." That gave me the chills. *She is possessed. What did I get myself into?* I thought. I still doubted that I could succeed in getting rid of that entity.

We met the next night and, after three subsequent sessions, following Ipupiara's instructions, her condition completely reversed. Felicia now wears and enjoys green clothes, grows plants at home, and more importantly, has moved on nicely with her creative career, started a relationship with a great guy, and has subsequently married him. Here is what she wrote me later:

"You can't even believe what has been happening to me. I am evolving so quickly and processing so many emotions that I'm like a roller coaster, but it's beautiful and exciting and at the end of each day I feel closer and closer to inner peace. The love is just pouring out of me. I want to smile and hug everyone, even strangers! I'm out of control with love and light! I love it!"

⚡ SHARK ATTACK

"Can you see my thirteen-year-old son Max? He's a good boy, extremely sensitive and musically talented, but he is going through a rough time right now. We just had a session with the famous John of God on his visit to New York; he told him that he needs a spiritual cleansing."

I was talking on the phone with a woman with a heavy Russian accent. A few days later when she and Max arrived, her son was clearly distraught; he complained of a recurring bad dream that he had had again the night before.

"Can you tell me your dream?' I asked, curious. He shifted in his chair uncomfortably. I prodded him further and he reluctantly obliged.

"In the dream a small skinny man wearing black clothes, with an ugly face, went after me relentlessly. There was something gay about him," he said uncomfortably. "He did not do anything bad to me, but he made me feel scared and it felt very eerie and uncomfortable. This dream comes to me even during the day and disturbs me all the time. I want to forget it. Can you take it out of my head?" It was clear the young man desperately wanted to pull these elusive forces and thoughts out of his head.

I did both a candle reading and a palm reading. His hands revealed a very sensitive person, a natural healer. "You are right; sometimes Max gives me amazing massages on my lower back and it really takes the pain away," his mother chimed in from the back of the room.

I asked Max to stand in the center of the room so we could start the healing ceremony. With trago in my hands I blew into the bottle, creating four long whistles to evoke the spirits. I closed my eyes and "looked" at his spiritual body. The vision that appeared startled me. A huge blue and gray fish—more like a shark—swooped down with great speed from the ceiling and made a U-turn before it hit the floor and swooped up to merge with the kid's body with an amazing force. *Wow, what was that?* I wondered. I took a deep breath, opened my eyes, and asked Max, who stood there waiting and quiet, "Tell me, Max, if you had a choice, what kind of animal would you be?"

He looked at me, surprised by this strange question, turned his blond head to the left in shyness, and then a small, devilish smile emerged on his lips: "A shark!" he said confidently. Wahoo . . . Goosebumps covered my body.

I shared with them the vision I had just experienced. All three of us were amazed. "And why would you like to be a shark so much?" I asked.

He took a moment, chose his words carefully, and finally said, "I guess I always liked them because they are big, strong, and powerful, and they can protect me from the bullies in my school."

After the ceremony we sat around my altar. "How do you feel?" I asked him.

"I'm okay. I feel more relaxed, maybe stronger, and calm . . . good," he smiled.

I went on to explain to him and his mother the concept behind the power animal's spirit in the shamanic tradition. I also asked him to set up a small altar so he could continue to meet with his fearless shark before going to sleep and ask for his protection. Maybe even get a picture of a shark and put it on the wall, or wear amulet to remind him of his true power and nature. He loved it.

I was left wondering about that dream he shared with me earlier. Was the small, skinny man a representation of one of the kids who bullied him? Maybe it was another male figure in his life. Maybe it represented the fear of part of himself. I would have to wait for that part of the mystery to reveal itself.

≈ A Grandmother Extraction

My client Audrey, a striking dancer and choreographer and a published poet in her early fifties, came to me one day perplexed. "There are too many conflicting agendas in my life right now. I need to consolidate and concentrate on one thing. I feel fragmented, as if I'm blocked creatively. I don't know what is stopping me. I start a project and then stop. Nothing seems to flow as it used to."

When I read her candle I had the strong feeling that what she

needed first was a healing to break her three-pack-a-day cigarette habit. I asked her to remove her clothes and stand in the center of the room for a La Limpia ceremony. Concentrating, I called on the mountain spirits and my teachers for assistance. I blew trago, pounded and brushed her with green leaves, smoked her with strong, fragrant copal resin, extracted the negative energy out of her with the brown eggs, and then stepped back.

I was startled by a vision that unexpectedly arose behind her. From the center of her spine, in a quick swoosh a misty white trail jerked out of her. Quickly it ascended and disappeared into the heavens. Unprepared, I caught a glimpse inside this mist of an old woman. "Her grandmother," was the message I got. Immediately I understood. The woman in the vision was thin and her dark eyes desperately sad; her face was pale and she had long, white, disheveled hair. I was totally surprised by the image, to say the least. I took a deep breath, shook my head in disbelief, and went on to clear this unexpected energy. I strongly blew tobacco smoke on different parts of Audrey's body and continued to create a solid protection shield around her with healing stones in my hands.

As the session ended I discussed this exceptional event with Audrey. We were both surprised by the spontaneous spirit extraction. From behind the tables he said, "It is very interesting. You know, my grandmother, my mother, and as a matter of fact I myself believe the rest of the women in our family all felt powerless, which I think led us to alcohol, cigarettes, and sexual addictions."

The next morning Audrey called me. "I wanted you to know that immediately after the session I went downstairs and, as was my habit, I lit a cigarette. It tasted terrible. I threw it down. I lost all desire to smoke. I couldn't even put a cigarette in my mouth. It's unbelievable!"

A few months later Audrey finished a poetry book and was having great success with her choreography. She felt like her creative block was lifted. And a few years after that when Audrey came back for another session, she brought a photograph that had been part of a trove of old family albums.

"Here is my grandmother," she said laughingly, pointing at the photo.

"Yes, that is exactly the old woman I saw during your first healing session," I told her.

"I would love to have another session," she said, "but I'm afraid you will remove my coffee addiction, and that I am not willing to do. I love my coffee."

⚡ HER MOTHER'S CLAWS

I received this e-mail from Lana in Ohio following an article about my work that appeared in the *New York Times:*

"I am healthy and approaching eighty years old. I have been married for fifty-seven years . . . Sadness and grief dominate, as my mother had a younger brother and her father beheaded by the cossacks during a pogrom in Russia. . . . My poor mother never released her grief—it was central to her depression. . . . I'm told that my mother's spirit continues to grieve and that sadness surrounds her. Apparently the spirit is walled off by a silolike structure that rises above her. I'm told that I am afflicted as well with endogenous depression, with less fight in me to overcome darkness than I used to be able to exert in my daily existence. I think I need my mom taken away from me. . . . Otherwise, I am a happy person, a retired registered nurse."

Lana flew to New York with her psychologist husband to get treatment from me for her chronic depression. We had two double sessions and she went back home lighter and happier. She wrote, "Our work has produced good changes, with those issues being resolved—REALLY! It revealed the stark nature of my impediments to 'ignite' the Sacred Fire."

But there were still bouts of depression remaining and so she asked me to perform a long-distance healing. "Maybe I need a spirit extraction," she suggested. I usually prefer to perform ceremonies in my client's presence, as I believe it to be a more intimate and powerful experience, but I agreed this time, as I had already worked with her and knew her quite well by then.

As Lana lay back in a reclining lawn chair in her backyard in Ohio, I closed my eyes and started rattling. In a few seconds I felt a sharp pain in my right shoulder blade. The pain was digging deeper. I scanned her body and I could see that it was her pain. I was a bit surprised, as we had not discussed it before. I stopped rattling and asked her if she was experiencing a pain in her right shoulder blade at that moment.

"Oy, Itzhak, yes, I have had that pain for most of my life," she said.

So I did not make it up . . . I breathed easier. I closed my eyes again and called my spirit guide to help me find the source of her pain. Immediately I saw her mother's fingers digging into her flesh right where the pain was. I introduced myself to her and asked her to please let go of her poor daughter so she could be free and happy. But her mother refused to have any of it: "She is my daughter," she exclaimed. I continued trying to persuade her. She cut me off and sternly said, "I won't let her go because I don't want to let go of anyone I love. I need them. Do you know what happened when I let go of my first boyfriend? I lost him forever! I will not allow my daughter to separate from me, ever!"

I listened to this and then told her, "Your daughter will love you even more if you set her free." After a long back-and-forth, reasoning with her like this, she finally relented and released her daughter.

"How do you feel now," I asked Lana afterward.

"I feel great. The pain is gone! Wow, I'm sorry to have put you to such hard work."

A few months later I received this e-mail from Lana:

"Since the last phone session I had with you, my husband and I have had a sweet, caring relationship. No more arguing—after all, we are now eighty years old and yes, still sexually attracted to each other and in love. My husband and my two cats continue to sustain me."

⚡ THE WHITE DRAGON

"My husband, Roberto, has recently been diagnosed with pancreatic cancer. It's stage 4, and we are looking into alternative support in addition to the medical treatments he is undergoing. It's great that you are working in the Quechua/Inca tradition, as Roberto is originally from Peru. There have actually been a few rituals in the past weeks in Peru where he's been the focus. But something in the same time zone/geographical location would be helpful at this time to be sure."

Roberto's wife, Kathy, wrote me this e-mail, to which I responded, "I will do my best—it is in Spirit's hands." We set a time to meet.

On the scheduled day Roberto arrived with his wife at his side. He was tall, slender, and frail, with long, smooth brown hair. He wore stylish black round glasses, like some celebrity, and behind them were the most loving eyes I have ever seen. But they also held distress. I invited him to sit by the altar across from me. He saw me looking at his glasses. "Somebody famous once advised me that if I ever wanted to be recognizable I have to wear something outlandish like this. So I did, and it worked," he smiled. He then told me calmly, in a soft Spanish accent, with no trace of fear in his eyes and with a half-apologetic smile, "I don't have any illusions. I am not afraid of dying. I'm not a fighter; I accept my destiny. Everyone has to go sometime, and maybe this is just my time." I looked at this man and wondered, *Is he enlightened?*

"Before we do the healing session we need to do a candle diagnostic reading," I told him. "Do you agree?"

With a lot of concentration and intention Roberto slowly brushed the white candle over his fragile body and then handed it to me while I chanted. The room was quiet with anticipation. His wife sat on the couch watching closely. I took a few minutes to observe the flame. The disease clearly could be seen in his body as a big, dark blob in the lower part of his abdomen. It had already spread massively to the rest of his body, creating a heavy cloud of negative energy. From the configuration of the blue flame and its flow at the bottom it was clear that Roberto was extremely connected to Spirit and had strong intuition and dreams.

"I am sure you are constantly having many visions and dreams," I said, looking up at him.

"Yes, it's true, but I buried those abilities down deep within me." He lowered his eyes and fidgeted with his thin hands.

"Did you have an imaginary friend as a four- or five-year-old?" I asked.

He moved uncomfortably in his chair and raised his eyes. "Yes, when I was a very young boy in Peru I had an imaginary friend. It was a white dragon. I was very different from the rest of my intellectual, businesslike family and I was embarrassed to share it with them as no one believed me and, even more so, they ridiculed me. I buried him within myself and forgot about him until now. Thank you for connecting me with him again," and he began to weep as if a dam had just broken open.

We sat in silence awhile. Then I took a look at his palms. "You are very sensitive but also an independent, free-thinking man, maybe even stubborn." The words just came right out of my mouth. "You are full of passion with a great need for expression. The source of your creativity comes from your profound intuition, the feminine energy. You seek intimacy in relationships, and I see that you are not concerned so much about making money. Am I correct so far?"

"Yes, you are right about that," he chuckled and looked at Kathy, who smiled in agreement.

"What is it that you do for a living?" I asked.

"I'm a filmmaker. I've made documentary films about creative artists in Europe and in the States. I'm also very open to all kinds of spiritual practices."

At this point from her seat on the couch Kathy interjected: "My husband is very humble—his films have been exhibited at many international films festivals and have won many awards." Roberto chuckled and smiled humbly.

"I'm happy you made a connection with your white dragon. It is your power animal in the shamanic tradition. It signifies spiritual and magical life transformation. He is a powerful warrior who can blow fire out his nostrils at his adversaries. His character is one of strength and courage. Can you connect with his power to defeat your sickness?" I asked as I prepared him for the healing ceremony.

"I don't know how to," he hesitantly replied.

"Let's just try. Close your eyes and see if you can meet him now, ask him to help you defeat your sickness."

And so he did while I rattled from across the altar. At the conclusion of the rattling Roberto smiled broadly and thanked me. "It was so wonderful to meet my white dragon. Thank you for this gift." We then proceeded to do La Limpia portion of the ceremony. "As I perform the ceremony please concentrate on the white dragon and ask him again to help you." To my surprise, because he was so frail, Roberto was able to stand strong for the duration of the twenty-minute-long ceremony.

"How do you feel now?" I asked afterward.

"Much lighter, calmer, and happier. I saw the white dragon again—and I think I know the source of my sickness," he added knowingly. It seemed as if the ceremony had moved him deeply; there was some resolve in his voice and I could see that his face had changed.

Following our session, his loving wife wrote me an e-mail:

"Querido Itzhak, just to say muchas gracias for your healing touch and sensitivity working with Roberto this afternoon. It was a powerful session and I'm hoping he's taken in some of what you said to him, and also did with him. He needs to claim his power, to be an active participant, to call in the white dragon to slay this beast . . ."

Roberto came to my office for another session, and then I saw him again in his apartment when he was bedridden. Although his physical body was deteriorating rapidly, his spirit was strong and he was contained and full of light. Standing by his side, surrounded by get-well cards, prayers, and ritual objects from many traditions, we spoke about his work, the famous people he had worked with, and the last film he and his wife had made, which had premiered recently. We also spoke about great books, philosophy, and art. I mentioned that previously I had once had a fine-art career that ended many years ago. "You must paint again," he said.

"I create in a different way now," I laughingly replied. We had become fast friends. I told him that I wished I'd met him many years ago and we laughed at life's strange journey.

At the end of the cleansing ceremony he was peaceful and a big smile spread across his sunken face. "It was really a very powerful ceremony, thank you," he whispered, and I left.

After I returned home I got this e-mail from Kathy:

"Thank you again for another powerful and meaningful healing session for Roberto. His engagement with you has been very important for him (and me). It's great to have these times with you, especially before he goes back for his next chemo. The white dragon was very happy to have your presence this morning. He is sleeping so peacefully this evening."

Some weeks passed and I heard from Kathy again—Roberto was in a hospice and had requested one more ceremony and ritual before I left for a trip abroad. When I entered Roberto's hospice room it was clear this would be our last ceremony.

He was quite lucid and emotionally very open to reflecting on his life as he faced this last phase of the journey. Roberto was glad to see me and we held hands and had a heartfelt conversation.

"Do you have any regrets before you leave?" I asked him. He smiled and laughed and with a mischievous look said, "There was once a *New Yorker* cartoon. It showed a man on his deathbed. There was a priest by his side asking him the same question. The patient answered: "I wish I had worked harder." He burst out laughing, holding his bloated belly. And then he said seriously, "I want you to promise me that you will start painting again." I held his hand, looked into his beautiful brown eyes, and made him a promise: "I will paint a special illustration in the book I am working on."

"Oh, that will be wonderful," he smiled victoriously. I set up my shamanic tools and altar to perform the cleansing ceremony by his bedside. He was ready and was smiling. It was comforting to see him surrounded by so many well-wishing cards and prayers sent by his family and friends and various shamanic and spiritual objects from around the world that Kathy had brought from home. It was around noon; the sunlight came pouring in through the big southern windows, illuminating everything. Somewhere in the middle of the ceremony something unusual happened. As I was ready to blow the agua florida on Roberto, the white dragon appeared. Joyously he was playing hide and seek above his bed and making big somersaults in the air. I was delighted to see the vitality and humor of this magical creature, having so much fun as his owner's body lay so broken. The white dragon gleefully told me, "I'm not ready to leave yet, I want to play some more. There is so much more I still want to do here!"

"But Roberto is ready to leave his body," I said to the playful dragon.

"Give me six more weeks," the dragon said, continuing his swirling around the hospice bed. He disappeared when I finished the ceremony with the sharp whistle of the ocarina.

I was truly confused by that surprising message. This was really unexpected, as Roberto had already spent the longest amount of time in the hospice of anyone, and the staff was expecting him to go through his transition at any moment. We hugged and said good-bye, as if it were to be the last time we would see each other in this short lifetime. I packed up my belongings, and just before leaving the room I hugged Kathy and to her great surprise told her that I would see them when I returned from my trip abroad in six weeks. She looked puzzled, as if she did not understand what was I was saying. Yes, it did not make any sense. Caring for him for all those long months was incredibly rewarding but also an intense and exhausting task that she performed lovingly, with great devotion, creativity, and perseverance. But this could crush anyone.

And so it was. Almost six weeks later, the day after I landed in New York, I got a call from Kathy, "The white dragon is still with us," she said with a sparkle in her voice. "Yes, I would love for you to come."

I went for one more visit. Unable to eat or even open his eyes,

Roberto was still with us, whispering loving words as he traveled back and forth between different realms. Three days later his soul passed on exactly as his power animal, the white dragon, had said he would. I was not yet consciously aware of this, but late that evening I felt some kind of communication from the white dragon and sent Kathy an e-mail just as it turned into the next morning—January 11, 12:34 am.

My message was a very simple one:

"?

Blessings,

Itzhak"

"It was quite a journey, to be sure and, as you say, it was in the hands of Spirit," Kathy wrote back in an e-mail a few days after Roberto's passing.

14

 ⫶ ⫶ ⫶ ⫶

Aztec Seeing

*The common eye sees only the outside of things, and judges
by that, but the seeing eye pierces through and reads the
heart and the soul, finding there capacities which the
outside didn't indicate or promise, and which the other
kind couldn't detect.*

Mark Twain

I first experienced the technique of Aztec seeing with a visiting Aztec shaman and I have since used it successfully many times in my own practice.
This modality of bodywork is used for diagnosing and healing the mind,
body, and spirit. It enables us to tap in to body-stored memories, bring
them to the surface, and rebalance the client's mind, body, and spirit energies. Again, how we "see," no one knows for sure. We just have to listen
deeply to our hearts, trust our intuition, and have faith in the process.

The premise of this work is that our physical bodies store in different parts and organs the many events of our life. Aztec seeing allows you
to unravel incidents and memories the client never previously shared or
told you about certain relationships the person had. In this modality
you and your client are required to simultaneously share what you each
"see" or feel as it is happening. I teach this technique in my classes with
people who have never done this kind of work before, and it is extremely

successful in bringing out useful insights. So here is how it works:

The client lays on her back—this can be done fully clothed—either on a table or on the floor. You then put your left hand, the receiving hand, lightly on the client's navel, close your eyes, and open yourself up to receive messages either by feeling or through visions.

On the human body the navel represents the center of the universe and the source of life. There are more than 70,000 nerve endings that converge in the navel. In addition, at the center of the palm there are more nerve endings than almost anywhere else on the body. This meeting of these two highly sensitive energy centers in turn connects us to our nerve impulses, which come from the brain. The nervous system is what is responsible for our emotions and thoughts as well as our body movements.

You then feel the energy that flows in to the palm of your hand and listen to messages that come in. Keeping your left hand on the navel, you lay your right hand lightly on the solar plexus, or heart center, and wait for messages about the overall energy and emotions. Then you move your right hand to the right side of the navel, the place that represents the body's masculine energy; then to the place below it, to the place that represents the life force, or sexual energy; then to the left side, which represents the feminine energy of the body. The purpose of this is to check in all four directions, going in a circle around the navel. Once you are done you proceed to lay both hands on the chest, neck, head, and legs.

During this entire process the client and you should be sharing your visions, memories, and feelings. As I said, I use this technique often, seeing relationships between the clients and their parents and best friends, people's homes, landscapes, places of work, and many more associations.

There is one special session that used Aztec seeing that is deeply etched in my mind.

ᛉ NOT-SO-SWEET SIXTEEN

Laura, an elegant woman in her early fifties, an executive secretary in a large company, has been a client of mine for a few years. Laura was born in the United States but moved to Europe as a young child. As an adult she moved back across the ocean. She never married or had children although she desperately wanted to have a family of her own. In one of the sessions we wanted to unblock some resistance she had to a possible new relationship she was forming. I recommended we do the Aztec seeing ceremony. I took some time to explain the ceremony as it was our first time doing it together, and encouraged her to share her insight as I performed it.

She lay on the patchwork Lakota blanket and closed her eyes, never suspecting that a long-hidden secret would be revealed. I took a big breath, laid my left hand on her navel, and closed my eyes. I could feel tingling nervousness building inside her. My right hand started to move up to her heart center. I noticed shortness of breath—a sign of fear—she was almost panicking. As my right hand traveled over her left side, an image of her as a sixteen-year-old girl surfaced; the girl looked sad and ashamed. A message, a revelation, unfolded in my mind. I wasn't sure I should even share it with Laura, but I trusted that Spirit would send the right message even if I didn't understand why. I asked Laura, "Did you have an abortion when you were sixteen?"

She gasped and held her breath. Her face reddened and her body tightened, then a stream of uncontrollable tears and loud moaning started to flow out of her. I waited for her to calm down and after this unexpected emotional release I continued.

"I also see a blond, thin, seventeen-year-old boy with bad acne on his face. Was he your boyfriend? Did he leave you? Is this true?"

The secret was out now: "It is true. I never told anyone about it. No one. I didn't even tell my mother. I managed to get the money and had the abortion secretly. My boyfriend—you described him so accurately— did not want to have anything to do with it. It was the darkest day of my life. It broke my heart and I have never trusted men again," Laura whispered in a desperate voice as she wiped her eyes.

"Would you give that new man a chance?" I asked her.

She thought about it for a minute. "I think I will this time," she replied, and a slight smile came across her suffering face.

15

USING SHAMANIC
VISION IN BUSINESS

It's only with one's heart that one can see clearly.

ANTOINE DE SAINT-EXUPERY

In my shamanic work I see many people who are high up in the business and financial world, lawyers, entrepreneurs, and those who are self-employed. Using the shamanic toolbox enables them to reach higher, resolve tension and problems with the people they are working with, gain insight to the core of their personal problems, and increase their bottom line. It also helps them create a vision for their companies and themselves. After all, these are the people who are the leaders of our communities and, as one of them once said to me, "I have a great responsibility. I am in charge of half a million people's lives."

Business leaders and shamans share many of the same critical virtues. They must be warriors to stand for what they believe in, they must be intuitive to see the big picture and forecast events and trends, they must possess special emotional and spiritual powers to inspire their communities, they must have strong problem-solving skills, and they must focus on practical results. As a shaman you will be surprised at how easily you can apply these virtues in a business setting, and how you can use the qualities you have developed on the shamanic path to inspire and encourage the people with whom you work.

Every company, just like a person, has its unique mission or life purpose that reflects its goals and aspirations. A company's culture and spirit determine its business activities and the ways in which the company delivers its message and markets its products. Using ancient shamanic techniques you can align the unique spirit of each individual who works for the organization with the company's management goals, and in doing so the company can maximize cooperation and financial success. This can create a healthier, more supportive internal team environment, as it can help resolve interpersonal conflicts. There are many examples of companies who run according to higher standards of ethics, contributing to the good of their employees, communities, and environment and often enjoying an improved bottom line. Their ethics create an increase in the popularity of their brands and they obtain more brand loyalty from their consumers.

As I have mentioned, I too had my feet in both the shamanic and spiritual worlds. For many years I owned an advertising and design agency where we created award-winning branding, marketing, and advertising for small and large corporations. To be honest I had always felt uncomfortable and sometimes guilty for practicing in one of the most manipulative industries, which promotes unnecessary consumption and waste. It was a real challenge, which a few times I could not stomach. It was a vision in the Ecuadorian Amazon that finally gave me peace. In it the ayahuscha spirit revealed to me, "There is no difference between the practices of a shaman and an advertising man. The difference is in the intentions." She went on to recount the similarities. As the guilt lifted I started to accept only clients whose companies' intentions I believed in, and I refused a few big clients that sold products or services that were against my conscience, sometimes to the dismay of my employees and family.

My shamanic teachers had their feet in both worlds, too. They could not understand why a person wants to give up a day job and become a full-time healer. They were convinced that it is necessary to keep a balance between the material and spiritual worlds. In doing so they feel the healer stays connected to the client's life experiences and can develop true compassion. One teacher is a farmer, a vendor, and hat maker; the other was a teacher and museum guide. One was a grass cutter and carpenter. They did not feel ashamed by any means about their physical work outside of the healing rooms.

☡ THE DEVIL'S WORK

I had been teaching seminars and performing healing sessions in Florence, Italy, twice a year, in the spring and summer, for many years by the invitation of Alessandra, who herself is a shamanic practitioner. So I had worked with many people from all walks of life and classes, including important business people. One day a new client arrived, a businessman in his fifties. "He is from one of the richest families in Florence," Alessandra told me later. He was totally taken by surprise by the healing session's revelatory powers and insight into his childhood abuse and business career.

An hour after our session he called, "I would like you and Alessandra to come and make a presentation to the local chapter of the Young Presidents, a group I belong to." They are top business owners under forty-five years old. "We meet in one of our member's hotels. Can you come?" he asked, and we agreed. This sophisticated, rich, and skeptical group of well-dressed men and women was surprised as I suggested that instead of a long lecture we could do a shamanic journey, so they could experience it for themselves. They agreed, to *my* utter surprise.

They lay down on the carpeted conference room floor and I taught them the shamanic journeying technique. At the end of the first journey they learned how each of the power animals they just retrieved perfectly revealed their personality, individual managerial style, and qualities. The hotel's owner retrieved a turtle, as she carried the weight of her family and business responsibility on her back, proceeded forward slowly, and needed to be grounded. The funeral home owner received a lion because of his need to be truly independent, his territorial tendencies, and his method of observing from above to protect his family and business. The fabric company owner received a wolf, symbolizing his need for close family relationships and teamwork, his use of sharp intellect and instincts, and his yearning for freedom. The gym owner received a snake, letting him know his power was in shedding his old skin to embark on a new transformation toward a bigger vision. And so forth.

Then they journeyed back to their newfound power animal with a simple question, "How can I improve my business?" At the end of that journey each of them received great insight and answers, which they said they were going to implement in their businesses. As we munched on the delicious buffet spread afterward, the group enthusiastically decided to hold a weekend seminar later that year for the entire chapter and their families. Moreover, the woman who owned the hotel and thirty-two other hotels around the world invited me to hold similar sessions for all her executive management teams in each of her hotels.

But that was not to be. Unfortunately a priest, who was notified by one of the participants who felt guilty, cut the group's enthusiasm short. He warned them that the church would have to excommunicate them if they continued to practice "the devil's work." No need to say they stopped communicating with Alessandra in Florence and with me.

⋋ Business Rejections of the Value of Shamanism

A year after our experience with the Young Presidents, another incident showed me how some business people and societies, against all common business sense, are still in the grasp of religious fanaticism.

Alessandra and I had planned a seminar in an old monastery on a hill overlooking Florence. The monastery was not getting much use because of a lack of community participation, so they were now renting the old picturesque estate to other groups to cover their upkeep costs. When we arrived straight from the airport to check the premises, Alessandra went to the office to iron out the last details of the weekend. I went outside to breathe some fresh air and admire the panoramic vista from the large parking lot. It was quite a pastoral day, a little chilly with blue skies; the enthusiastic chirping birds erased the memory of the long, grueling flight. The famous Duomo could be seen at the center of the sprawling ancient city as the Arno River twisted lazily beneath me. It was just like a perfect Italian renaissance oil painting.

After a while, when Alessandra did not come out to get me, I went back to the office looking for her. As I entered the monastery I was greeted by loud arguing in a screechy Italian voice I did not recognize. The only word I understood well was the name of Galileo Galilei, which was repeated a few times. The two women were in a powerful shouting match with reddened faces over a man who died in 1642. "What's going on?" I interjected.

"She doesn't want to honor our contract," Alessandra said, fuming.

"Why?" I asked in disbelief. "We already paid for it."

"Because we do 'the devil's work' and she said her community objects to us doing a seminar here. She insists that Galileo was wrong and it was right to condemn him as a sinner and let him die."

"What? She still believes the Earth is the center of the universe, and she probably believes the Earth is flat, too?" I asked astonished.

"Yes. That's right," Alessandra said in resignation as her hands flew sideways in disgust and hopelessness.

"Let's talk to her superior," I suggested as I saw that nothing good would come of talking to this woman and we could be in big trouble.

Finally, after a back and forth conversation with the woman in charge, she agreed to honor the contract they had signed and we went on to hold a beautiful seminar.

ᘐ Wooing a Client

What was supposed to be the final meeting was going nowhere. Mr. Cranfield and his marketing director were sitting across from me at the conference table, questioning me over and over again, seemingly not satisfied. How could I prove to them that we were the perfect advertising agency for their fledgling auction house? I racked my brain. We had already negotiated and agreed on the terms of the retainer in our last meeting. This was our fourth meeting and I didn't know what else to say or do to convince them that my agency was the right choice for them. We came highly recommended by Mr. Cranfield's wife after doing great work in print and TV advertising for her company. I showed them our portfolio. We discussed case studies. I assured them about our media-buying power, but I could feel there was some hesitation, something he needed to ask me but was unable to do so. As a last resort I decided to turn to my power animal.

While Mr. Cranfield was taking a short break I sat back in my chair, closed my eyes, and called my power animal, the white dove. She appeared and I hurriedly asked her to help me by telling me what I could do to fulfill Mr. Cranfield's wishes and win his account. She said, "Offer to present him with a whole advertising campaign." I was surprised because earlier I had insisted that our agency would not do any speculative work for new clients because they could easily judge us based on our past work.

When Mr. Cranfield walked back into the room, I turned to him and said, "Mr. Cranfield, I know what you want and I'm willing to give it to you. What if I come in next week with an advertising campaign to show you what we can do for you? Would that make you happy?"

He smiled sheepishly. "That would be great. I was afraid to ask you to do that." He was relieved.

In the end our campaign and my agency were not chosen. "You are too creative for our company," they told us. "Maybe we could use this creativity in our new division or for special projects, though," they added.

Regardless of the outcome, the ability to get to know our challenger's wishes in such a short time was an excellent experience, one that confirmed for me the use of shamanic journeying in a business setting.

☷ A New Approach

"Itzhak, I admire your group's organization. How do you do it? You are only a few people, and doing such a great job," Johanna said to me about the NY Shamanic Circle one night after our monthly circle. I looked at her with total surprise. After all, she had been one of the leaders of her well-established organization for many years and I always admired their activities. "I want you to come to our board meeting and help us," she continued.

"I would love to; it would be a great honor indeed," I replied. "But maybe instead of me talking, we can use the same shamanic tools we just used tonight. Let's journey to your organization's soul and see what spirit would say."

Johanna, a bright-eyed, petite woman with full gray hair thought about it for a while. "Okay, that sounds possible. Let me talk with the board. By the way, have you done this before?" she asked.

"Yes, once in Israel. It was very interesting; the results were unexpected."

She looked curious. "Tell me about it," she asked.

"I was asked by a spiritual organization, based by the Dead Sea, to try to resolve their personal conflicts, arguments, bickering and, most of all, their inaction. Some of them lived in a commune there, and some were dispersed across the country. During our first gathering, as they shared their journeys it became clear to me that they needed to dissolve their organization and go their separate ways so they could be true to who they were at the present time and not hang on to an old dream. On our second meeting in Tel Aviv I laid out my analysis. They understood and accepted it with sadness."

"Interesting," Johanna said. "I hope that won't happen to us."

A few weeks later the entire board of directors was lying on mats in a circle on the cold floor of a big auditorium, journeying first to retrieve their power animals' spirits. We talked about the meanings and teachings of each of them and how they related to their management style and character. "Now let's ask your spirit guides for insight about what steps your organization needs to take to make it more successful in today's world," I suggested. As the drumming came to an end, they shared their journeys and my partner and I took notes. At first none of the journeys made any sense to them and they were puzzled. "Let's meet in two weeks and we will give you a written report with a business plan to revamp your organization based on your journeys," I said to the group.

When we met again I gave them the rather detailed plan looking at the following aspects of their business: what age group they already had—60–80; what age group was their target market—25–50; what message they needed to craft in order to attract new younger members— shake up the old intellectual image with something more upbeat and accessible; what kind of events they needed to produce—those based on more current social and environmental topics and more experiential, not just lectures and films; what to serve at these events—light vegetarian refreshments; where to advertise their events—social media, electronic newsletters, member incentive programs; what kind of website they needed to create right down to the font size—not too much copy, more images, and larger fonts.

We handed them copies of the printed report. Johanna was surprised. "You found all of that in our puzzling journeys?" she asked.

"I can't tell you exactly how we did it but we pored over every detail in your journeys, as each of them is a symbol and has meaning. We look not only at the stories, we decipher and extract the true meaning behind the symbols," I explained.

They implemented most of our recommendations and it worked. They attracted a younger audience and their organization continues to flourish.

EPILOGUE

⩘ ⩘ ⩘ ⩘

WE ARE ALL SHAMANS

Learning from my clients' life stories and from my own childhood, I believe that as young children we come into the world highly open to the world of magic and mystery. We are even encouraged and receive applause for being creative and intuitive—right up until the time we are forced to "grow up," and then bit by bit we learn to conform to society's expectations and codes by suppressing our feelings and our imagination. To be safe and accepted a child learns that it is more important to adapt to the limited conventional educational systems—a system that emphasizes the "follow the rules doctrine." Instead of encouraging out-of-the-box thinking, igniting the passion of self-discovery to expand consciousness, it rewards the logical, rational, scientific mind, serving as a soldier for a well-run society ruled by big corporations and institutions.

Still, despite all the programming to conform it is not unusual to hear some of my clients and students say, "I can't believe I dreamed that he was coming to visit us and two weeks later he appeared." Or: "I went to the store looking to buy a black scarf but there were only yellows and reds. Then for no apparent reason I wandered to another section and saw the exact black scarf I had my mind set on." Or: "I had a strange feeling this person would call me and the phone rang; it was she." Or: "I had a feeling I must call him right now. I stopped the car and called. He was going to be in the office for only five minutes and I caught him in the nick of time." Or: "I had a feeling I knew that city from long ago, as if maybe I was born there." Or: "Oh, I was just talking about you and here you are."

It is important to realize that one can develop these dormant abilities in a methodical way. Just like going to a gym to develop strong muscles, we can develop our intuitive "muscles" and increase the power of our "sixth sense" transmitter and receiver signals. The less you resist those experiences and the more you practice the more successful you'll become. The more successful you are the more you will believe in yourself. The more you believe in yourself the deeper your understanding of the universal energies will become.

Here are a few suggestions to help you develop your intuitive skills:

▲ Devote a certain time of the day to a period of meditation to quiet your mind and develop deep listening.

▲ When seeing images in your mind's eye hold on to them and watch them develop without holding any judgment. Carefully examine what you see and how you feel about it. Check the surroundings, hear the sounds, listen to the messages, and ask your spirit allies to clarify your visions.

▲ Learn to softly gaze over peoples' energy fields and pay attention to the messages you receive, both mentally and physically, and don't discount and judge them.

▲ Join a shamanic drumming circle or some other supportive group in which you can regularly practice and develop your latent gifts. You'll be surprised to see that there are many people like you.

▲ Take a few workshops with shamanic teachers or other intuitive people whom you trust.

▲ Find books that incorporate stories of "unnatural" phenomena. They can help expand the mind's possibilities and inspire you to go further.

▲ Take notes of your life's strange "coincidences," accidents, or flukes. Nothing happens without a reason; learn to embrace it.

▲ Notice patterns in your own and others' behavior and in nature.

▲ Withhold judgment of your visionary experiences. Stop denying them, whatever they may be.

▲ Keep a diary of unusual events. Write down everything you see without censoring it.

▲ Verify your visions. Don't be afraid to call the person you had a vision of or a dream about, even if you might feel like a fool.

▲ Surround yourself with a supportive community of like-minded people with whom you can share your experiences so you don't feel isolated and ridiculous.

My visions, stories, and personal experiences are not unique. Many of my fellow shamanic practitioners from many cultures around the world encounter similar stories and maybe even some that are more amazing. I believe, as Ipupiara told our New York Shamanic Circle on many occasions, "We are all shamans. I am no different from or better than you are. Just because I wear feathers on my head, have long hair and a ponytail, wear a strange poncho and colorful clothing, and speak in a funny accent doesn't make me a more powerful shaman."

I truly hope reading this book will encourage you to claim your birthright and set you on a fascinating life journey. We are truly all shamans.

BOOKS OF RELATED INTEREST

Shapeshifting
Techniques for Global and Personal Transformation
by John Perkins

Shamanic Awakening
My Journey between the Dark and the Daylight
by Sandra Corcoran

Plant Intelligence and the Imaginal Realm
Beyond the Doors of Perception into the Dreaming of Earth
by Stephen Harrod Buhner

The Secret Teachings of Plants
The Intelligence of the Heart in the Direct Perception of Nature
by Stephen Harrod Buhner

Plant Spirit Healing
A Guide to Working with Plant Consciousness
by Pam Montgomery

Ayahuasca Medicine
The Shamanic World of Amazonian Sacred Plant Healing
by Alan Shoemaker

The Shamanic Way of the Bee
Ancient Wisdom and Healing Practices of the Bee Masters
by Simon Buxton

Original Wisdom
Stories of an Ancient Way of Knowing
by Robert Wolff

INNER TRADITIONS • BEAR & COMPANY
P.O. Box 388
Rochester, VT 05767
1-800-246-8648
www.InnerTraditions.com

Or contact your local bookseller